Praise for *The Power of Days*

"Filled with determination and an unwavering spirit, the founding story of Days for Girls comes alive in this remarkable book. Its message of courage and resilience offers valuable insights into how to overcome obstacles in order to create a lasting impact in the world. This inspiring and essential read is a call to action for anyone committed to creating positive change and a more just and compassionate world for everyone. I wholeheartedly recommend you read this book!"

—Cynthia Kersey, author of *Unstoppable* and founder and CEO of Unstoppable Foundation

"Mergens uses her immense talents as a writer and storyteller to destigmatize the topic of menstrual health, offering a blueprint for others who want to catalyze change for a fairer and more equal world."

—Raj Kumar, founder of Devex

"Celeste Mergens takes you on a journey of resilience, hope, and healing in this inspiring and uplifting memoir."

—Jen Gottlieb, keynote speaker, author of *Be Seen*, and cofounder of Super Connector Media

"I was brought to tears many times as Celeste reveals the unbelievable and heartbreaking reality of the unmet needs and injustice that millions of girls and women worldwide experience every day of their lives. I found myself cheering out loud as she and her dedicated companions worked to shatter stigma, shame, and taboos, turning periods into pathways of healing, new growth, and opportunity. A humble champion and advocate for women around the globe, Celeste Mergens honestly uncovers a tragic problem that we all need to hear about and help to solve. Her unique story will touch your heart as Days for Girls reclaims precious lost days of education and equality, and replaces them with days of dignity, safety, and freedom. Celeste Mergens exemplifies mission, purpose, and contribution at the highest level. This book will change and inspire you!"

—Cynthia Covey Haller, coauthor of *Live Life in Crescendo*

The Power of Days

The Power of Days

A Story of Resilience,
Dignity, and the Fight for
Women's Equity

Celeste Mergens

BenBella Books, Inc.
Dallas, TX

The Power of Days copyright © 2023 by Celeste Mergens

BenBella Books, Inc.
10440 N. Central Expressway
Suite 800
Dallas, TX 75231
benbellabooks.com
Send feedback to feedback@benbellabooks.com

BenBella is a federally registered trademark.

Printed in the United States of America
10 9 8 7 6 5 4 3 2 1

Library of Congress Control Number: 2023005838
ISBN 9781637743744 (hardcover)
ISBN 9781637743751 (electronic)

Editing by Laurel Leigh
Copyediting by Elizabeth Degenhard
Proofreading by Madeline Grigg and Rebecca Maines
Text design and composition by Jordan Koluch
Cover design by Morgan Carr
Cover photograph © Mite.org
Printed by Lake Book Manufacturing

A portion of proceeds benefits Days for Girls.

**Special discounts for bulk sales are available.
Please contact bulkorders@benbellabooks.com.**

To my forever family who teach me anew the power of love every day.
To our global family who believe in and work for new possibilities.
Your capacity, dignity, commitment, and strength are astounding.
This book is dedicated to the future that is possible when we all come together.

Contents

Prologue   1

Part One

Chapter 1   I Am Not from Here   7
Chapter 2   Pathways and Sidewalks   9
Chapter 3   Her Wild Bow   13
Chapter 4   Wrong Answer   17
Chapter 5   Migration   20
Chapter 6   When I Wake Up Falling   24
Chapter 7   The Man Who Painted Wild Horses   27
Chapter 8   Takeoff   29
Chapter 9   Stay   34
Chapter 10   Inconvenient Arrival   37
Chapter 11   Paper Walls   41
Chapter 12   The Shed   45
Chapter 13   Precious Scars   49
Chapter 14   Sticks, Stones, and Gravity   50
Chapter 15   Turtles and Islands   53
Chapter 16   A Seat at the Table   59

Part Two

Chapter 17   Learning in the Round in Kenya   69
Chapter 18   The Tracks to Kibera   75

Chapter 19   They Wait in Their Rooms   78

Chapter 20   What Dreams May Come   81

Chapter 21   The First 500 Girls   85

Chapter 22   The Birth of Days for Girls   90

Chapter 23   Hearing Their Stories   96

Chapter 24   No Remorse   99

Chapter 25   The Chief of Dagoretti   101

Chapter 26   Home Again   105

Chapter 27   Space   110

Part Three

Chapter 28   Zimbabwe or Bust   117

Chapter 29   Body Wisdom   121

Chapter 30   The Power of We   125

Chapter 31   A Bus to Botswana   131

Chapter 32   I Never Knew   138

Chapter 33   The Facts   143

Chapter 34   Getting to Kgotsu   146

Chapter 35   What Woman Would You Have Me Say No To?   149

Chapter 36   Movement   152

Chapter 37   Cutting   156

Chapter 38   The Secret Hidden in Our DNA   166

Chapter 39   When the Stakes Are High   170

Chapter 40   Men Who Know   174

Chapter 41   Every Girl. Everywhere. Period.   177

Chapter 42   A Single Page   182

Part Four

Chapter 43   The Wisdom of Those We Serve   189

Chapter 44   Then Get Up   196

Chapter 45   Failing Forward   201

Chapter 46   Speaking Up for Periods   207

Chapter 47   The Power of a Crowd   211

Chapter 48   The Earthquake that Shook Up Periods   219

Chapter 49   Untouchable   225

Chapter 50   These Are Not Mountains   228

Chapter 51   What Color Is This Dress?   230

Chapter 52   The Longest Layover   235

Chapter 53   Periods Don't Cause Banana Blight   249

Chapter 54   The Part That Saves Lives   258

Chapter 55   An Unfortunate Liability   261

Chapter 56   The Terminator   265

Chapter 57   The Women of the Cloud Forest   271

Chapter 58   What We Fear More than Death   276

Chapter 59   The Price of Pencils and Pads   280

Chapter 60   Time in the Zone   288

Chapter 61   Cambodia   300

Chapter 62   Resilience   311

Chapter 63   The Power of Knowing   318

Chapter 64   The First Lady, the Minister of Gender, and the Royal One   323

Chapter 65   For the Girls   330

Epilogue   334

Acknowledgments   337

Prologue

"CELESTE? IS THAT YOU? CAN YOU HEAR ME?"

The headmaster of the orphanage that was stretched beyond capacity shouted over the crackling phone connection from Kenya.

"We are in great need. We are completely out of food, and we have been for days."

Despite every effort, the growing need born of the crisis in Kenya had already become greater than any of us supporting the orphans' educational center could provide for.

Eight months earlier, on New Year's Day 2008, Kenya's worst ever ethnic violence had been sparked by a tightly contested presidential election. Within minutes of the announcement of President Mwai Kibaki's victory, protests erupted in the streets alleging a stolen election. Hate speech and bitter accusations perpetuated by the two competing political parties fueled the anger on both sides.

Kenyan officials banned political rallies and protests, warning that they would crack down on anyone who threatened law and order. Suddenly, friendly neighbors forgot their trust, focusing instead on differences of opinion and the narrow divide between votes. Fires burned. People who might never have dreamed of perpetrating violence torched buildings: one a church with women and children locked inside. Each candidate blamed the other. The peace and stability of Kenya went up in smoke.

A call from our friend and Kenyan driver, Paul, was the first to put us on high alert. "My brother has just been shot in the leg with an arrow from a crossbow. We are taking him to the hospital now. It's gotten bad here. Please pray for us," Paul said as he made his way through the chaos to get his brother to care. My husband Don and I had been with Paul in Kenya only a few weeks earlier. Now violence had spread all the way from Nairobi to Kisii and even north to Paul's village near Nakuru, where his father had been chief.

Eventually, the violence displaced almost half a million people.

The population of the orphanage and education center swelled from an over-crowded 420 children to a reported 1,400 orphaned and abandoned children—all packed into the crude, corrugated-metal facilities. I say reported, because I still cannot comprehend how it could be possible to fit that many bodies into the space available. This orphanage and academy were not my family's program; we and our friends focused on helping communities be more self-sustaining else-where in Kenya. But having come to know them, I had joined other supporters in responding to their needs. My hope was to find and rally support for solu-tions that would help them sustainably thrive instead of surviving day to day. Then came the frantic appeals to address the rising need for more food, clothing, school supplies, and blankets as the number of those seeking shelter grew.

And now this call.

I desperately wanted to help feed them, but there were no more resources I could send. Far away, back in the States, Don and I, along with friends, did all we could to support them as the need grew. Car-washing fundraisers. A golf classic. Our personal resources. We had nothing left to send.

As a woman of faith, I did what remained. The thing I knew I could count on. I had survived on faith all my life, like water and air, trusting that I am held. I dropped to my knees, pleading fervently for a way to help the children. "I'll do anything. Just tell me what to do to help." But nothing came to me. Not even a bad idea, like the time we organized a garage sale in the fall at the far edge of town to raise money for the school, and it snowed. Only two people came.

I fell asleep still pleading.

At 2:30 AM I awoke with what felt like an urgent news ticker running through my mind with a question so unexpected that I literally gasped: "Have you asked what the girls are doing for feminine hygiene?" I had never thought to ask that, not even once, and no one had ever brought it up. What *were* they doing?

Jumping up from bed, I ran to my computer and sent an email to ask. I didn't expect an immediate answer. Smartphones were not everywhere back then. Sur-prisingly, the reply came almost instantly.

The email read, "Nothing. They wait in their rooms."

Nothing? How was that possible?

I could picture in my mind the bunk beds crowded end to end and side by side in dimly lit rooms. Children had to climb across other bunks to get to their own. Two or three girls shared each level of the beds, so that fifty children slept in a small area. I was already concerned about and trying to address the over-crowding and lack of safety of such an arrangement. And there were even more children now. How did they possibly wait in their rooms?

The answer arrived the next morning. During their periods, the girls sat on pieces of cardboard, missing school and remaining isolated—for days.

How had I never asked before?

This new awareness alarmed me so much that it took a full two days before I stopped urgently seeking funding for both food and menstrual pads long enough to think: *Pads are not even what I was asking about.* Nor had I considered the fact that in our family, we referred to menstrual care products with a code name: turbos. As in, "Honey, could you pick up some turbos for me when you're at the store?" I don't recall how we arrived at the term, but feminine hygiene was not part of my vernacular at the time.[1]

I had concentrated my efforts on resources I already understood increased the resilience of a community, solutions they could own themselves: education, water, irrigation foot pumps, sanitation, solar options, agriculture, and health. Now the thing that was shrouded in silence—menstrual health—was added to the vital list of practical needs that were urgent to the power of three.

The shame and shrinking confidence of not having menstrual care products was familiar to me—I had experienced it as a teen, tucking folded toilet tissue, always fearful that the sliver of a solution I had devised might fail me before I checked it again. But my family didn't talk about periods, and neither did any of the girls that I had met in Kenya. Now the question for me was not whether we should respond, but rather how I had never asked before. Certain things are basic to survival: air, water, food, connection, and the dignity of days.

In the early hours before sunrise, I refocused on how to get funding. The

---

[1] As of this writing, the term is currently "menstrual care products." Interestingly, this important focus has many ongoing debates over terminology.

girls needed food; they also needed a way to leave their rooms and go to class. If I could raise enough funds, we could buy a short-term supply of both food and disposable single-use pads, but what about next month? If they had to choose between food and pads, I knew and understood that the need for food would win.

I wanted nothing more than to help. Hunger hurts. Every thought tracks back to food, derailing even sleep. This call for help felt like a train striking me from behind. I should have heard it coming.

Part One

Chapter 1

I Am Not from Here

Nevada State Park, 1967

THE LULLABY OF THE ROAD HELPED ME FORGET THE CROWDING IN THE back seat of the 1955 faded blue Chevy Bel Air four-door where my three sisters and I tagged along with my mom and the man I knew as my father. He was on the hunt yet again for "greener pastures"—searching for a better job and a better life in yet another, then another, place.

We moved from state to state thirty-two times before I was thirteen years old. Roadside rest stops and state parks served as our temporary homes along the way. Stale day-old tuna fish sandwiches, dry on the outside, mushy in the middle, would "do us" for days.

When I was around five years old, at one of the state parks, I was admiring the sparkle of the sun-drenched sidewalk, feeling its warmth on my bare feet when the glint of a rhinestone collar on a small white dog caught my attention. The flash of its collar twinkled up the matching leash to the manicured hand of a woman holding a perfectly good half-eaten apple. She stared down at me before throwing the fruit into a nearby garbage container. It had been a while since I had eaten a meal. All I could think of was how delicious that apple would feel in my insides. I was working on a plan to rescue it from the dumpster and still find a way to climb back out when I felt the woman looking me up and down. Her nose crinkled as if I had just offered her a day-old unrefrigerated tuna fish sandwich. Her eyes narrowed.

"Where are your shoes, girl?" she asked.

I stood as tall as I could. "I'm toughening my feet," I said. This stranger didn't need to know we were "in between" homes, and that I had the unfortunate habit of wearing my shoes out on the sides, or that even though my mom shaved down the heels to level them, my latest pair were beyond rescue. Where were my shoes? I hadn't left them behind in the car or scattered on a patch of gravel—I had no shoes.

It was as if I suddenly stood in front of a mirror and saw myself reflected through the woman's eyes. When she looked at my bare feet and clothes much too small for my undersized frame, she saw a little girl, unkempt and unworthy. I looked down at my dirty feet. For just a moment, I saw myself the way she did and I felt small, poor, and ashamed.

A sudden warm assurance came over me; I was more than what she saw. I wanted to tell her as much: "I am not from here. I am not what you see!" But when I looked up, she was gone.

That moment scratched at me for years. I used to think of that woman as Cruella de Vil, the villain from one of the few movies I watched as a child. It wasn't until recently that I finally saw the woman's momentous part in my life as a gift. At that young age, I was shown a truth: we get to decide who we are. Was I simply a poor girl living wherever we landed? Or was I more?

That still, small assurance sustained and guided me. I was not my clothes. I was not my hunger. I was not my physical appearance. And I would later go on to learn I am neither my abundance, positions, nor intellect. For better or worse, none of us are. We are not our economic circumstances; we are not our possessions; we are not our trauma. It is not our circumstances, but our responses, that shape and define who we are. I somehow knew then—and I know even better today—that each one of us is far greater than we can possibly comprehend; each one of us has something to contribute. We all matter.

There are many unusual remnants of those years on the road. To this day, I can't eat tuna sandwiches. I eat apples through the core so that only the stem remains. I am uncomfortable eating in front of people unless everyone has food—which can be very inconvenient, especially while traveling. Those same experiences likewise left me interested in people and places in a way that leaves no desire to stand in judgment of them.

I call that moment with the woman and her apple a gift because it went on to become a touchstone, a hope, and a prayer to survive the difficult years ahead.

Chapter 2

Pathways and Sidewalks

History, despite its wrenching pain,
cannot be unlived, but if faced
with courage, need not be lived again.
—Maya Angelou

Ashland, Oregon, 1972

PIECES OF STRING, DYED AND KNOTTED INTO PASTEL MACRAMÉ BRACE-lets, were my undoing. It had come to the attention of my fourth-grade teacher, Mr. Wright, that I was selling them to classmates to raise money for a home for my sisters and me to run away to. We had discovered a derelict cabin in the woods. Scant partial walls propped up the roof, which was held together more by moss and sky than boards. This became my first attempt at a home of our own. My hope rested on the possibility of safety from the temper tantrums of the man who sometimes tolerated us—my father. In the weeks that followed our discovery, I focused on making enough money to buy boards and buckets to hold water for drinking and washing. This cabin would mean no more moving on. It could be a roof of our own without the flood of parental storms.

Bracelet sales turned into a small cluster of coins inside my school desk. I weighed the sum total of funds raised for "our house" in my palm. Not yet enough for a single board.

Mr. Wright took me aside after class to tell me that he'd called my mother in so we could chat. My mostly quiet mother often let doorbells go unanswered for fear of talking to strangers; when she walked with us to the playground at Lithia Park, the gravel of pathways and sidewalks had her full attention—anything but the faces of people passing by. Though it is worth pausing to point out that she took us to the playground, and that we miraculously now lived in a place that had one. But she rarely visited our school. The mother I knew would rather play with rattlesnakes than talk with teachers. Right on cue, she came into sight, though it took me a moment to register that it was her. She walked tall and smooth, dressed in a Jackie O.–tailored dress I had never seen before, with her hair perfectly styled.

This unknown mother talked to Mr. Wright with a soft southern accent that was as new as the dress. "Oh, she is such an imaginative child! Yes, it is a gift. No, there are no problems at home. She will not be selling any more bracelets. Thank you for your concern." They laughed. Then she took my hand and I followed, more astonished than irritated, wishing I could always follow this mom home. She didn't say a word on the long walk up the hill, first along the sidewalk, and then the edge of the dry storm drain, carefully avoiding lawns. I kept staring at her and her perfectly coiffed hair, and the sway of her step. When we got home, she silently disappeared into her room. I never saw "that mom" again.

—

That was the year we developed the habit of living in one place. I was ten. The GI Bill had helped our family buy a house of our own, a single-story rambler at the top of a dead-end hill. It was warm and solid, with many windows. The sort of house where no one would suspect a thing. After school, my sisters and I would walk up the last steep part of Iowa Street. I always entered the house on guard, my emotional antenna outstretched to read the temperature of the room as we entered. Who was home?

It could be my easily triggered father inside, cropping up unexpectedly. He had begun traveling alone on asphalt road construction crews almost as soon as we'd bought our home. His varying work schedule meant we never knew when he might be home. Being in his presence was like observing a hornet, predictably painful but only if he noticed us. What I never could predict was which version of our mom we would find when we came through the door.

Some days, we found the one who would suggest quickly cleaning the house and then going to Lithia Park to play. At other times, the one who drove the accelerator to the floor of the car, taking us on a high-stakes ride of road versus rage. Other days, it was the musical one who coaxed beautiful melodies from anything with a string.

Once in a while, I found the version of my mother that troubled me most—the one that was a little girl.

She would be curled up against her bedroom wall, her arms wrapped around her knees, rocking back and forth, a metronome composed of body and wall. As I slid down next to her, a small child's voice spilled out the horrible things she was hiding from, as if in real time. She recounted being stabbed in the nose with a fork because she tried to take a helping of food before her oldest brother. Or being forced to spar with her siblings. Two by two they were called out to enter a ring formed by mostly unwilling witnesses, and forced to fight until one of them fell. The fallen and the victor were then forced to watch as two new victims were called out to replace them in the ring. My "child-mother" next to me rocked harder when she told of being hung in a gunny sack from a fence post if she refused. She told of the time her two-year-old brother was fascinated by the blue propane flame under a pot of boiling water, so her father dipped the boy's hand in the water to show him what hot was. She whispered when she described the way men rotated through her mother's house, and how she and her sisters were taken as the fallout of her mother's appetite for ravenous men.

But the incident that seemed to haunt her the most was the time her mother beat her so badly that she was unconscious for eight days. Her eyes would finally find mine when she told of how she only realized she had been unconscious all that time because her teacher asked her where she had been. When she woke up, no one in her family acknowledged they were glad she was still alive. I hugged her close whenever she got to that part.

She polished each of the worrying stones of memory as I huddled next to her, witnessing the things that had left her vulnerable—stuck and out of order, the little girl that needed to be heard. I put my arm around her and tried to soothe her, not old enough to grasp that I was hearing things a child shouldn't hear. My attempts to protect her from the nightmares of her past added the weight of her stones to my own burden. She became like my sisters, another of the children I had to protect. It had been a long time since I had been the child in this family.

Years later, I was attending college, walking along another sidewalk—this one filled with hope for what was possible in my future—when it hit me: my mother was split in two. During her eight days of unconsciousness, she wasn't in a coma. That period marked the moment she couldn't stay together anymore. Her only defense had been to leave behind a part of herself for a time. It was that very piece of her I would sometimes find slumped against her bedroom wall.

It didn't occur to me when I was young that life behind our closed doors was so far from normal. My sisters and I were stuck in survival mode. We loved our parents and wished they knew how to love us, too. There was no fantasy that things were ideal. I simply couldn't afford to wonder what life was like for other girls at school, who always had pencils and clothes that fit, nor could I dwell on the fact that they likely didn't come home to find their mothers had become children in their absence.

She was a fragile-winged phoenix, coming and going right before our eyes, glorious, and pure in heart. Ashes, ashes, we all fall down.

Chapter 3
Her Wild Bow

Where words fail, music speaks.
—Hans Christian Andersen

Ashland, Oregon, 1972

OUR MOTHER'S DEFAULT SETTING WAS EYES DOWN AND VOICE SMALL, but her violin bow was a force of nature. It spoke for her, wild and strong where she was often painfully shy. Her music helped her manage to survive. Now that we had our own address on Iowa Street, she joined the symphony. She was so gifted that the symphony allowed her to bring my three sisters and me to rehearsals, concerts, and even the celebration parties of orchestral events. She kept a newspaper clipping featuring a photo of a rehearsal moment, a percussion member crashing a pair of brass cymbals just behind my sister Janie slumped in a chair. My sister slept on. We were raised in a loud and crashing home; the cymbals were far more melodic.

There were quiet moments too, like when my mother sewed orchestral skirts for us on her antique treadle Singer sewing machine. She hummed to the rhythm of the dancing bobbin and needle, a few straight pins pursed between her lips. I stood next to her, tickling my palm against the bristled burgundy velvet embedded within the sewing machine tabletop. That machine was treasured. It survived numerous downsizings; as we moved from place to place, it was always carefully packed in the limited space of the small trailer we towed behind us. Fabric pieces became a skirt for each of us, perfectly matching her own concert-length dark blue, with three satin ribbons spread across the waistbands. We wore them to her concerts, and to our local church when she could get us there, her ever-present entourage of four.

She would occasionally be hired to clean the home of one of the leaders of the Rogue Valley Symphony in Oregon prior to events. My sisters played tag outside while I helped my mother inside. There didn't seem to be much to do. I was mystified that someone actually paid us to dust invisible dust from pretty things on shelves and to turn the corners on toilet tissue before we left the re-sparkled bathroom. Often while we cleaned, caterers were setting up for post-concert celebrations. They wrapped boxes in linen and placed them on tablecloths—terraces for their landscapes of silver trays filled with colorful hors d'oeuvres, accented with impossibly curled vegetables fashioned into ribbons and flowers. I deconstructed their staging in my mind to try to figure out how they did the things I missed while in another room. Not much dusting got done when catering was setting up.

In my college years, those acquired skills for napkin folding and arranged table displays all came into play when I got a job in event catering. I was equally comfortable doing dishes or directing the flow of people and food—one of the many gifts that came from my mother's love for music.

She taught us all to play the violin, too. Though never as eloquent in the language of strings as she, I still owe a lot to her bow. It wasn't only catering, design, a love of classical music and events that I learned at her side; I also learned the power of "we."

My mother could fill a room with a dance-inducing jig, a mournful anthem, or the theme from *Sesame Street*—"Sunny day, sweepin' the clouds away"—with equal ease. But the moment the orchestra all came together, the room had the potential to transform with a power that sang through your very insides. The cacophony of tuning instruments transmuted to a transcending wave of sound. It wasn't always perfect. At rehearsals, the conductor would bring the room to a stop with a tap of his ivory baton, and ask them to repeat the offending measures. Sometimes he even called on the first chair—the premiere musician for each instrument's section—to play the problem spot correctly so others could hear it, and then everyone joined back in. They didn't have to get things right the first time.

Every instrument mattered; their music was made more powerful by their differences. Each musician supported the others in something bigger than themselves. I witnessed how one person would raise their instrument, an individual working on their own splendid tune. Then another, and another until many individuals became one movement of sound and the roof could barely contain the fullness of it. Strings of notes were brought to life in *The Firebird* by Stravinsky, or the score of *Peter and the Wolf*. Once, they featured the vocal artist from the original Walt Disney movie narrating from the edge of the stage as they played the score live, while the animated movie played on a giant screen just behind them. The magical experience that filled the room with notes, laughter, and applause of delight stays with me to this day.

Her music, their music, held power and I took it all in. Coming together, whether in music or in crucial conversations, can be a powerful thing. But it requires learning to hear others. It takes practice to create something bigger than yourself, but it is only possible by working together.

I also learned a new language from the musicians, a language stretching past the edge of survival I had known. Not from their music, but from how they connected. They were confident even when they were questioned or asked to start again. Instead of taking offense, they sought to understand. Their ability to bridge gaps in understanding was built from where they came together in creation and support of one another. It was like watching Da Vinci's engineering feat of sticks and ropes, a bridge of safety come to life. Years later I would learn that there are words for these skills: social capital.

Poverty has its own language, like place and time. It marks an expectation on your tongue and mind. It is more than a lack of financial resources; poverty is a multifaceted social issue. According to the book *Bridges Out of Poverty*, "The ability to leave poverty is more dependent upon other resources than it is upon financial resources . . . an individual must suspend their 'emotional memory bank' because the situations and hidden rules are so unlike what they experienced previously." Ample emotional, mental, spiritual, and physical resources are all important to becoming self-sufficient. Not to mention a support system to count on when you are at the edge of financial disaster and short-term assistance is all it would take to save you from a fall. Many do not have that lifeline of support.

Understanding various societal codes of conduct increases the likelihood that someone will be able to rise out of poverty. You don't have to assimilate, but

I learned that I needed to understand. While I didn't yet know the power of a mentor, I did begin to pick up on the new social cues surrounding me. Watching the patterns of people became one of my favorite pastimes. People in the orchestra, parents at church who smiled at and listened to their children, and Dr. Peterson, the woman who served as both my school principal and my sixth-grade teacher, all held their own important clues. Relationships, role models, healthy coping strategies, and knowledge of "hidden rules" are all important parts of building the foundation needed to rise and remain out of poverty. Surviving transitions and diversity in environments takes strong decoding skills. Each interaction added a new word to my social vocabulary and gave me hope of new possibilities. By paying attention and practicing new social language over time, I became equally comfortable with the rules of engagement of both poverty and financial abundance. I became bilingual in economic stratospheres while my mom made her wild bow sing.

Chapter 4
Wrong Answer

Life is ten percent what happens to you
and ninety percent how you respond to it.
—Charles R. Swindoll

Ashland, 1974

THE SMELL OF HOT TAR STILL ENVELOPED OUR DAD WHEN HE ARRIVED home four days earlier than expected from his latest construction contract. He added a six-pack of Pepsi to the fridge as he told my mom, "It's time to move on. These jobs around here aren't worth my time." Somehow, in the days that followed, my mother, the shy, intelligent woman that I was most familiar with, got him to agree to stay and go back to college instead. He could finally have a career he felt was more worthy of him. The GI Bill could pay for that too. As promised, she did his papers, read and summarized his books—everything, except take his tests. At twelve, eager to help, I read a few of the books too.

He even had the son he had always wanted: the newborn of my mother's stepsister, a heart wish granted to us because he was born addicted to heroin. The baby smiled at us even as he spat up blood. We took turns holding him. He taught us to hold each other more. A priceless gift to every one of us.

It all worked, until the day our dad came home from class with a brand-new yellow truck with big fat tires and an engine that vibrated the air with a mere tap of the accelerator. My sisters and I ran around the truck celebrating. Mother stared at him. "Where'd you get the money?" He had arranged to sell our house. The house that had finally kept us in one place for two glorious years.

But that wasn't all; he wanted a divorce. He was moving in with a college student he had met at school. Message delivered, he got into his yellow truck and drove away.

People gave us their condolences. That confused me. Why would I be sad about him leaving? To be honest, I was relieved. No more holding our breath until the next torrent hit. Though I had gotten adept at taking his beatings without falling into grief. Like the time he lined us all up and demanded a confession for something we didn't even know about. I stepped forward; best to get it over with. He unlatched his belt and started welting me with it. I refused to cry. He hit me harder. My sisters started begging, "Just cry. Just cry!" I would not. Not this time. He hit me again. The belt slung me to the ground. He started to kick me with his steel-toed work boot. My sisters' cries rose higher. And then it stopped. He had walked away. He never hit me again.

Now, he was walking away from all of us. This man was not worth grieving over.

I didn't know then what I know now, that cycles of violence end in one of three ways: serious harm or death, the victim or perpetrator withdraws, or the victim stands up. I didn't know that yet, but I felt it. We were free.

The smile on my face stayed for days.

We were moving back to Oklahoma. Adventure awaited us. Before we left, the bishop of our church visited with my mom and then called me into his office. "Me?" I asked, puzzled.

"Your family is going through a lot. How are you doing?" he asked.

I marveled at how often people asking that question looked so concerned now when they didn't ever ask before.

"Good."

He pulled his chair around next to mine, leaning forward. "Tell me something. When you are married someday, if your husband hit you, what would you do?"

I thought for a minute. "I would go to my room and try to figure out what I did that caused it."

"Wrong answer."

"What?"

"No husband should hit any family member, ever. If you tolerate it even once, it sets off a cycle that continues. Girls who grow up with abuse in their home often subconsciously marry a man like their dad so they can prove that things would have turned out differently if they were in charge. Don't fall for that trap. Be on the lookout. Promise me you will decide now. No matter what, you will not accept physical abuse in your home. Otherwise, this pattern will continue in your life."

I tucked his counsel away and packed it with me as we followed my mom onward from place to place.

Chapter 5

Migration

You don't drown by falling in the water;
you drown by staying there.
—Edwin Louis Cole

Oklahoma, 1976

THE BLANKS IN MY MOTHER'S RÉSUMÉ WERE FILLED WITH THE CARE OF children. Solid pay does not come easily to a single mom who must balance two jobs, four daughters, and one newly adopted son with zero support from her ex. It proved to be just the formula for working herself to exhaustion on a daily basis. The mountain-sized load of responsibility she single-handedly tackled was also the answer to why everyone had expressed condolences when they learned of the divorce.

She remarried two years later at the recommendation of many who said this new man was a good man. A kind man. A family man. A hardworking provider. She could trust him; I heard them say it. I wanted to believe it, too. Her white wedding dress was a flag of surrender. He moved in.

The neighbor's cockroaches fled to our house the week our new stepfather moved in. At night, when I turned on the kitchen light, the short round insects scattered across the floor and showered over me from the ceiling. I screamed, shaking them from my hair and arms. My newest stepfather laughed and said, "The neighbors must have sprayed."

The next day we sprayed too, passing them on to other houses before I wiped down our Tupperware containers. The sponge collected stiff-winged tiger-eye bellies under curled-up legs. I rinsed away the peppery smell of them and scooped dead fish from our aquarium—the unintended victims of the insecticide.

Our new stepfather introduced us to scrubbing sponges and taught us that freezing batteries extend their shelf life. He also taught us the superior nature of homegrown organic tomatoes grown in compost-filled recycled tires. His hardened muscles endorsed the protein shakes he churned in a green blender, "for strength."

I was sixteen years old the day he went after my sister, slamming her head through the plaster wall, a single shout stopped his solid arm. The thud of her pale head filled our house as I yelled, "Stop!" He turned his face to me in slow degrees. I prepared for rage. He smiled. His eyes widened when my voice lowered, my body a vibrating drum. "Don't—ever—touch her again."

—

We were not safe with this man. Once again, I plotted to find a way to provide and make a home. Nothing had ever proven that I could look to anyone else to find a way out. I no longer had to rely on selling bracelets at school to help my family. I followed our newest stepdad to the roofing construction site he worked on and offered to help straighten up the worksite for free. After the first day, they hired me to help on-site. On the fourth day, under the searing heat of the Oklahoma sun, I noticed how roofing crew members had to stop frequently to trudge up and down the ladder for more shingles. Noting the pattern, I balanced a bundle over my shoulder that weighed nearly half what I did and climbed up to deliver them just as a crew member turned to get more. Both men on the rooftop stared at me, mumbled thanks, and got back to work. After several trips up and down the ladder, it was accepted without comment that I would deliver the shingles. I got a raise. I started strategically placing bundles, and became the swift "shuttler," laying single shingles in position ahead of the nailer. I got another raise. Eventually, I was promoted to the top crew, which meant roofing brought a lot of support to my family.

The same promotional pattern worked in sheet metal too. I started out cleaning floors, then noticed how slow a man was going as he worked a metal press. I asked him to show me how he did it, then offered to give him a break for a bit, "just for fun," promising to keep up with his daily count pace while he was gone. His entire quota for the day was finished before he returned. The supervisor noticed, and I was added to the sheet metal crew. I got another raise. I learned to weld. I got another raise. My family still had the support of the newest stepfather, so I was able to put away a little money for college, which I saw as my only way to support them long-term.

Visitors to the shop took a full three beats to recover from seeing a young woman when I lifted my welding helmet visor. The same shock accompanied me to college. On my first day of class in engineering, a young man turned around in his seat and asked, "So what are *you* doing in engineering?"

I answered without hesitation. "I've always loved and excelled at math and science. My favorite teacher advised engineering. You?"

He turned back around to the front without another word. I was, at the time, an unexpected element in all the worlds I chose. Never believing in barriers to what a "girl" can and cannot do. That stance would, in the future, translate to breaching barriers for taboo subjects on a global scale.

—

I first learned about engineering when I was twelve, in the pages of the stacks of books I brought home from the library every night. Six cranks of the battery-free flashlight that I won as a premium for my newspaper route meant I could keep reading. I'd fall asleep after my arms tired of balancing the book and light. One of those late-night books featured a boy who built his very own ham radio, an amateur radio that could bounce communication signals far enough to talk with people in China and in the space station. He had built it himself to connect with the network and grew up to be an electrical engineer. That's when electrical engineering got added to my list. Today I hold ham radio license KE7RXK.

Before high school was out, letters of collegiate acceptance came in from both the Massachusetts Institute of Technology (MIT) and Brigham Young University (BYU) in Provo, Utah. Not realizing the prestigious opportunity that acceptance from MIT was (a book at the library listed it as emphasizing engineering) and wanting to be closer to my sisters, I chose BYU. I was fortunate; Brigham Young University is a top-tier school. Many students are never introduced to alternatives. They don't know that universities are as unique as fingerprints, and they may find the academically rigorous and creative space of Cornell, formal historic Oxford, global Georgetown, the laid-back pace of a smaller regional college with fewer students and a more personal touch, or the innovative challenge at Stanford to be just their speed.

I was just happy to be on target. Getting into college, check. When I got to BYU, I listed electrical engineering as my major and spent an entire day at the BYU testing center testing out of as many general education courses as I could, ready to dive straight into engineering and graduate faster. The plan for our future was finally starting to come true. I imagined that my mom would be alone again soon, but stability was in sight if I could just work fast enough to make it through school.

Sixteen credit hours of electrical engineering and two part-time jobs filled my waking hours. And suddenly dates, lots of them, but school and work came first. For the sake of my siblings, I focused on my studies.

Then one day the phone rang.

My mother was calling to tell me that my latest stepfather—the one that slammed my sister's head into the wall—had just attacked and molested two of my sisters, and it was all my fault.

Chapter 6

When I Wake Up Falling

When someone shows you who they are,
believe them the first time.
—Maya Angelou

Utah, 1980

EVERYTHING THAT HAD FELT IMPORTANT MOMENTS BEFORE DISSOLVED.
"What? Where are they? Are they okay? Can I talk to them?"

My mother's voice grew shrill. "Talk to you? They don't want to talk to you! This only happened because you left us. It's your fault, and we all know it. They hate you." She hung up.

I couldn't argue.

The newest stepfather had been with us for a while, and although he was as hardworking as his reputation led my mom to believe he also had a temper worse than his predecessor's. He was dangerous, but I knew how to read the flames of dangerous men. I specialized in calming him down by distracting him, getting him to discuss the things he felt himself an expert in. Besides, the topics he was interested in were interesting to me. If his voice started to rise, I would run to the room where the disturbance was to keep him distracted, not wanting him to wake their new baby. Even with the addition of my newest sister, I hoped my mother would choose to move on soon. Instead, in my absence, this latest husband had turned my sisters' bedrooms into his hunting ground.

I risked the expense of a long-distance charge to call her back. I begged to talk with my sisters. "No. They will never speak to you again." She hung up.

The grief I'd managed to hold at bay for years waded closer, a gaping whirlpool in the making. It drew me into its undertow in a way that left the air squeezed into a mist of gray. I rolled up in a ball in my bed, missing classes and calling in sick to work for a week. Then two. Then three. Then a letter came in the mail. It was from the attorney of the man that I had known as my father, my mom's first husband. He was legally disowning me. Which never happens to anyone in the United States in this century, as far as I know. But the state of Oregon had garnished all his wages for back payment of unpaid child support. Years of it. He was desperate.

This document was his way to minimize his losses, claiming he did not owe any support to my mother for me. In it, he declared that I was never his daughter, that I never considered him a father, and that he could not be held responsible for my care. And further, the letter cited what (prior to updated privacy laws) his full parental access to my academic records allowed him to see: my compounding days of absence from classes. He used this evidence as final proof that he owed no support. The man had been an absolute no-show for years. Now this letter, his kidney-punch attempt to sidestep parental debt, was added to the sharp uppercuts of my mother's calls. A letter weighing mere ounces was the blow that took me down.

A few days later, I became a college dropout. My grants were lost. After years of trying, my hope to ever break out of the trap of poverty and violence that I was raised in blurred to invisible, as pointless as ink in rain. I slid into darkness, waiting to dissolve. If not for faith in God, and the smallest whisper in my heart that there could be good to come, I would have taken my life.

I had only one place to go. As predicted, my mother had just moved again, leaving her husband for a duplex only ten miles from where I was. She was happy, almost giddy, as she pulled in to pick up the Dropout and my two boxes of possessions, tokens of my surrender.

My sisters barely looked up from the blaring TV as I entered their new home. No hatred, no anger, no welcome. We were all pasta in an overcooked bowl, on the verge of mush. Looking into their faces, I realized that although I could barely breathe I had to get up and try again, even if the world was still gray with loss.

A few weeks later I mustered the strength to go to the military recruiting office.

"You've come to the right place. Can I get you some water? Coffee?" The U.S. Navy recruiter in front of me wore a white shirt, its sleeves pressed at attention, each collar lapel featuring a different emblem pin. A colorful ribbon badge pinned just above a pocket spoke of rank, honor, or prestige. I didn't know which.

"Water would be great," I said, straightening the cuff of my own sleeve.

"So, your dad served in the Navy," the recruiter stated, looking at notes I assumed were from our previous phone call. I didn't correct the relationship he assigned to the man that I had always known as my father—the man who had proven again and again to be more step than father—but the reference to him now felt like a bayonet plunge. The recruiter looked up and smiled. "A family tradition. And you just left engineering. Is that your goal? To go back and finish?"

"Is full tuition really part of the benefit?"

"Not only is it a benefit, but you can also start your contract time while attending college, depending on the track you select and qualify for. Is that what you want?"

"Yes," I answered. "Absolutely."

"Well then, let me get the paperwork started. There's a quick exam. No problem for someone like you, I'm sure. I'll be right back."

As he left, I noticed the large framed poster hanging on the wall: *Navy. It's Not Just a Job, It's an Adventure.* I'd had enough adventure. I wanted something as dependable as a metronome. Regulated. Steady. Something to keep me afloat.

The recruiter called when my exam results came in. "It looks like you could qualify for any program here that you'd like. Have you thought about which you'd want?"

I asked instead which branch was the hardest.

"The Marines," he said.

"Marines it is."

Next, I started to book an appointment for a physical. Ironically, in light of what would later become Days for Girls' mission, it was a menstrual period that kept me from being a Marine. While I waited out a cycle, as recommended by the clinic, to fulfill my physical exam requirement for signing, my mother called my biological father (not the bully I had understood to be my father): the one I did not know. "Do you still want her? You can have her now. She's joining the Marines."

He bought a plane ticket for me to fly to meet him.

Chapter 7

The Man Who Painted Wild Horses

The unexpected moments
the music, the mistakes
and the misty surprises;
makes a life.
—Soumojit Dutta

San Diego, 1967

WHEN I WAS FIVE, I DIDN'T KNOW THAT THEY WERE *HIS* WILD HORSES that ran pounding across the painted canvas in front of me. The oils brushed into flying manes across a desert, free. He and my mother talked quietly at the end of the hallway. She kept saying, "*No,* you had your chance." Every time she said it, he looked over at me, so much love showing in his eyes that it was enough to keep my focus off the horses for a moment. I had never seen love like that. His green-flecked eyes shone. When he turned back to my mom, I went back to all the wild horses. I didn't hear him approach until this stranger knelt next to me and asked, "Do you like the painting?"

I could barely look away, but answered, "I have never seen anything so beautiful."

"I painted it," he said.

"You did?"

"It isn't my finest work," he said, looking intently at me.

All those wild horses, the wind nearly leaping from that desert, the sun far from sight but still radiating warmth across the rippling flanks. He stood up, reached into his pocket, and took a five-dollar bill out of his wallet. He then glanced at my mother, who stood silent and sullen but nodded her head in approval. He pressed the money into my hand. "This is for you. Go buy a pretty new dress, okay?"

My mother pulled me along by the hand as I stared back at the man that she left without another glance.

My mother and I picked out a brand-new red plaid taffeta dress with a white slip. I wore it home, twirling at every opportunity. As we walked in the door, her husband asked where I got the dress. I stopped twirling. My mom ran to the back of the house. His face reddened, his voice a rising quiet threat. "Take it off. Now!! Take off that dress!" I stood as still as I could, my arms upraised as he jerked it off, shouting over my head, "You stupid women! None of you can be trusted!"

He ripped at the dress, dropping it to the floor. I couldn't even close my eyes. He slammed his way out the door, but I didn't dare pick up the dress. Which turned out to be a good decision because he whirled back and snatched it, leaving with it trailing from one hand.

Now, all these years later, my mother was finally telling me that the man who raised me with his iron fist, steel-toe boots, and sharpened words was not my father. I should have known, because every photo of my sisters and me was an ideal illustration for the *Sesame Street* song refrain, "One of these things is not like the others." I once asked my mother why I didn't have freckles like my sisters. She answered, "You do. You're just one big freckle."

On the day she told me that someone else was my father, I knew instantly, it was the man with the wild horses.

Now, we would meet again.

Chapter 8

Takeoff

You can't reach what's in front of you
until you let go of what is behind you.
—Delores Thornton

San Diego, 1981

MY DAD HAD WAITED ALL MY LIFE FOR THIS MOMENT. IT TURNED OUT that while I moved from place to place, my biological father and his brother James would track my latest whereabouts through my Aunt Loise. My father reached out to my mother, again and again, asking if he could see me. My mother had always refused. Instead, she sent him tiny school photos, each a needle in his eye for abandoning her. He had an album full of them.

They had been childhood sweethearts. When he learned she was pregnant at seventeen, his mother sent him away. His family knew of my grandmother's reputation and possibly feared that my shy and wounded mother was like her—thirsty for men. *How did he know this baby was even his?* No matter what their thoughts of my mother were, the greatest barrier between the young couple was that my father was betrothed to someone else. While betrothals are not as common in the United States as in other parts of the world, my father's family are of Spanish, Mexican, French, and Irish heritage, and the predominantly Spanish customs of the family ruled that day. Fulfilling a promise to a beautiful girl he had known all his life was an easy choice. So, he married Argentina, beautiful and even-tempered, his second cousin, betrothed to him at birth.

Heartbroken, my mother swore that he would never get me. He made his choice and now, he had to live with it.

It brought little solace to her that when I was a toddler, my Grandma Ballow saw me for the first time and wept. The family resemblance was so clear that she exclaimed, "She's ours!" Perhaps this is why, to this day, my mother's walls are lined with photos of my siblings' families but not mine. I am the needle in her eye. The reminder of what she had hoped for but had been denied, to love and be loved by the one I so closely resemble.

Looking back, I realized that my mom and the man I thought was my father once tried to tell me the truth during an unheard-of trip to McDonald's for an ice cream cone, just the three of us.

"We have something to tell you," she said.

My stepdad chimed in, "You were already there when I married your mom."

I was confused and completely missed what they were trying to tell me. How could I be there before?

Before you judge my lack of insight too harshly, in fairness, I had not yet had "the talk." I didn't know anything about how babies happened. It also never occurred to me that someone could have a baby outside of marriage. Such possibilities were never discussed.

Yes, I was eventually educated about sex at school. My introduction was not in the classroom, but rather in the cafeteria line. It happened a few weeks after the McDonald's incident, and a few weeks before the official class at school.

A boy I had a crush on was making a joke using crude anatomical references. I was aghast. Perhaps an old-fashioned term, but one that seems absolutely appropriate for how I felt at that moment—aghast. "That's rude, Scott, and it's not true! My mother and father would never do such a thing!" As he laughed, others joined in.

Another boy asked, "How many kids are there in your family? And you think they didn't . . ." He was interrupted by his own laughter as well as a growing group of kids standing nearby. "She thinks that sex doesn't make babies!" More laughter.

"What do you think brings babies? A stork?"

I dropped my tray back on the counter and ran all the way home, including up the steep upper part of Iowa Street. I slammed through the door. I told my mom what the kids had said.

She looked at me blankly and said, "I knew we should have told you."

—

We often think of maturation and sex-ed as an awkward class in fifth or sixth grade, but all over the world, it is actually an important piece of understanding that brings greater wellness and safety. Ignorance is not bliss. There were a lot of things I didn't know when I was twelve. I certainly didn't yet know that I was the daughter of forbidden childhood sweethearts. And now, to keep me out of the military, I was flying to meet the woman who was willing to take me in as wild oats sown by her husband before they married. How would she feel about me coming to roost in her nest? How would the rest of them feel?

My unknown family, the ones I was gaining in the wake of losing so much, were waiting at the gate of the San Diego airport when I landed. Grief smothered me like fog as I prepared to greet them. I said a silent prayer: *Please don't let them see my wounds, or at least let them love me anyway.*

"There she is!" A tall and lanky young man called out, "I'm your brother Jimmy. We were worried you had missed the flight. Sorry we are late! Aunt Susan hit a huge piece of metal with her car. It could have hit the engine, but it just hit the tire. We're fine. I'm your brother Jimmy, did I tell you that? You play guitar? I do, too! Maybe we can play together. Can I carry that for you?" His dark, curly hair framed his face, which was as friendly as it was handsome.

"I'm your Aunt Susan," the woman standing next to him said, looking like Miss Hawaii, pausing from waving at people long enough to scoop up a relative stranger. Both she and Argentina were dressed with elegance and smelled of designer perfume.

Argentina stepped forward next and hugged me. "Welcome. Do you have luggage?" she asked.

"No, this is it," I answered, managing a smile at the circle of eager faces. There was no need to stop by baggage claim. I had only a small bag and my guitar.

The journey to the airport parking lot was a friendly Q & A tennis match that was at once wondrous and terrifying.

—

My father was waiting for me when we reached their home. "You're here! Sorry I couldn't meet you at the airport, baby girl. Concrete day. It's a big project or I would have left before it was even finished. Now I can take an extra day off."

A shallow creek ran nearby the house. Eucalyptus trees stretched high over-head, filtering the light through their leaves so that shade and light flickered playfully in his green eyes.

My Aunt Marilyn, my dad's trendy youngest sister, offered me one of the lounge chairs near the creek, then curled up on the one next to it. "Tell us about you!" she said.

Argentina smiled. "I'll get started on some dinner. You three enjoy some time together." She and Aunt Susan went inside.

I was a foot away from my father.

It felt like I had been dropped into a movie. "Well, I love painting," I said, then looking at my father added, "Like you! Do you still have the painting of the wild horses?"

"Oh, that thing. I don't know. I may have given it to someone."

We shifted from story to story, laughing. It was easy to be with them. Soon, I was telling them about how I worked in sheet metal and roofing. He, or maybe it was Aunt Marilyn, told a story about the time he caught a monkey and suc-cessfully smuggled it back home through customs. I asked about the peacocks strutting behind us. He answered that he loved birds. We couldn't help but laugh even at grim stories, like the time he fell off a construction site roof and hit the edge of a tar mixer and broke his back.

"Anything to get a break," he said. He painted every story with broad strokes of humor.

He still looked at me with the same loving eyes that I had remembered. I noted that he looked at everyone that way.

The rest of the family arrived for the barbecue. It felt like art come to life. Festive mariachi rhythms rose as the warm wind curled through the tall cacti. The picnic tables held bright cellophane-wrapped terracotta bowls of green guacamole and chunked tomatoes. In the cooler rested large ripe watermelons. I mingled with the family like I was never lost from them. I watched as they moved together in a comfortable dance practiced over years of family gatherings. Clapping and stamping to the music in their Gucci boots. My grandmother, my abuela, brought even more bounty to the table as aunts called to cousins tagging cousins, and uncles grilled carne asada on an open fire. The contentment of their invitation to participate in their family clashed with the regret I felt for all the years I had missed. My grandmother, the one who, before she first saw me, had once said I could not be theirs, handed me a slice of watermelon. "Taste this, Corazón."

Chapter 9

Stay

For there is always light, if only we are brave
enough to see it—if only we are brave enough to be it.
—Amanda Gorman

San Diego, 1982

MY FOUND-FAMILY INVITED ME TO STAY. MY DAD AND ARGENTINA'S house was still under construction, so arrangements were made for me to be with Aunt Susan and Uncle James's family. They opened up three-year-old Yvette's beautiful room to me, with its plush blush carpet and California closet. I didn't really need much closet space, so my things didn't displace her clothes neatly arranged by color and category.

Despite my new family's warmth, or maybe because of the reassurance of it, I quickly sank to the feared depths of my particular entanglement. Right when it felt like it mattered most that they could know me for who I was, I would soon be unable to be anything but the "Sorter-of-Hard-Things."

For more than three weeks, I stayed in Yvette's queen-size sleigh bed, wearing the beautiful hand-painted floral pajamas they had provided me, and prayed my way back through the knots of my life. As I puzzled through what I had experienced, recollections showered over me like pieces of ash. I refused to blink or look away; instead, I confronted the emotion of them, trying to witness it all in new ways. I prayed, pondered, and cried, not necessarily in that order. I captured new insight in tear-smeared journal pages. I felt the pain in waves. I slept. I read scripture. I slept. I wept. I prayed. For weeks. It's a wonder they didn't send me away. Instead, Aunt Susan would check in. "You okay? I brought you something to eat." My father was blessedly absent for my visit to the bottom of my personal entanglements, though she told me that he regularly called her and Uncle James about me.

I wasn't conversational, nor witty, nor even, I'm sure, particularly good at being thankful. But they didn't ask me to be anything. And they didn't ask me to leave. I was an intruder that could have been considered a family mistake. Who has that kind of patience for a relative stranger? Thankfully, they did. It was a miracle of unconditional love.

I dove in deeper. The process was like scraping abandoned, hardened wads of gum pressed into my insides by a myriad of moments, a few still sticky despite the passage of time. I had been trying for years to get the wads to all fit back into their foil wrappers, but they never really belonged to me. I could drop them now.

The checklist of realizations started to add up: yes, the parents I grew up with never understood me. Yes, I was painful for them. I was impossibly active and curious; I still am. They wanted quiet and slow. I loved to go fast, sing, and create things. In first grade, I rallied the neighborhood children to produce a circus and invited everyone to see us perform in a nearby abandoned lot. In fourth grade, I convinced my classmates to use weeks' worth of recess to act in a play that I made up with the catchy title, *The Real, Real, Real Wild West*. I called my mother to meet me at school and bring her makeup bag. It was an "emergency." She came! And was shocked to learn that my teacher, Mr. Wright, watched our performance and decided to arrange an assembly presentation for the whole school, and it would begin in forty-five minutes. My mom almost fainted when I told her that she was in charge of everyone's makeup. But she stayed. I don't remember any of the lines now, but I do remember overhearing my mother later telling my stepfather that I said, "Work with me, people," quite a lot just before the play began.

A couple years later, my mother only learned about my latest backyard production—a dramatic choreographed piece (I can't even tell you where I got these ideas) with my patient sisters as primary dancers—after I brought her one of the last hand-drawn tickets I had made, the rest of which I had already passed out to our entire neighborhood. To my mother's great despair, people came. Afterward, one of our neighbors asked if she would allow me to participate in Oregon's Shakespeare Theater's Summer Internship program, an opportunity usually reserved only for select college students. She assured my mom that she would take special care to personally watch over me. My mother declined. My stepfather, who had the final say, had said, "We won't have one of ours hanging out with hippies!"

I was the alien among them, the kryptonite to their publicly shy nature. They couldn't figure me out. "You and your books, and the way you talk! Tell her to shut up, Margarett." That doesn't even count my questions about history and science, or my ideas for how we could be financially solvent, or the time I asked at age twelve if I could be in charge of the checkbook, certain that I could manage it better. When we needed groceries, they instead bought jukeboxes and other heavy things we could not carry with us.

I think it is fair to say, they found me completely obnoxious. The more they tried to hold me back, the harder I worked at showing them my plans could succeed. The harder I worked at pleasing them, the more it tormented them. And it struck me, in Yvette's room, with my tears, my journal, my prayers: they were jealous. My own parents were jealous. It was an impossible realization until that very moment. Nothing I could ever do would change that. Only my sorrow, failure, or disappearance would please them. They were broken while I refused to be. The state I had been in for weeks would have pleased them. It was then I decided to survive this, too. No, more than that—I was going to be me and love it. I got dressed, brushed my hair, and left the room.

Chapter 10

Inconvenient Arrival

Life is simple. Everything happens for you, not to you.
Everything happens at exactly the right moment.
Neither too soon nor too late. You don't have to like it . . .
it's just easier if you do.

—Byron Katie

San Diego, 1982

JUST WHEN I WAS READY TO FACE LIFE ON MY OWN TERMS, INCONVEniently, I met the love of my life.

Don Mergens was flying home to his family after two years serving a mission in Montana when I left Yvette's room. A few days later, while his family celebrated his return, I was soaking in inspiring speeches at a young adult conference, replenishing the warm reassurance that I had counted on my whole life: we are not alone. We are all loved. There is a purpose for our journey here. I left that day with a new decision: going forward, I would own the gifts of the experiences I'd had without flinching, and view them with gratitude, no matter what.

On the way home from the airport, Don announced to his family that he was not going to date for a while. He just wanted to focus on school. His mother was pleased since he hoped to follow in her footsteps and become a medical professional. But three days later when Don walked into church, a place that I had long held as one of my anchors, he says that he looked up, saw me sitting in the choir, and knew instantly that he had found his soulmate.

Don tells it best. He heard the prompting so clear that it was as if it were spoken aloud: "That's your wife."

"Go on!" he said to himself. He heard the prompting again. He leaned over to his dad and said, "Do you see that girl sitting in the middle? She is going to be my wife."

Don says that his dad looked up to the choir and then back at him and said, "Honey, I hate to tell you this, but she is way out of your league." Don, in characteristic good cheer, replied, "I know it! But the Spirit told me that she's my wife!"

"Then you need to pursue it," his dad said.

Don was smart enough not to let me in on it. I wasn't thinking about dating or marriage but was focused on discovering my own path forward and learning to breathe again.

He found me in the foyer after the service and invited me to have lunch with his family: "You have to eat, right?" Then, he suggested going to a visitor center for the afternoon. From there, we walked along San Diego's embarcadero as the sun set until lights shimmered over the bay. After he drove me home, we sat on the bumper of his car still catching up like best friends after years apart. We were so caught up in hearing each other's stories that we didn't notice the time until the early morning chill of March hit. It was 3:40 in the morning before we went our separate ways. It was a movie moment: the air sweeter to my lungs, the door floating on its hinges. It took a while, but I finally fell asleep, still smiling. We saw each other every day after that.

When I moved out to Dad and Argentina's house a few months later, Don traveled back and forth every evening in his silver VW Jetta for months. Even though I lit up as much as everyone else when he walked through the door, it frightened me. How my very skin felt more alive when he arrived. How I found myself eager to remember to tell him a certain something that had happened during the day. The closer I got to him, the more uncertain I was that I could maintain the wall of protection I had needed all my life. From time to time, I would declare that we should probably take a break. His face would soften in regret, but he never objected, leaving without complaint. He called it "pumping the brakes," and he says it was the hardest part of waiting for me to catch up.

My abuela loved Don immediately. She loved cooking for as many people as possible. He did, too. Her smile spread all the way to the twinkle in her eyes. And she smiled quickest when Don walked into the room. His dark hair perfectly combed over his golden-brown eyes, with a smile as quick as her own. In my new family, there were apparent comfort zones. Men gathered outside barbe-cuing, drinking beer, and talking shop. The women sat inside cooking and chat-ting together over coffee. Don split the difference, coming in and out, and the women loved it. He always took extra time with my grandmother. Unbeknownst to me, she was coaching him on how to win me over.

Both of them encouraged me to play guitar with my brother Jimmy outside near the red bougainvilleas on the patio, while they plotted in her kitchen.

Don asked me to marry him under a full moon, near a palm tree, in the open space between the house of my loving abuela and the white stucco home of my father, both people still miraculous to me. There, Don knelt on one knee and gave the most beautiful proposal, though I do not recall a single word of it because—don't hate me—I said no. Or at least I didn't say yes. I said I needed time to ponder and pray about it. For me, a yes would be forever. Don and my abuela were both devastated. Don has never let me live it down.

—

My mother arrived in San Diego shortly after the proposal with her newest hus-band, a dirty-blonde glue-sniffing addict named Ken, and my two youngest sib-lings. Don offered to fix her failing car. He adjusted the timing belt, gave it a tune-up, and replaced the headlights before topping off the engine with oil. She took me aside and told me they would be looking for a place nearby, and invited me to move in with them. I could help her with babysitting when she got work. I agreed to help.

"Do you think this relationship with him is going anywhere?" she asked, pointing to Don.

I watched him leaning over the hood of her car, replacing the spark plugs. "He's amazing. He's kind, intelligent, and deeply spiritual in a way that leaves him more concerned for others and what is possible than preoccupied with him-self. I'd rather spend time with him than with anyone else. He's my best friend, but how can I trust . . ."

She interrupted, "He's too good to be true. You just need to realize that you will never get everything you want. It just isn't out there. Not even in him."

She left, calling out the window, "I'll call you when we get our place." My beloved little brother and spunky youngest sister, born of the husband before this one, waved from the back window, unaware of the dangers of new stepfathers. I sighed. I had no choice but to follow them.

I was given a cot on the enclosed side porch of their small white house with a large dead lawn. On the very first night, I was startled awake. Ken was standing in the dark at my bedside. He silently retreated back into the house when I gasped and quickly sat up. I held vigil on my cot, clutching my knees in front of me, sleepless for the rest of the night.

The next morning, I told my mother how he was reaching for me when I woke. She said there was no danger with Ken; what was wrong with me? Don came to get me as soon as I called.

My mom slammed the door, my siblings huddled behind her as I left. This time, there would be no going back. I was finally certain that I had to choose, and I was choosing a future of my own now. One that could include both safety and love.

—

A few days later, Don and I were driving when I mentioned in passing being his wife someday. He slammed the brakes.

"Did you mean that? Are you going to be my wife?"

I laughed. I hadn't even realized what I just said. A heartbeat later I answered, "You know, I guess I *did* mean that!"

He cranked the steering wheel hard to the left.

"What are you doing?!" I asked, grabbing the handhold above the door as we did a U-turn mid-intersection.

"I'm going to tell someone before you change your mind," he said, suddenly fiercely focused on the road ahead. I laughed again. Who could blame him?

When my grandmother heard the news she jumped up and down, banging pans together in celebration. Don, whose voice alone was enough for anyone to fall in love with, was humming nonstop, and I joined in, our voices a perfect match. I had chosen. It was Friday the thirteenth, the day I would luckily say yes to the best thing that ever happened to me. We were married four months later.

Chapter 11
Paper Walls

When water turns to ice, does it
remember that once it was water?

Whidbey Island, Washington, 1998

THE LOVE DON AND I HAD FOR EACH OTHER GREW TO INCLUDE THE miracle of six amazing children. The wondrous Devin, Dane, Ashley, Breanna, Raymond, and Reed, each unique and remarkable. Love, laughter, and laundry, in that order.

Our home in Freeland, Washington, where people gathered. The neighborhood kids spilled in the door at any time to join us.

Once, one of Devin's friends showed up for breakfast for the fourth day in a row. I laughed and asked, "So, are you moving in?" To my surprise, he said yes. We told him that he better call his mom to get her okay. And with that, we had an extra son for a few months. He wasn't the only one to stay. Exchange students, foster kids, and enough joy for us all. In between the work of life, I planted flowers in the front yard while my children played games nearby. It wasn't perfect. It was better than that; it was family. Home. It was everything I always hoped it could be.

I was thirty-six years old and securely surrounded by my family when a dream swept in like a stealth tsunami, leaving me awash in sadness that rose up in waves threatening to drown me. Some memories lurk in the fiber of your being just out of sight. This one had been waiting a long time.

Ashland, Oregon, 1970

I was eight years old when we lived in the broken house, with cardboard for walls on the inside and newspaper for insulation, at the top of a hill off of old Highway 99 outside of Ashland, Oregon. We were there when we got the news that my mother's stepfather had died. He had wrecked his truck, and been trapped inside. My aunt had been thrown clear into the barbed wire at the road's edge, leaving her deeply cut but alive. I went to the room my sisters and I shared and cried as loud and hard as I could. At one point my mother said, "I didn't know she felt that close to him." I upped my effort. I remember it all clearly because I was so afraid. I was afraid someone might suspect how happy I was that he was gone, but I didn't remember why.

Our house had four rooms: two bedrooms (one for our parents, one for us kids) and a bathroom with a clawfoot tub with a rust stain around the drain and a broken chain that used to have a rubber stopper attached. A single room held the space between. Against the far wall was a sink and almost-cabinet, while a small wooden table with five found chairs and a roadside sofa filled the rest of the space. My three sisters and I shared a bunk bed that swayed with a tiny hint of danger when you climbed to the top, not really risking falling, just a quiver that put you on alert.

The top bunk was my favorite place to be if I was inside, though I far preferred being outside running, digging for old bottles and rocks, ever in pursuit of an arrowhead. I had gone on a school field trip to a small local museum where they showed us minerals and arrowheads. The Shasta tribe in Oregon and northern California fashioned arrow-point weapons chipped from obsidian and flint stone by striking a series of skillful blows at just the right angle. Dad confirmed that arrowheads were to be prized, and a person who could find them around here would be lucky. When he talked about arrowheads he looked happy. I wanted so much to find an arrowhead to give him.

He was a man who wanted sons. He had four girls. I wished I could be a boy for him. Instead, I settled on searching for an arrowhead. I loved the open adventure of the outdoors. Back then, if school was out, kids could roam free until the sun neared the horizon. For that matter, for us girls, school was not always part of our mandate, though I loved learning as much as I loved the hills. In our family, moving kept school to a minimum, and in between, we could just say we didn't feel well, or that we didn't have something to wear, which was often true, and it was also a perfectly good excuse to go find arrowheads.

This "wood-on-the-outside, cardboard-on-the-inside" house had a roof that didn't leak except in one corner of the kitchen. It sat on property that stretched the length of the cascading hills with giant boulders to explore and climb, spotted with a few scrub pines scattered like haphazard needles in a pincushion. An irrigation ditch ran through the property, and Dad warned us of the many ways the water could suck us into nearby grates we couldn't see and drown us, or cut us in two. The "cut in two" threat worked, and even on hot days we stayed on the ledge, lowering buckets into the ditch and throwing in leaves to race in the current but never venturing in. Nearby, under an oak tree, I tied a few pieces of old plywood onto an abandoned metal box spring that my sisters and I used as a trampoline.

We had been in this place for almost a year, and it was heavenly exploring the hills. But on the day the call came about my step-grandfather's death, the joy of the box-spring trampoline and even the hills held no power over my duty to cry. This felt urgent in a way that few things in my life had ever felt. I kept up my deliberate mournful display as if my life depended on it. It must have been torture for my family. I don't know why they didn't come in and say, "Stop it! The rest of us are trying to live out here."

At some point, I must have decided it was enough. After that, my newly deceased step-grandfather became the shadow of gray that threatened me whenever anyone brought up his name.

I didn't recall all that he had done to me. But decades later, I was suddenly walking around with the ghost of his memory threatening to overtake me. I could barely catch my breath for the energy of holding it at bay. Friends stopped mid-sentence in conversation to ask if I was okay. "I don't know what's wrong," I'd say. One friend suggested I contact her counselor Janet, a professional whom I could conveniently call from home.

Janet's voice was calm, a decibel short of cheerful. During session three, she asked a question that blew down a barricade inside me. What the question was is lost to what happened next. I was alone in my room; light streamed in from a wall of windows in front of me framing the waters of the Puget Sound sparkling in the near distance.

"It was in the shed."

Chapter 12

The Shed

If you continue to carry bricks from your past,
you will end up building the same house.
—Unknown

Washington, 1998

THE ANSWER SURPRISED ME. IT SPRANG FROM THE GRAY PLACE THAT stood between me and an anger I could never afford to stoke, let alone feel. But it sparked before I saw it coming and torched the wall on the other side of the gray before I could even take a breath to call it back. Suddenly, it was as if I was seven years old and trapped in the shed again.

Trigger Alert: Violence and Abuse

Before you follow me in, please know that I am not in that shed anymore. The man that you are about to witness is not in the shed either. Less than a year after this event, he was crushed in a truck that rolled over and over before he was relieved of his life. You will find proof here, and my witness that if you survive and heal, devastating trauma can be transformed. If you don't want to follow me in, you can skip ahead to chapter 13. You have options. We all have so many options, no matter what our circumstances are. You have the power to shift any experience. What you tell yourself matters. Jump ahead if you wish, knowing that the good news is that surviving is always a powerful choice. Or stay with me and see for yourself.

Oklahoma, 1979

When I recalled the moment in the shed, the room rewrapped around me so clearly that the dust on the Coke bottles stacked in wooden cartons in the corner of the shed looked 3D. I shared what I was seeing with the calm voice on the other end of the line. My step-grandfather invited me to see something in his toolshed. I followed him in. He backed between me and the door and shoved me to the dirt floor. The memory had no sound, only motion. No voice, only space. His rough hands smelled of diesel when he covered my mouth to stop me from screaming, bruising me into the ground. I kicked with all the strength I had until the pain pinned me, stabbing me into stillness and I was left with nothing but to leave—floating, focused with all my might on dust motes that floated too, haloed in the sunlight coming in the one window above the workbench. My mother looked in from the slight edge of the shed door just before it was over. For the briefest moment I hoped for rescue. But she moved out of sight as quickly as her glance had flicked away.

When my attacker was done, he pulled what was left of me off the floor, saying, "Tell anyone and I'll do the same to your sisters." He pushed me forward to the abandoned commercial washers and dryers stacked just outside the shed. My hands cupped at his demand, and he poured scoops of stainless dimes from the coin boxes into my palms. "You're the winner," he said.

—

I never told anyone. Not even when my mother had to take me to the doctor because I had a severe urinary tract infection and hadn't "been quite myself" in weeks. As I write this, it only now occurs to me that when the man I called Grandpa took me to the general store in Salina, Oklahoma, to choose a present to spend dimes on, I was not alone. One of my sisters had dimes too. I chose a string and colored rock mosaic art kit of a turtle. She chose a barrel full of plastic red monkeys.

Silence seldom protects anyone.

The hour appointment went by in a wail. I sobbed harder than I had ever cried. My whole body trembled as I felt it all anew. I rocked with the ache of it. The counselor said, "You're safe. You're here in the present. I want you to take extra care of yourself today. Take a warm bubble bath if you'd like. Drink plenty of water. Call me at any time if you need to. Perhaps cancel any obligations that you may have for the next few days so you can feel and process this fully. And Celeste, good job. That was deep and important work. It takes courage to open the door to these things. You did it. Now it can start to heal."

When I went into the bathroom to wash my face, the mirror reflected a swollen upper lip. I drew a warm bubble bath and discovered my upper left arm and chest had speckled bruises where I had just recalled being pinned down. How? I was not hitting myself as I recalled the incident. How could my body appear almost as if it had just happened?

Later I came to learn that the body remembers. I found the work of Dr. Paul Pearsall and his book, *The Heart's Code*. In his research, he discovered that heart transplant recipients knew inexplicable things about their donors that they shouldn't have been able to know. His work argues that memory is held not only in our brain but also in our cells, in every fiber of our being. Others have found the same:

> *We have learned that trauma is not just an event that took place sometime in the past; it is also the imprint left by that experience on mind, brain, and body. This imprint has ongoing consequences for how the human organism manages to survive in the present. Trauma results in a fundamental reorganization of the way the mind and brain manage perceptions. It changes not only how we think and what we think about, but also our very capacity to think.*
>
> —Bessel van der Kolk, MD[2]

At our next counseling appointment, I told Janet about how my body had shown marks of past trauma. Shown time-lapsed tattoos rising to the surface. Shown circulation returning to a cut-off part. She acknowledged the phenomenon. It was all a big *aha*. Trauma is held in our very DNA. It's in the mind tapes we have to undo, it's in the wounds we have to take responsibility to heal, it's in the decision that is ours to make: whether we will break the chain to shift the pattern or continue to suffer the effects.

---

[2] Bessel van der Kolk, *The Body Keeps the Score: Brain, Mind, and Body in the Healing of Trauma* (New York: Penguin Books, 2015), 21.

According to Dr. Bessel van der Kolk: "As long as you keep secrets and suppress information, you are fundamentally at war with yourself . . . The critical issue is allowing yourself to know what you know. That takes an enormous amount of courage."[3]

Our body holds knowledge, experience, and trauma. It even has the ability to contain an overwhelming experience until we feel safe and secure enough to let it out. Until we are able to process our trauma, our body holds it for us. Left unprocessed, however, trauma is free to creep up and give us an anxiety smackdown, self-sabotaging surprises, or a depressive slam from what feels like nowhere. This is proven to be true even for generational trauma. We cannot move forward stronger than ever until we confront the demons of our past.

—

In time I learned to pause whenever I felt a wave of unexpected grief or strain for no apparent reason. I committed to asking myself where the emotions came from, and trace back to what happened just before the feeling in hopes of finding a clue. Taking time to notice familiar mind tapes and replace each with new refrains: *I am strong. I am intelligent. I am worthy. I am here, safe, right now.*

Several days after recalling what had happened, I worked up the courage to ask my mom if she remembered seeing me in the shed. She said she remembered being worried that she had seen something that might have been happening, but she asked my stepfather whether he thought there could be a problem, and he said no.

Maybe I should have felt anger. But I didn't. I felt grief. A huge *why?* rolled under my skin, but I also felt her loss. Her vulnerability. She had seen me—and she hadn't been able to see me in that shed. It was a place she couldn't go. She had been wounded by men like my step-grandfather, and so she couldn't see me there or else she would have had to face the painful memories of her own rooms. Rooms that had left her split in two.

---

[3] Ibid.

Chapter 13
Precious Scars

There is a crack in everything,
that's how the light gets in.
—Leonard Cohen

Wherever you are, whenever you are reading this
YOU NOW HOLD SOME PIECES OF THE PUZZLE OF MY FAMILY'S LEGACY.
The experiences of many are far worse. I wondered whether I should share all of these details. Was it important? Helpful? Would you be able to see beyond the trauma and recognize the gifts of strength that happen when you survive? Would you see my mother as an intelligent seeker? The creative beauty? Or the fractured woman struggling to stay out from between cracks, tripping from silent, to musical, to flaring defensiveness? Could your answer be equally "all of the above" for her? For each of us? Do we have to be unflawed to be worthy? My mother's wounds and brilliance taught me to see the possibility of between. The art of precious scars.

The Japanese art form kintsugi mends broken pieces of pottery with gold. There is no attempt to disguise the damage. The cracks are highlighted and refined rather than a reason for disposal. The cracks themselves transform a broken cup into a jewel. Sometimes, in repairing things we increase their value. This is the art of resilience. Each of us can seek and find positive ways to cope with traumatic events, learn from negative experiences, and take the gifts from them—and witness for ourselves that all our experiences make us each unique, precious.

Chapter 14

Sticks, Stones, and Gravity

These mountains that you are carrying,
you were only supposed to climb.
—Najwa Zebian

Whidbey Island, 2002

THE GRAVITY OF THE SHED GRADUALLY LOST ITS POWER OVER ME, ONE
orbit of release at a time. I forgave myself, as mystifyingly all those who are attacked must do. I forgave my mother. But could I forgive the man who hurt me
most? Surprisingly, it was not the man in the shed; I had opted for making him
obsolete. The result of opening that door wide—he held no more power over me.

The man I struggled to forgive was the first of my stepfathers, the dad I grew
up with, the one who had tossed me against floors as casually as dirty laundry.
The man who spat construction site profanity in every direction around him,
though by far the most festering of his words was his refrain reserved just for me:
"Shut up, stupid girl."

In the home that Don and I created, *shut up* and *stupid* became the "S"
words, topping the list of the profane. Our children all knew—use the S words
and I would arrive at their sides like a heat-seeking missile. "Nope. We treat each
other with respect in this family. Try again using kinder words."

As much as I had hoped to escape the black-hole wobble of uncertainty of
my stepfather's imprint, it often sucked me back in. An upper limit to my atmo-
sphere that I yearned to heal. It was that particular piece of darkness that called
to me: *Ready or not, here I come.* My dreams featured him showing up at the bottom of a sandy cliff, kicking the base of a rickety ladder of pieces of driftwood

and stone that I was trying to knot together, desperate to scale the steep cliff. I'd wake up in a sweat.

It was a dream that carried both shine and shadow. I took on a now familiar constellation: *Feel pain. Pay attention. Pray. Journal. Surrender. Try to release. Repeat.*

And then one day it happened.

Like slinging past the pull of Jupiter, I could see light cresting from a direction I had never spotted before. I could own this particular pain. I was the one that was holding the tether. I was a grown woman. I didn't even need a dad. I could release him. Perhaps he had done the best he could. At this point, what business of mine was it that he chose what he did? I could not change it. But I could choose my response.

There is a space between experience and response when we decide what category the experience belongs in: personal, affirming, deforming, or none of our business. I discovered that I could reopen that gap and change my mind. I could move it from scarring to claiming my strength and safety. His problem. Not mine. I had survived. I had my own orbit now. I could let it go.

It wasn't an affirmation. It was the burst of a supernova that had been just out of sight, waiting for me to release the chain. I watched the dueling moons of derision and defensiveness pass through each other and move on, barely objects of interest.

My stepfather called me two days later.

"Celeste? This is your dad. How do I get to your house from the ferry?"

I stared at the beige phone receiver in my hand with its tangled cord. "Ferry? What ferry?"

"The Whidbey Island Ferry. I'm here to visit you."

It had been twelve years since I had seen or heard from my stepfather.

Within forty-five minutes he stood on our porch looking much smaller than I remembered him. My children crowded around me, curious about this man they had never met that I called Dad. He wore a baseball cap, fashionable jeans, and a new-looking pair of tennis shoes, with a fishing pole balanced against one shoulder. "Fishing, anyone?" he asked.

"Yes!" Dane shouted, running to get his own pole.

"Good to see you," I said, welcoming him in.

Later that night, while Don grilled up the fresh-caught fish on the barbe-cue, I made a simple salad and washed the dishes left from lunch and visiting. I watched the best of my stepfather play out in front of my children. He charmed them with his monkey face, puffing his cheeks while he tugged on his ears. They fell into laughter. He laughed with them. After dinner, I was back at the dishes, and Don and the children were downstairs getting ready to show him our family videos, when he stopped on the other side of the counter from me, the sun setting in the windows behind him.

"How'd you do it?" he asked.

"Do what?" I said, placing another dish into the dishwasher.

"How'd you become such a great mom after we treated you so bad?"

I started to answer, "You were doing the best you . . ."

"No," he interrupted. "There is no excuse for what I did, and I'm here to make up for it." With that, he walked downstairs to join my family.

He only stayed a few more days and we would never see or hear from him again, but I saw the miracle and the pattern. Sometimes the star we wish on doesn't shine until we no longer need it to, and we let go.

Chapter 15

Turtles and Islands

There are only two ways to live your life.
One is as though nothing is a miracle.
The other is as though everything is a miracle.
—Albert Einstein

Whidbey Island, 2004

FEW CREATURES SEEM AT ONCE AS WISE AND ADORABLE AS TURTLES TO me. Which is how *turtles* became the term I used for my children—to remind me that the new speed of my life would, for a season, need to be theirs. So much living in each step: slowing to Galápagos tortoise speed to listen. Running to keep up.

Our six children were an integral part of all the activities of our days, which included building businesses and volunteering in our community. Our pace quickened as they grew. If I volunteered, they volunteered. They took on community clean-ups with us. They helped with Parent Teacher Association activity prep, including a community-wide festival I volunteered to lead. But at night, while they slept, I carved out time just for me. I filled that time with research, reading, and another life-long joy, writing. Letters to friends, family, editors, and politicians; five chapters of a novel; and a picture book about planets.

I liked to pretend that while I was writing, my sons never played "giant squirrels" on our neighbor's rooftop when they were supposed to be sleeping, but alas. When our neighbor complained that the boys were running on top of his house at night, I would go downstairs to check and find them innocently curled up in their beds "sleeping." It drove our neighbor to distraction until he installed

a giant motion-activated light sensor, and it stopped. Years later, the boys con-
fessed that it was them.

There was also the time they took one of my best sheets and lit the road on
fire. When I learned about it, they said, "Mom. We live on Whidbey Island.
There's nothing to do at night. The other kids either smoke pot or do pranks. So
obviously, we lit the road on fire." But in fairness to them, they get credit for visiting the lonely, and helping doorbell-ditch groceries and goodies at the doors of
those in need. To keep us all out of trouble, they also helped launch a nationally
renowned writers' conference. Well, that wasn't how it started, but it turned out
that way.

You know when you find the perfect taco truck, or a gourmet genuine sushi
genius tucked in a strip mall, or the best ice cream ever, and you just have to
share it with your friends? For me, experiencing the premier Maui Writers Conference was like that. After years of staring at their ads in *Writer's Digest* and a
series of miracles—I arrived! I loved every minute of the conference and returned
home wanting my other writer friends to try it, too. It wasn't just getting to swim
and "jump rope with God"—a perfectly suited phrase used by locals describing
the thrill of diving porpoise-like over Maui's ocean waves again and again. It was
also the gift of swimming in creativity with other writers; opportunities everywhere; agents, editors, and bestselling authors sharing their greatest tips. For a
writer, it was nothing short of scrumptious.

Gifted friends in my writers' group had been unable to attend. What if I
could bring the experience of the conference to them, to our whole community,
sans waves and volcanoes? I had just seen the best. It would take planning and
systems to make it easy for others to help, but I could see how the pieces could
come together Whidbey Island–style.

—

For starters, I prepared twenty notebook binders, each containing a playbook
for unique assignments needed to build our first event. Fanning them out on the
table a third time, I straightened the edges while waiting for the strangers who
had responded to my community service call for volunteers. The doorbell rang
twenty-two times that afternoon!

Most were excited. Only one said, "What makes you think this will even work? Do you have the funding for it? You'll probably go broke." She didn't even wait for the meeting to start before leaving. I may have encouraged her not to take the risk. The others selected a notebook and sat down to meet one another and hear the vision. Those who were most interested were almost as excited as I was. But the woman who couldn't believe it could happen was not alone. I had approached the Whidbey Island Arts Council and one of them asked, "Where would you hold it? We don't even have a convention center or hotels."

He had a point. Even today, much of the Island's population is rural and agricultural.

One of the council members leaned back in his chair. "What are your credentials to do such a thing?" Unbeknownst to them, they had just stirred up my secret sauce. Tell me I can't do something that I can already see, and my entire being responds, "Watch it happen."

Eighteen months later, Don and friends hung a banner spanning the main road into the seaside town of Langley that read *Celebrating Writing.* The volunteers, my family among them, worked together as 280 people enjoyed the first-ever Whidbey Island Writers Conference. It broke even financially the first year and garnered wide acclaim by its third. The conference thrived, bringing with its success much-needed tourist revenue to the south of the Island in the off-season.

The very things that made some residents feel that it couldn't happen became the reasons it would go on to be seen by many as one of the best writers' conferences in the United States. Our lack of a convention center was overcome by using South Whidbey High School's state-of-the-art auditorium, even though this necessitated arranging alternatives for events planned during the school day on Friday. As a result, unconventionally, we had Author Fireside Chats: attendees spent the day as guests at some of the finest homes on Whidbey Island while bestselling authors, esteemed poets, agents, editors, and scriptwriters came to visit them. It wasn't turning lemons into lemonade; it was lemon meringue with a swirl. It was magical.

—

I have often found in my life that when things are most challenging is exactly when creative alternatives can best take you to the next level. Things you might never have considered can grow out of the challenge itself. If you can rise above the first wave of panic and get to asking what *is* possible instead of getting caught up in what is not, entirely new options and opportunities appear.

Year by year conference teams assembled, dreaming of the authors we'd love to come join us, and planning, each person choosing a role that played to their strengths. We created an event that eventually brought as many as four hundred people annually from far and near to celebrate writing and expand their knowledge and connections. My family volunteered at every event for the next seven years. They were patient with the massive daily communications, team correspondence, and event preparation throughout the year. At the event itself, Don and the children were among the many remarkable volunteers who ran errands, served as hosts, and gave directions. My children served as ushers and snack room attendants, though, if we are to be honest, the necessary supply of Oreos, strawberries, and deviled eggs was increased in direct proportion to their stewardship. They grew up as the conference grew. Family and friends were the last to leave, sweeping the floors on our way out. We laughed about the good memories as we drove home, my voice hoarse, my feet sore, my mind already unpacking what worked and what could be improved, all the while floating with joy.

Between conferences, the work of the writers' association brought me back to something I had given up on long ago: completing my education. My friend Andy recommended pursuing a master's degree in creative writing and literature; I had never completed a bachelor's. Was that even possible?

A letter made all the difference. In my application to Goddard College's MFA program, I shared how only catastrophe could have disrupted my love of learning and the hope a college education held for me, but my commitment to showing up 100 percent was unending. What was next was in their hands. The dean himself called to invite me to join them. A letter, an essay, aptitude, test scores, and life experience all counted in the tally: the sum, a second chance.

Soon I was back in school, this time while raising six children and running a world-class writers conference. I was still immersed in motherhood, the best vocation of all, but now I also experienced the joy of creative academic accomplishments.

My workload tolerance would make a Microsoft manager blush, not necessarily a good thing but always my natural pace. Even in high school, my calendar was packed. But now the allure of accomplishing so many tidy checklists and being there for my family was a combination that drove me to work well into the night and to rise early while they slept so we would have time together during the day, a habit that is still part of my daily routine.

I woke up every day asking myself, "What if you are the luckiest woman in the world?" I had a loving family, a great vocation, and lived in a beautiful home overlooking the waters surrounding Whidbey Island. It was heavenly and a stark contrast to my experiences as a child living in poverty.

But then a gentle prompting surfaced within me, an unsettling of sorts. A feeling that I should step away from directing the writer's conference. Step away? What a strange thought. Why would I do that? Everything was going so well. I loved the team and the impact the conference was making. Only a few months later, a simple misunderstanding led to a crack in our team. Contention broke out and my usual ability to connect and bring open discussion failed. Everything that had flowed so well now felt like slogging in mud. Then a feeling of calm set in. A feeling as small as a whisper: *Ready to step away now?*

At the next board meeting, I resigned. I wished that I had let go before this "brick-over-the-head" moment. Still, I agonized: Why was this happening? I didn't understand. That night I doubled down with what I know has always held me, personal prayer. *Please. If I can do something to make it all work, please tell me how. But I surrender. I'm letting go.*

I couldn't imagine why, but I was sure it was absolutely time to step away.

Waves of grief kept crashing.

I had let go, but I hadn't. Because I had made a serious mistake. Somewhere along the way, the conference had become part of my identity. I was Celeste Mergens of the Whidbey Island Writers Association. Stepping away was heartrending.

What next?

In truth, my life was full. I was finishing my master's degree, and I had the most rewarding and challenging vocation there is, being the mother of six busy, fun, and dynamic children. So how could I possibly feel rudderless?

The Dalai Lama said, "Remember that sometimes not getting what you want is a wonderful stroke of luck." And singer Garth Brooks sang, "Sometimes I thank God for unanswered prayers."

I promised myself that I would never again fall for the trap of allowing something I did to become my identity. That's when a new and unexpected gift came to me: knowledge that not only are we not our difficult circumstances, but we are also not our roles, jobs, awards, or titles. We are far more. Our journey is defined not by the steps along the way, but by our response to them. When a door closes, or even when we choose to close it, we can walk down the hallway and trust that the next step will become clear.

Today, from this side of the experience, it is clear to me that if I had not closed the door on my chapter with the writers conference, I would not have been available for what happened next. It certainly didn't feel like it at the time, but that door closing carried a tremendous blessing, one that was about to open up the pathway to finding the mission and work of Days for Girls. In fact, the door to my "what's next" had already cracked open over a year earlier when I was miraculously invited to attend an event celebrating an equivalent to the Nobel Peace Prize: the World Food Prize.

Chapter 16

A Seat at the Table

Whidbey Island, 2003

THE NEWSPAPER CLIPPING IN MY HAND WAS SLIGHTLY CURLED AT ONE edge from rereading it. The article heralded Dr. Pedro Sanchez, the winner of the 2002 World Food Prize. I had never heard of the prize before, but I had been puzzling on and studying how to help people overcome hunger since I was a child. Now Dr. Sanchez and his team had cracked the code for reducing hunger and restoring rainforests. Just two of the many reasons he won the heralded prize recognizing individuals who have increased the quality and availability of food in the world, reducing hunger.

Almost every paragraph of the announcement fit in with some of the puzzles that were ever in the back of my mind. What if we could find ways for communities to confidently manage their own resources in ways that helped them thrive? The saccharin aftertaste of well-meaning helpers who see people as poverty leaves them feeling worse off. This man and his team focused not only on practical, effective ways to solve some poverty, but they did it in ways that included those they serve. The article got added to one of the file folders in my desk: *Solutions to Poverty*, after *Author Contacts*, *Child Development*, and *Favorite Home Designs*. Dr. Sanchez's work addressed four of my passions: reducing childhood hunger, food scarcity, environmental wellness, and inclusive leadership.

A globally renowned soil agrologist, Dr. Sanchez and his team took on healing the barren red clay hardpan where once diverse rainforests teeming with life stretched into the sky above Costa Rica. Clear-cutting had deadened soils, shaving away vital nutrients. Or so it was until Dr. Sanchez and his team discovered ways to amend the soil and reform hardpan to be productive enough for crops, and even to begin to regrow forests.

They discovered suitable solutions by listening to those they sought to serve. In Tanzania, his team tackled the thief that turns forests to deserts: desertification. His team didn't shame people for cutting down trees but rather focused on asking about the needs that led to cutting them. They learned that the local people understood that as trees became more scarce there is more risk of the desert swallowing their lands, but if they could not cook their food and keep their children fed there would be no next generation to protect. Cassava, a local starch staple, is often toxic unless cooked properly.

In response to this challenge, Dr. Sanchez's team introduced fast-growing trees that would provide a windbreak and shelter in the first year, and produce necessary firewood in the second without depleting slower-growing native trees. They found a local flower that could be dried and added to the soil, replacing the need to import expensive fertilizer. Dr. Sanchez and his team were helping in practical, effective ways because they cared for and respected the community enough to ask, listen, and respond. Imagine a world where everyone listened and leaned in to create suitable, sustainable solutions that addressed problems in ways that brought healing and new growth by supporting the leadership of those facing the challenge.

"Meet Dr. Pedro Sanchez in person" was added to my wish list. An internet search found multiple university engagements he had attended, but not where he would be. After a while, I gave up on seeing him lecture in person and decided to write a letter to the World Food Prize instead. I thanked them for bringing awareness and support to best practices by recognizing his work and that of others like him. I commended their efforts and explained that I had not been able to find a way to meet him in person, asking if they would please pass along my admiration and appreciation to Dr. Sanchez for not only what, but how, he and his team had accomplished so much.

A few weeks later, a letter and packet of information about the World Food

Prize came in the mail. I ran my fingers over its elegant pages featuring remarkable global changemakers and participants: government agricultural ministry representatives from around the world, humanitarian and former U.S. President Jimmy Carter, scientists, economists, and, yes, Dr. Sanchez. I searched the registration sheet for the cost to attend; unable to find any, I called the World Food Prize office to inquire.

The woman who answered the phone hesitated before asking, "You have received an invitation to the World Food Prize?"

"Yes."

"Then you are our guest."

Surprised, I murmured something unintelligible and thanked her. Their guest! How was that possible? Someone must have decided that I should get my wish to meet Dr. Sanchez.

Later that night our family gathered at one of the picnic tables at the beachside park in Freeland near our home on Whidbey. Our youngest sons, Ray and Reed, broke off pieces of hotdog buns and tossed them to swooping seagulls as I told my family of the amazing news.

"I was invited to the World Food Prize!"

Our daughter Ashley looked uncomfortably concerned. "Gee, Mom, I know that we tell you how good your chicken pesto sandwich is, but it's not *that* good." We all laughed, because in truth I am a terrible cook, managing to cook only a few dishes well. Her concern was well-founded. Don is the cook in our family, and a good one. To this day, I believe we are invited to parties primarily so he will bring his salsa verde. I assured my daughter that no cooking would be involved; the event was a convening of thought leaders to create change around the issue of world hunger.

Des Moines, Iowa, 2003

The wonder of arriving, standing behind esteemed delegates, many dressed in their finest colorful traditional sarongs, dresses, and suits nearly took my breath away. I whispered to Don, "How did we get here?"

"We drove here from the airport."

"You know what I mean."

He smiled, then added, "You were born for this."

Flags of many nations graced the foyer high overhead at the Marriott Hotel in Des Moines, Iowa, where we checked in before joining other delegates for the opening session. Don left after the opening event, leaving me to enjoy the rest of the day's sessions featuring speakers and reports on resources, developments, and programs successfully reducing hunger. Even their very name focused on the solution of greater food production and access rather than the problem of hunger. I filled my notebook with things that were of great interest to me. It was heavenly. As I met gifted individuals from around the world they would ask what position brought me to the summit. My answer? "I am here in the capacity of number one fan."

Don joined me at the first of several celebration dinners. He and the man who sat next to him talked about skiing. Best mountains, best runs. The joy of it. It wasn't until the man rose to speak that we had any idea that Don had been talking to Dr. Norman Borlaug, 1970 Nobel Peace Prize recipient and founder of the World Food Prize. During their entire conversation, this tall, distinguished gentleman had not mentioned his role, nor his prestige. He humbly introduced himself only as Norman and chatted about skiing. Impressive. The next day we were invited to attend the induction of the newest World Food Prize winner, Dr. Catherine Bertini.

Dr. Bertini is a woman intent on turning the world of hunger and poverty upside down. She led the World Food Program for ten years insisting that she didn't want to hear why food that was meant to provide sustenance at the most desperate of times was rotting on the docks or in storage, unable to get to those in need. She wanted answers for reaching them: by boat, balloon, or elephant, whatever it took. She wanted to know how it would land where it was needed when it was needed. No excuses. She flipped the budget to emphasize delivery over administration and encouraged her team to focus on what was possible—analyze obstacles and find ways to meet the need.

Her team learned that the military in Afghanistan had been confiscating and selling or redirecting relief food instead of it reaching the intended communities. In response, they conducted a survey asking the community to list ten things they themselves would do with more resources. Women in the community named family and community benefits for nine or even ten of their recommendations. The Afghan men that were surveyed named between one or two items outside of things listed for themselves. The team shifted to finding ways to support more of the community by supporting the women. It was decided to provide "bakery" grants, providing grain, oil, and funding for small clay ovens. It worked. Food and resources started flowing where they were intended, to the entire community.

But soon, the Taliban announced they were taking over the businesses, and women would no longer be permitted to own bakeries. Catherine, whose entire focus was on ensuring that food got to where it was scarce, without excuse, stood the Taliban down. No bakeries? Then no more grain. It took a painful ten days before the Taliban backed away from the demand and the women's bakeries were reinstated.

When Dr. Bertini stood to accept her award at the House Chamber of the Iowa State Capitol, Don and I were miraculously seated in the chamber room between the CEO of National Public Radio and a World Bank representative. Catherine announced that she would use the funding to set up a girls' education and toilets fund. She explained that school toilets were often kept exclusively for boys, a tradition that made it difficult if not impossible for the girls to attend school. She intended to build bathrooms and help girls stay in school. She shared how doing so had already proven successful. Dr. Bertini also implemented programs that helped girls attend school by giving them a measure of cooking oil at the end of a school week, the equivalent of up to a week's salary in value. Her program turned a food substance that might have been distributed for free into an incentive for families to allow their girls to attend school. Brilliant, humble, and kind, she was another exemplary leader.

As Don and I descended the enormous spiral stone staircase down to the equally spacious capitol rotunda where the celebratory dinner was being held, we stopped short. There was no assigned seating. Where should we sit? In every direction, there were dozens of large round linen-covered tables. A large clear globe lit from beneath sat in the middle of each. We didn't want to take prime seating from others more officially attending. In the end, we selected a table tucked under the prominent spiral staircase. We were there only a few minutes when a woman took the seat to my right. As we introduced ourselves I was asked the now familiar question, "And you are here with . . . ?" Others joined us as I shared my capacity as "number one fan" of the Prize, adding my esteem for and hope to meet the still elusive team of Dr. Sanchez.

The woman's eyes fairly twinkled as she said, "We are Dr. Sanchez's team." I looked up and there was Dr. Sanchez standing directly across the very large table from me. Amazing? Yes! Unlikely? There were about seventy tables in the large room, so doubly yes. I'd call it miraculous. He took a seat. I couldn't hear what he was saying but I had been soaking up, noting, and memorizing significant segments of all of the sessions, including the Millennium Village report that he and renowned economist Dr. Jeffrey Sachs had given earlier. And now here we sat continuing the conversation among his amazing team.

At one point someone lamented that it was "too bad that people back home didn't care." I asked what people at home did care about. A man who introduced himself as a former U.S. undersecretary of agriculture answered, "Mostly football."

"What if you asked sports figures to be your public voice and let them share how much reducing hunger matters?" I suggested.

The conversation transitioned to funding initiatives in the United States. At the time there was a U.S. Postage Breast Cancer stamp; part of each stamp sold went toward breast cancer research. I suggested that perhaps there could be a "stamp out hunger" stamp. The people nearest me asked, "Who are you with again?"

The woman to my right gave me her card, inviting me to consider joining their team. I was floating on air and, although no formal invitation ever came of it, I did leave with a notebook full of practical positive solutions, amazing connections, and a lingering sense that I might have something to contribute when it came to addressing systemic issues of poverty. A few weeks later, our friends Jim and Andy Clay had a question for Don and me: "Would you like to come with us to Kenya?"

We would be heading to Kenya to help them plan to build their new Clay International School campus in Ngomano as part of Project Education, Inc.

"Are you kidding? Of course! We'd love to go," I said.

I like to tease my friend Jim that what has happened since is all his "fault."

Part Two

Chapter 17

Learning in the Round in Kenya

The quieter you become, the more you can hear.
—Rumi

Kenya, March 2006

IN THE MOONLIGHT JUST OUTSIDE OUR ROOM IN WOTE, KENYA, TWO men talked quietly in Bantu, a local clicking dialect. A hummingbird language of shifting sounds. Too excited to sleep after the drive from Nairobi, I listened, quietly mimicking the resonating hum, click, and pop of the Bantu outside. My mouth and throat failed miserably at the attempts. I listened enviously to their flutter of words until sleep came.

The dusty drive from Nairobi had required a stopover halfway to our destination in Ngomano. It was a simple guesthouse, really a café with a row of rooms stacked above and behind it, but each room had a fan, bed, mosquito net, towel, two pillows, one sheet, a heavy blanket, and the thing that made it luxurious by local standards, a private bathroom with hot water. Still the heat of the night made sleep an on-again, off-again challenge.

Morning departure was early after a breakfast of hard-fried eggs, toast with orange marmalade, half an orange, and my newfound favorite breakfast beverage in the world, chocolate Milo. I was introduced to it in Kenya, where they serve it with hot goat milk. Warm, rich, and not too sweet. I learned to pronounce it Mee-low, only later learning that other places refer to it as My-low. It, like many other words, was introduced to me through the lilt of a Kenyan accent. How we relate to things is so often shaped by our introduction to them.

—

On the way to Ngomano, red dirt roads transitioned from standard roadways to ribbons of carved ridges with gaping ruts so deep that the driver asked us to get out and walk for a bit, concerned that it was too risky for occupants. No one complained. It was a beautiful day. We walked past thorn acacia trees. Bright yellow southern masked weaverbirds dipped in and out of their dangling tear-shaped nests. The flare and dash of them among the trees were rivaled only by single-use plastic shopping bags that fluttered from branches and clustered in roadside brush and in muddy tangles against rocks. The amount of plastic puzzled me; people and dwellings seemed few and far between. Where was all the plastic coming from?

Our new friend Julie Ndinda, who was born in Ngomano, explained that local Kamba people have a tradition of beautiful handcrafted carrying baskets called *kiondos*. They are woven with care as a bride's gift to take with her to the home of her husband. But baskets were left at home now in favor of the perceived status symbol of purchases: single-use bags. With no real disposal solution, plastic grew to be a compounding problem.

My mind started cascading through ideas: Could they be melted to manufacture something useful locally? Perhaps sandal soles? Stools? Woven into beach mats that could be sold elsewhere? A friend would later buy me a *kiondo* made of single-use bags, but no amount of kiondos would make up for the number of plastic bags that were left fluttering in the bushes and trees. In 2018, Kenya, like more and more places in the world, wisely banned single-use plastic bags.[4]

We hopped back in the vehicle, only a few hours to go.

—

Drought had turned the soil in Ngomano to dust and cracked curls where mud had been. The river was dry now, only stones and sand dotted with holes

---

[4] Days for Girls followed suit. Replacing the Ziploc bags in our DfG kits with new washable, moisture-proof carrying bags became our choice to leave the fluttering to birds, not bags.

hand-scooped by children remained. Children perched within them, digging for muddy water cup by cup to fill and carry their cans to homes miles away. Wells in Ngomano are costly, needing to be drilled deep enough to avoid hitting arsenic-laced water. Julie knew firsthand how much the drought affected her homeland. Her husband, Benson, was leading the Project Education, Inc. program there in hopes of improving things.

We passed round thatched huts, home to children who ran after us shouting *"Muzungu!"* as we waved to them.

"What does it mean?" I asked Julie.

She chuckled. "White people. Though it is translated as 'chicken running with its head cut off.'"

Local families seemed to favor small, round clay and thatched huts. Julie explained that they felt round structures allowed rare breezes to swirl through them easier, giving people relief from the scorching heat. In square buildings, the breeze is stopped. The wisdom of such a design seemed obvious after that. I recalled the many abandoned buildings and projects, all along the route. Was it insufficient funding, lack of community buy-in, or perhaps even failure to incorporate local design that led to their abandonment? Julie said it was all of those things.

When the red road reached the village of Ngomano, it was not obvious that we had arrived. There were two loosely constructed lean-to shops featuring what appeared to be only a few essentials balanced on slim boards and dangling from nails. A spotted goat tied to the closest shop bleated a greeting, but no one else seemed to be there, not even in the shops, except for Julie's mother, who smiled and offered candies to each of us. "Everyone is waiting at the school," she said.

One more turn and the school property was in sight. The women, dressed in brightly colored fabric wraps, came into view just around the next turn. Their head wraps were the only thing between them and the searing sun, but despite the heat they broke into their traditional greetings as our vehicle approached. Their parade of welcome surrounded us. At the front, an elder woman kept the beat with a tin whistle held within her teeth. Shaking her shoulders, she stomped, her traditional beaded coin belt clattering like tiny tambourines. We piled out of the vehicle to join the processional dance. Stomps. Trills. Smiles and undulation. We tried to join them in song, mimicking the words they repeated but ended up merely mumbling in tune, later learning that the words were English, with the lilt of their Kamba tribal dialect. Our ears were not yet attuned to the accent. We had far more to learn about listening on many levels.

The local Kamba project leaders walked the length of the slope of the school acreage, showing us potential classroom sites. It seemed fitting to ask if the classrooms should be traditional round structures, which they chose to do. I was so focused on envisioning the potential of round classrooms that I ran straight into an acacia branch. One of its thorns, sharp and sturdy enough to pierce a tire, had no trouble piercing my nose. I pulled it out as I hurried behind the others.

After lunch—a stew of beans, rice, and corn called *githeri*, served with fresh chapati, round tortilla-like bread used to scoop up the meal—it was time to start building classrooms. Many in the community were on hand as we began to sketch possible building locations in the dirt. The team became a living compass: two sticks with a string stretched between us. One stick was held tight in the middle of the proposed building site, another person measured from there to the intended size, then another walked the circumference, stretching the string taut until a full circle was etched into the ground. Circles bloomed in the dust. Soon there were only two locations left to complete.

"It's time to rest," one woman said, gently guiding us to the shade of trees as others had already started to do. We chatted with those who spoke English and smiled with those that didn't. Perhaps a half hour later, I decided to jump up, convincing one other to join me. After all, there were only two circles left. We could do it in just a few minutes even in the blaze of midday.

The community watched with quiet interest from the shade. We wilted within minutes as we finished the last two circles before retreating, red, thirsty, and now aware of the wisdom of their timing for shade. I was being Muzungu. I committed to being less so in the future. Our hosts wisely arose only after the heat subsided a bit before starting to dig together, expertly managing traditional hoes to carve the foundation space in swift expert chops. All in preparation for the brick walls to come.

A few of us turned our focus onto the purchase of a brick oven and clay bricks for classrooms. Local leaders pointed out a similar brick oven on the neighboring property, a beehive-like brick dome structure stretching perhaps as high as ten feet.

Don asked how much it would cost to build a brick oven for the school's construction. "Six thousand U.S. dollars," was the reply.

That was a lot, but the oven would be used to build several classrooms.

"How much are the bricks themselves for these first few classrooms?"

"Six thousand U.S. dollars."

Pointing to the neighbor's oven just up the hill, I asked, "What if we rented their brick oven? They would gain income, and we would save, allowing more funds for classrooms and supplies."

The local brick mason answered without any change of expression, "This will not work."

I spent the next fifteen minutes, as the Kenyan heat continued to bake us all, diplomatically explaining in every way that I could how such an arrangement would be a win-win, but the answer remained the same: "It will not work."

More community members were now gathering in preparation for working together, a requisite of the Clay Foundation, as this school and the stewardship of it would be theirs from the first brick. They looked on patiently. The discussion continued. But we couldn't just all stand there negotiating brick ovens.

The local builder changed the subject. "Where do you want the oven to be built?"

No one answered.

The property was on a slope, so the oven should probably be built on the high end of the property so it would be easy to transfer the bricks down the hill. Oh, and not too close to the classrooms because we wouldn't want the heat from the ovens to make it hotter for students as additional classrooms were built. "Right? What do you think?" I asked.

Calmly, the builders again said, no, that wouldn't work either. Frustrated that my communication was so lost in translation, I finally asked why. The answer came swiftly from a few people speaking at once; the bricks we would use to build the classrooms *were* the oven.

Bricks are formed and stacked in the shape of the oven. A fire is built in the tunneled opening at the base where it is stoked and partly covered as the bricks cure. So, we could not rent the neighbor's oven. And it was not wise to build the oven far from the classroom sites. The oven was made of the actual bricks used to build the classrooms. They were one and the same. I wasn't being patient with them. They were being patient with me.

It turns out that you can't have your oven and your bricks too.

———

The rest of the afternoon went smoothly. We were on the same page now. Don started allocating funding.

We would have the pleasure of returning again and again with others to share potential solutions with the communities, letting them select their preferences, implement new ones, and return to report their progress and desires. I learned to listen first. Ask second. What did they see? What did they want? Culture, language, and even whether you are distracted or not when you hear something can affect vital understanding. For years to come, the oven lesson held under the baking sun would go on to serve me and Days for Girls, the organization that I would soon found. Listening, really listening, not only honors the wisdom of those you serve, it also saves resources and time, and builds better outcomes. I would soon learn things that were far more difficult to hear.

Chapter 18
The Tracks to Kibera

To pay attention. That is our endless and proper work.
—Mary Oliver

Kenya, October 2006

DAYS LATER WE WERE FOLLOWING WAITHAKA, A MIDDLE-AGED KENYAN dignitary, who was far outpacing us all despite one of his shoes being elevated by more than two inches to level his gait. We hurried after him along the railway tracks above the slums[5] of Kibera. One of the largest slums in the world, it stretches down from the tracks into the horizon like a sea of rusty corrugated metal. I was distracted by the lively and resourceful trade all around us. Women sat along the railway with colorful shawls spread before them covered with tiny dry silver fish, small tart oranges, or a few fresh tomatoes for sale. A man dusted his shoes for sale lined up in the dirt beside the track. Others carried sticks dangling with wares that ranged from batteries to sunglasses. Children balanced colorful plastic bowls on their heads, each bowl filled with fruit or freshly roasted peanuts wrapped in small paper cones.

---

[5] The term slum has become a bit controversial to some people over the years. While some have argued that the term should be abandoned, so far, every replacement term seems to be either incorrect or becomes synonymous with the word slum. Changing the name does not bury the issues, nor reduce the complications. After consulting with friends and associates who live in or near slums, all of whom assured me that they refer to their own communities by the term slum, we are using their term here. See also: https://www.bloomberg.com/news/articles/2017-10-10/the-case-for-retiring-the-word-slum.

We were there to learn more about a sustainable healthcare model as a potential solution to present to the community in Ngomano. We were in pursuit of sustainable solutions to assess, propose, and, with the community's selection, perhaps implement. Waithaka shifted our trajectory, leading the way down a well-worn path toward the rows of long shanty buildings to visit a clinic model owned and operated by nurses. A nurse had just prescribed an ointment for an eye infection to a patient. She greeted us warmly as she opened the privacy curtain and saw her patient out. She and nine other nurses who owned similar clinics spread throughout the slums shared the cost of bulk purchases of medicines and supplies to keep costs down. A doctor rotated between the clinics, weaving his motorcycle through the labyrinth that is Kibera to consult on more difficult cases. These nurses built their businesses offering quality care and medications that their patients could count on as legitimate rather than counterfeit ones found at some clinics. Counterfeit medications are a significant global issue that can, of course, have serious consequences. They look cleverly similar but contain fillers, some of which are toxic. I would experience it myself in Bangladesh a few years later.

This clinic model appeared to be just the kind of solution we were looking for: sustainable options, affordably stewarded by the community, as practical and suitable as they were effective. We were discussing what we had learned when Waithaka invited us to make a detour to visit a school and orphanage that he had been supporting in nearby Dagoretti. I was initially hesitant at the thought of how it would feel to see desperate children, but I believe in saying yes to every opportunity. We all said yes! That detour would change our lives.

—

We could hear the singing of the hundreds of children before our SUV even came to a stop. They were lined up on both sides of the dirt drive as we approached the entrance of the school. Paul, our friend and Kenyan driver, slowed the vehicle to a crawl. A mob of children closed in behind us, some tapping the windows as we passed. We were all smiling and waving as Paul stopped, just as the headmaster and founder of the Centre greeted us eagerly from the building's rickety entrance.

The Centre was renowned throughout the region, and arguably the nation, for supporting talent. It encouraged athletes, artists, dancers, and education in communities where survival was often the singular focus. A row of trophies lined a high shelf in the headmaster's personal office, all awarded to the students who had excelled at talents: sports, arts, and academics, many at a national level. The narrow classrooms were filled with more than a hundred children in each. Wedged side by side on slim wooden benches, they somehow managed to remain focused on their well-worn composition books. All of this in a space held together by little more than two-by-four strips of wood and sheets of corrugated metal, the children, and the force of the headmaster who called himself Pastor.

Many of the children's parents had come to the slums in search of jobs and found only destitution, often leaving their children behind by death or desperation. And this place, where the children sang with such joy when they really had so little reason for the shine in their eyes, had taken them in. The children captured my heart.

Chapter 19
They Wait in Their Rooms

Resilience is all about being able
to overcome the unexpected.
Sustainability is about survival.
The goal of resilience is to thrive.
—Jamais Cascio

Lynden, Washington, 2006

WE COULDN'T CHOOSE ONLY A FEW, SO WE ADOPTED THEM ALL. OR, AT least our friends and family joined the many others who "adopted" the Centre itself, desiring to increase the wellness of the children there. It became a place that I regularly stopped by on my way from the Makueni district every six months, hoping to bring them the same kinds of sustainable solutions we focused on in Ngomano.

The solutions were simple but had long-term results.

Our friends Jim and Andy Clay and I had been completing intensive study of sustainable development best practices since our first trip together to Kenya. Jim and Andy enrolled in formal master's degree studies in global sustainable communities at Goddard College. Still paying off my first graduate degree, I opted to audit the studies with them. The list of books that we studied and annotated grew: Paul Polak and Mal Warwick's *The Business Solution to Poverty*; *The End of Poverty* by Jeffrey Sachs (whom I had met at the World Food Prize); and William Easterly's rebuttal, *The White Man's Burden*, highlighting the need for the global north to be conscious of how aid can cause unintended harm, were among the dozens of texts that we dissected and discussed together. That intensive exploration of best (and worst) practices led to ongoing research to discover keys to help communities own their own change.

Now we were introducing practical solutions and working with the community to strategize for long-term community-led options for our work in Kenya and the orphanage. Solutions such as rocket stoves.

Rocket stoves were one answer for how to improve nutrition at the orphanage. Two simple metal drums welded one inside the other, in essence, an insulated burning tube with a simple intake pipe at the bottom allowed preheated airflow and the ability to burn fuel far more efficiently than an open fire, which allows heat to expand in every direction. Bundles of scarce firewood were costing hundreds of dollars a week. The day that I received the photos from Masese, the second in command at the Centre, of the children smiling in front of two new rocket stoves, I smiled, too. Now they could cook the same meals using inexpensive sawdust and corn husks that cost approximately $11 a day—a huge savings on wood. The savings could then go into other things they needed. A simple solution with long-term return on investment, suiting the need they had identified. Repeat. On to finding the next solution for problems they identified.

I thought that I had found my calling in life. I could help orphanages be more self-sustaining and livable. The next eighteen months went by quickly as we moved to Lynden, Washington, and I researched and innovated ways to help and friends banded together to raise money to send support. I didn't yet know that orphanages are often one of the most corrupt and profitable businesses in the slums. And I didn't know that the upcoming Kenyan election, and the political, economic, and humanitarian catastrophe that would follow, would trigger awareness of a silent crisis I had never considered.

On the night that I awoke just three and a half weeks before returning to Kenya, with the question "what are the girls doing for feminine hygiene?" I became so focused on answering the question of how to free them from their rooms that it took me several days to pause long enough to reflect on what I was really asking. In hindsight I realized what I meant to pray for was "What can I do to help them have food to eat?" But what I asked was, "How can I help the children?" Leaving an open-ended question in prayer and meditation is risky, and powerful. I asked, and I got the answer. Period.

The children at the Centre were all preparing for upcoming national exams.

When you are an orphan, education is a vital ticket out of the slums. Exams are costly, and the cost for retakes are simply too high. Without education, the future for these girls puts them at higher risk of exploitation at every turn. The days lost to lack of menstrual care resources are crucial to the girls and so is the confidence lost when you can't quite make do.

My sister Sarah reminded me that she had leaked through her clothing many times in class until she made the decision to just stay home. A long-forgotten missing link in our confidence: toilet tissue folded in lieu of pads that were too expensive to keep in stock for our family of four teenaged girls. You just hoped that it would do. But it didn't always; like the time I stepped from the truck of a date and while saying goodnight discovered a stain on the seat. Humiliated, I rushed inside to get a cloth and soapy water, apologizing again and again. Embarrassed and saddened that I wouldn't be able to look him in the eye, let alone date him again. I stopped dating people at school and moved my focus onto building the future when my sisters and I would all have what we needed.

So how did I not think to ask what the girls at the orphanage were doing for menstrual care supplies?

Even if I was able to raise enough money for single-use disposable products monthly, and the Centre had other needs like food, they would surely use that money for food. Any of us would, and, sadly, it would be the right decision. A decision that far too many people around the world face—every single month. So, how could we help with all of these needs and ensure that the girls had something they could count on month after month?

Knowing what you can count on is a big deal.

Chapter 20

What Dreams May Come

Sometimes it is important to wake up
and stop dreaming.
—Larry Page

Lynden, Washington, 2008

GOOGLE WAS BORN OF A DREAM. CO-FOUNDER AND INVENTOR LARRY Page said: "I suddenly woke up, I was thinking: what if we could download the whole web, and just keep the links . . . I spent the middle of that night scribbling out the details and convincing myself it would work . . . Amazingly, I had no thought of building a search engine. The idea wasn't even on the radar . . . When a really great dream shows up, grab it!"

We all dream, but dreams are not all made alike. There are the commonplace random bits, disjointed playbacks of the subconscious sorting daily experiences. There are the kind that momentarily make you afraid of waking to the dark. There are also the ones that are personal visions of possibility. But I have also had the kind that I later realize are of symbolic significance. They have a certain light to them, and often I only learn their meaning over time. I ponder over the nagging recollection of them, like a puzzle piece tapping its toe at me until understanding settles in, clicking it into place.

And rarely, I have dreams that have a different feeling altogether; I can almost feel the air within them. They hold an intensity of color awash in focused filtering. That kind of dream usually recurs, returning sometimes years apart. Just a small scene without context, and each time I awake from those rare dreams I have no idea what they mean, often overestimating the severity of their meaning until they actually happen frame by frame—a real-life, not-so-instant replay. There have been only a few of these dreams. Those dreams have mattered a lot, but not all dreams have mattered alike.

Once I dreamed that our family discus fish was floating, limp and deathly pale, at the top of her aquarium, her side slashed. I awoke crying—over a dead fish in a dream.

"Lady" was more friend than fish. She came to our family the day my husband and I moved into our first house. I had set off to the pet store with a budget to buy a few neon tetras and cleaner fish for our family aquarium. When I returned, Don stared at the single narrow bag that held a solitary coin-sized discus fish. "She" looked sad and gray, almost translucent alone in the bag. I assured Don, "It will be beautiful."

In time Lady grew to be as large as a tea saucer. She was a vibrant turquoise color when excited or content, changing to shades of gray when distressed. She waggled at the top of the tank when I neared with her daily chip of frozen worm meal—a finned family friend, joining us for breakfast.

I awoke from the dream of her failed body and ran to the fish tank where I found Lady convulsing against a rock in the tank. Not dead at all as I had assumed from my dream. Her tank was just too hot. One of my children must have turned the tank heater knob at the top and mistakenly turned up the heat. I adjusted it and began trickling cooler water into her tank, hoping to intervene without sending her into shock. An hour later she was back to Lady blue.

Many would find the claim of a foretelling dream impossible; perhaps you do as well, or perhaps you too have dreams you have been grateful for. Anyone who knows me well knows that dreams have been part of my journey since childhood. Neither shaman nor clairvoyant, I can't predict when the dreams will come, nor can I conjure knowing. They have simply always been part of my experience, as much as knowing things I should not be able to know. Like the time, as a child, I looked at a man and declared, "You are broken inside. You are dying." It turned out to be true, but regardless, I learned that day there are some things you should keep to yourself. Besides, I seldom see such things. My dreams and seeing are both fickle that way. I have long held the theory that dreams and knowing are somehow part of the antenna system I developed to help me survive childhood. I had to be able to read a room before I went in, to prepare to navigate stormy outbursts that might be waiting inside.

—

We were preparing to return to Kenya, this time with experimental solar ovens for the Clays' project as well as a more sustainable well pump, while also seeking a way to bring dependable washable menstrual solutions to the girls at the Centre. A recurring dream started waking me several times each night. The dream featured Pastor, the director of the Centre school and orphanage in Dagoretti, the man whose dedication to, and presentation, of his project had been so convincing. A man whom I had come to trust and consider a friend.

He and his family lived with the children at the Centre, a detail that had always impressed me. I was touched by the fact that his family was humble enough to live where the children lived, and I interpreted it as a means to save resources and to serve and protect both his family and the children. This detail, and the children themselves, had gone a long way toward solidifying his credibility.

But then the dream started.

The dream was a five-second loop of him walking out of a room, tucking in his shirt as he left; a fleeting glimpse of frightened girls huddled in the shadows behind him; a feeling that they were not there of their own consent. And I would wake. Again and again a wave of nausea came over me as if I were seeing it for the first time. Every time I would slide from my bed to my knees and ask: *What does it mean? Should I stop helping the school? Is there something else I should be doing?* And every time the impression that came was *Pay attention. Keep working. Don't judge.* I didn't know what it meant, but I did know one thing: the dream was in full Technicolor with a cold wind blowing through it that put me on high alert.

This dream followed me through the day, replaying as I ran through the next three and a half weeks leading up to our departure to Kenya. Even as I sketched our first washable pad design on the trunk of my friend Renee's car and talked to people about the need that I had just discovered to recruit help in funding, sewing, and creating five hundred washable menstrual kits in just over three weeks, the dream followed. Many found the news that girls were going without pads to be inconceivable. It not only shocked them but left more than a few stating emphatically, "How could it be true in 2008 that anyone anywhere could be waiting in their rooms without what they needed for menstrual solutions?" They, like most of us, had never thought to ask. They too believed that a pad is easily available at the store. Or in your bathroom drawer. Since periods have been shrouded in taboo and silence, we just didn't talk about them, nor did the girls and women going without bring it up. Thankfully almost a hundred people started asking this question: How fast could we create a sustainable answer for the girls? Meanwhile, even as I tried to outrun the wind of the dream about the girls hidden in the shadows, it kept following me, leaving me its echo: *Pay attention. Keep working. Don't judge.*

Chapter 21
The First 500 Girls

You have to see the miracles for there to be miracles.
—Jandy Nelson

Lynden, Washington, Fall 2008

A SOCK DOLL WITH EMBROIDERED EYES WAS MY FIRST SEWING SPE-cialty at age eight. In time, I could create patterns for and sew almost anything I could see: a backpack, a wedding dress. I could make a yellow banana or a dragon for Halloween costumes, but I did not know how to sew a menstrual pad. Let alone a pad that they could count on month after month.

The first design was a bad one. I can say that because I designed it. It was made of white cotton because sanitary pads are white, right? It was designed to look like a pad, because it was, well, a pad.

The absorbent liners were six layers of white bird's-eye cotton stacked and sewn into an oval that looked like a pad. Which, in hindsight, was a really short-sighted idea. After all, who would want to hang a menses-stained, white pad-looking thing in their front yard to dry? I have asked that question all over the world at presentations and I have yet to see a single person raise their hand.

A second component was to serve as a moisture barrier that held the absor-bent pad securely in place to keep the pad system from leaking. The first version had a moisture proof barrier that we called a "shield," with a simple ribbon at each end that held the absorbent pad in place and snaps that held them securely to underwear. We call it a shield because it keeps the pad secure without the worry of leaks.

This pad system of shield and liners that could be layered made it possible for the pad to adjust to personal flow changes. In time the two together came to be affectionately known by "insiders" as a Days for Girls POD—a Portable Object of Dignity.

Two shields, six absorbent liners, a pair of panties, a bar of soap, and a bag to hold it all in made up our standard menstrual kit. I drafted a list of supplies needed, very simple sewing instructions, along with our target date, adding a small description of why it mattered, along with my phone number at the bottom. Friends, and friends of friends, and I began sharing copies far and wide. Their commitment wasn't about saving anyone; they personally understood the need and they were passionate about doing something to help in such a direct and tangible way. From the beginning the response was remarkable and proof of the power of people joining together. The power of we, not the power of me.

—

We had been able to raise just about enough money for food, resources, and also fabric, and a few supplies to make our new washable menstrual kits, but it was going to be close. The majority of the money had gone for food and other resources needed at the Centre. We would need help to reach the goal of providing washable pads for all five hundred of the girls at the Centre. Word of the project spread. Soon churches of different denominations, the Swan Foundation (a small family charity), and even a fraternity joined in to help. Many used their own fabric; others were happy to sew up what we had been able to purchase. Everybody was working together to help find the best deals for us on panties and soap.

But supplies were only half the battle; we had to sew five hundred of these new kits in just three weeks. Although the first kits were a much less sophisticated design compared to what we make today, it still took a lot of time and effort to accomplish so much in such a short time.

Dozens of women showed up carrying sewing machines, irons, scissors, and extension cords, their families trailing behind. "What did you say we're making today?"

Almost a hundred showed up at several congregations, machines coming to a halt as I told them how the girls were waiting in their rooms on pieces of cardboard, then bursting into double time immediately after I finished talking.

A steady flow of volunteers carried their sewing machines up steep stairs to join in sewing at a studio shop. Our machines hummed as I told and retold the story of how I learned of the need. In between I answered calls from those on the hunt for the rest of the supplies we needed picked up and delivered.

The Swan family foundation took on making a hundred kits all by themselves. Other individuals sewed on their own, individuals like Betty Ross. She was eighty-two years old when she and two of her friends took on making the first Days for Girls (DfG) pads. All three of them sewed pads and attached snaps until their fingers bled. At the time, the snaps that secure the wings of the shield to underclothes were sewn on by hand. I only learned about their pin-pricked fingers when she called, not to report the state of their fingertips, nor the need for more Band-Aids, but to say they were out of fabric and, if we could find more, they would keep going. Afterward, she tacked on a casual query into whether it was okay to bleach the few completed items that had blood droplets on them, or should she throw those away?

Betty and her two friends kept sewing, as did numerous other generous and dedicated volunteers. Betty's trio would go on to make almost twenty thousand Days for Girls Kit components in the years to come, and Betty would be integral to one of thirty-one iterations of Days for Girls pads. She even innovated her own pad, which became known around the world as Betty pads.

There was much for us to learn and do, but we dove in and started with what we did know: we had only mere days to go until a few of us would fly to Kenya to the five hundred girls who were waiting. There were a lot of late nights sewing. Three of our children were grown and on their own now and the other three were still in high school—young enough to have their own busy schedules and just enough flexibility to help. I was also prepared to bring the two solar ovens and solar light bulbs that the community had selected as the next phase of the solutions to test at the Clay International School as part of Project Education.

Don and I would be traveling with a few strong supporters of the Clays' project who would become dear friends. Our children Brea and Ray would watch over our fourteen-year-old Reed, who would care for our dog Max and the chickens while we were gone. We were also scheduled to meet with government officials regarding the possibility of a college being established in partnership with the Clays, all before going to the Centre.

Before our departure I asked Masese, "Who is teaching the girls about what a period is and how babies happen?" He answered quickly, "No one. You can." Not what I wanted to hear, although I had a hunch that would be the case. The very thought of educating the girls felt incredibly intimidating. Researching which organizations in Kenya or elsewhere offered menstrual and reproductive health education brought no results. Every Kenyan organization that I contacted offered to send a delegate to see our presentation. I politely declined and kept researching. It was enough pressure without observers.

Then Canada's Aisle (Formerly Lunapads) owners, who remain global menstrual advocates and friends, generously offered to share the content of a small booklet about menstruation they had created. With their permission, we replicated portions in a more compact version and volunteers printed and folded five hundred copies to leave behind with each kit. My days were now filled with rallying others to do what had previously seemed impossible: talk to unsuspecting strangers about the importance of periods, menstrual supplies, and sex ed.

The day before we left for Kenya, seven extra-large, dark green duffel bags were crowded in Jim and Don's outer office. Inside each bag were the results of valiant efforts of hundreds of people who had stepped up after only just learning about the girls in Kenya who waited in their rooms, missing school. Everyone was grateful for the opportunity to take care of the girls' basic needs. Together the volunteers had accomplished the impossible. Not only in creating the kits, but in talking to friends, associates, and complete strangers about something none of us had even thought to previously discuss: periods. The girls would have a product they could depend on in just a few more days.

There was only one problem. We were still fifty pairs of underwear short of the five hundred needed. We had no funding left, no supply left, and no time left to find any more. Darkness was falling as we worked to finish packing the last duffel. A friend, who had been helping double count each component, and compress the contents of each duffel for days, asked, "Now what?" She gave me *the look*—complete disbelief—when I told her that this had all been inspired and blessed and that I was sure the fifty pairs of panties would come in time.

The answer arrived the next morning.

A few weeks earlier, my friend Jill had been on vacation in Portland, Oregon, when she got the email about our period pad project. Unbeknownst to any of us, and without knowing our dilemma, she stopped at a Dollar Store and purchased all of the panties they had. Jill's son Ryan said the boys probably needed some too, so Jill added a package of four boys' briefs to the box. While still on vacation, and without knowing our deadline, Jill boxed and mailed it all to her husband's office, who had them couriered to us. A box of exactly fifty pairs of panties and four boxers arrived just as we prepared to load the vehicle for the airport. It was one of the thousands of everyday miracles that have happened with Days for Girls from the very beginning. We packed the newly arrived miracles into the last duffel, laughing with relief that every girl would have what she needed. We were officially as ready as we could be.

Chapter 22

The Birth of Days for Girls

Girls are desperate to learn and to lead.
I have met many of my brave sisters who
every day encounter incredible obstacles
to education, including war, poverty, and
even personal attacks. Yet their knowledge
for learning is never overwhelmed and they
continue to show up.
—Malala Yousafzai

Kenya, November 1, 2008

THE TRICK TO GETTING THROUGH CUSTOMS QUICKLY WITH EIGHT large duffel bags is to announce that they are filled with menstrual pads. Customs passed the duffels through without unzipping a single bag. It had only been three and a half weeks since we learned of the plight of the girls and here we were in Kenya with five hundred kits—a miracle in kindness, generosity, and determination.

After a few days of check-in at the Clays' school and Project Education Incorporated in Ngomano, we were ready for pad day. November 1, 2008, was a day that I am completely confident in saying changed the direction of my life. Paul drove Julie Ndinda, our friend from Ngomano who now lived in Nakuru; Susan Fleming of Goddard College; Janine Keblish, a volunteer with the Clay Foundation; and Don and me through the narrow dirt roads of Dagoretti toward the school and orphanage. Without a map, Paul navigated his way there, passing small makeshift corrugated metal buildings and unmarked roads. The roadside was filled with proof of determined entrepreneurship: a young man welding free-style, without the benefit of helmet or visor, surrounded by others watching on as he sparked a belly-up motorcycle frame balanced on a wooden block. People sold cell phone minutes, toilet seats, and plastic plates. You could purchase what you needed from the convenience of your vehicle simply by waving at the person who held the item dangling from a pole at the street's edge. The ultimate in convenience shopping. One child led a blind elderly man by the arm, his palm extended to passing drivers. Another sold Chiclets gum. Paul turned down the last dirt path and arrived at the school.

Once again, the greetings from the children were filled with cheer and song as we were steered to the large metal space we had arranged to rent for the occasion. It was the only place big enough to hold both health education and the kit distributions for the five hundred girls who would join us. There would have to be two sessions in order to accommodate everyone. The space was empty except for rows of well-used plastic chairs and a few stick-built tables. We lugged the first sets of duffels into the room as girls started to stream in, their excited voices echoing from the roof.

Don helped carry in the last of the duffels and then retreated outside to blow soap bubbles with the younger children and boys. Just outside of the meeting space near where the children chased bubbles was proof of another reason it was so important to provide a sustainable menstrual solution. There was no place to dispose of "disposable" pads. The single-use pads we had sent funds for until our arrival were now littered along the entire fence line adjacent to the latrines. They were curled up in the spaces of the chain-link fence and piled against the corner fence post. In fact, the pit latrines were being hand shoveled to remove the used products before the latrines could be emptied by the truck service. Worse yet, girls were retrieving used pads from the pile strewn on the ground at the end of the latrines to wash and reuse.

I hadn't thought of any of these issues. I felt like I should have. I should have known there was no disposal truck that arrived on schedule to take things "away." In fact, there is not anywhere to take them to, and in this case, it was blatantly obvious. Seeing that the used pads added to environmental and health issues, as well as to increasing stigma, we were even more grateful to have arrived with an alternative.

The first group of girls quickly filled the room, crowding onto a few worn plastic chairs and narrow wooden benches, borrowed from their classrooms. When we told the girls what we had brought for them, cheers echoed from the ceiling and walls.

It fell to me to present "the talk" about maturation, menstruation, and how babies happen. My attempts to delegate that portion of the presentation had failed. When I was a little girl, I wanted to be a singer, writer, or scientist. Never once did I imagine growing up to be a world expert in menstruation, sex, and global health. On that day in Kenya as I started my very first presentation to the girls, I was not yet an expert in any of those things, but I had gathered information and made a plan, dividing responsibilities with the team, determined to do my best for the girls.

The chatter of girls filled the room as they waited to hear what this was all about. I walked to the front and welcomed them, took a deep breath, and dove in. "Women are beautiful and powerful naturally. Today we are going to learn about how amazing our bodies are and what you can do to stay safe and strong. Are you ready?"

"Yes!" they shouted back. We didn't have a sound system, but they gave us their full attention. I explained that they had a wonderful muscular organ called a uterus . . . twenty minutes later they knew the basics of how menstruation worked, how babies happen, and how to take care of themselves during their period.

Some people worry that if youth learn about sex they will rush right out and start having it. So much so, we decided not to use the word "sex" on the flipchart page about sexual reproduction. Instead, we titled it "How Babies Happen"— equally accurate and far more likely to be seen as appropriate by teachers in classrooms. In truth, knowing the facts helps protect people from exploitation and unnecessary health risk. I think that I can speak for many people when I say that learning the "Facts of Life" left the majority of us saying, "Uh, no thanks." I have yet to know anyone who found "the facts" a reason to run out to try it immediately.

I was determined to teach the truth, with a strong measure of awe for the wonder of how our bodies work. No agenda, just facts. We hoped the girls would leave wanting to stay healthy and say no to sex before they were ready for the consequences, so they could say yes to a stronger future.

Strong health knowledge leaves all genders less likely to be exploited and more likely to understand the consequences. It's no secret that all over the world girls are often made the targets, and in some cases even used as scorecards for young men challenged to tally their masculinity with how many girls they can make pregnant. Sadly, it is the girls—and their babies—who are left to pay the consequences alone. In many places, young women are surprised to learn they have the right to say no. No one ever told them. That day I saw the enthusiasm and determination in the girls' faces, though I didn't yet know how broadly transformative this kind of education could really be.

Julie would discuss the importance of women in communities. Susan would cover hygiene. Jane, a recent graduate of the Centre, arrived just after we did. She was in college now and was greatly admired by the girls. She took on talking about standing up to exploitation. Janine would focus on finishing the setup of the kits and panties for the first distribution. We would all join Janine between our parts of the presentations and once the distribution began.

It was Julie's turn. Her broad smile turned serious as she told them about the older man from her village that had stalked her, and how she was afraid and embarrassed to tell anyone, but when she did speak out to her mother and family, they stood up for her and told him to leave her alone. And he stopped harassing her. She paused, looking into the attentive faces around the room. "You deserve to be safe and strong." They cheered as she walked back to the side.

We hadn't had time to coordinate much except to divide responsibilities for topics, so what Jane did next came as a complete surprise. She walked confidently to the front. A beautiful twenty-one-year-old Kenyan college student in a tailored powder blue dress. She looked around the room and then started a simple rap complete with finger snaps: "When a boy bother you, I tell you what to do. You tell him zip it! I said just zip it!" And with that, she took a tiny bow and returned to her seat without further comment except for perhaps the swagger of her hips as punctuation. Cheers and laughter poured out in equal measure.

Susan talked to them next about hand washing and hygiene. Julie, Janine, and Susan all helped show the girls how their new kits would work, which was tricky because there were two different versions. But we didn't hand them out yet. We saved that for last.

After we "talked facts," I picked up the small stack of eight-by-ten photos that I had brought with me. One by one I turned each photo around for the girls to see. The photos were of Kenyan women: women like Nobel Peace Prize winner Wangari Maathai; people like my friend Julie, who was present with us that day; a female Kenyan scientist. Then I told the girls there was another Kenyan woman who mattered very much, and I knew this because her needs are what had woken me up at two-thirty in the morning. I had tucked a mirror behind the photos and now walked slowly around the room, holding up the mirror so the girls could see themselves. "You matter. Your safety, health, and future matters," I told them. "We do not know if *you* are the next Wangari. Wangari did not know she would be who she is. You do not know what is ahead for you. Stand together. Study hard and know that a lot of people came together to make sure that you have your days back because you are important. Walk tall."

That poignant and tender moment was followed by what started out as an orderly distribution of the menstrual kits. Behind me, girls were now scrambling to get their own kits and the line to pick out the correct size of underwear was getting long. Janine, a former Ford model, who was tall enough to be clearly seen even when surrounded by girls from every angle, looked visibly distraught as she tried to ensure each girl received only one pair of panties, knowing that we had only exactly enough. Keeping things calm was an effort the whole team was now focused on.

Seeing that the team had things in hand now, I moved toward the door to encourage girls who had received their kits to start moving out, acknowledging each as they left. At that moment Don stepped in and snapped a photo of the first group of girls to receive what would soon be known as Days for Girls kits.

That photo captured the moment Days for Girls was born. Girls in red sweater school uniforms held up their menstrual kits and smiled, though my smile was bigger still. I was overjoyed with relief that they had what they needed now, but that feeling quickly shifted when one said, "Thank you so much. Before you came, we had to let them use us if we wanted to leave the room and go to class."

The din in the room made it difficult to be sure that I had heard her correctly.

Her companions were nodding in confirmation, but I prayed that I had misunderstood, or at least that she hadn't meant what I feared she meant. I looked around, suddenly aware that they could actually be at risk in sharing this with me.

There was a crowd of girls trying to move through, and another group waiting to come in. There was no way to focus with the level of sound and confusion in the room. I hurriedly asked a few of the girls to promise to meet me afterward so I could hear them fully. Could they come meet with us at our hotel later with others who could serve as witnesses? We offered to have Paul come back and pick them up. I watched them leave, realizing this wasn't just about pads, or even getting their days back as I had envisioned. It was about dignity, safety, and freedom.

Chapter 23

Hearing Their Stories

I remind myself every morning:
Nothing I say this day
will teach me anything.
So if I'm going to learn,
I must do it by listening.
—Larry King

Nairobi, Kenya, November 1, 2008

THAT EVENING FOURTEEN GIRLS AND A FEW YOUNG MEN CROWDED into our hotel room upstairs where Janine, Don, and I waited to meet them. One of the teachers, Aggrey, had come with them. We offered them soda and cookies and then invited them to share only what they themselves had experienced or witnessed. I would take notes.

Nothing I could have expected prepared me for what they shared. They were not only being asked by the headmaster, Pastor, and some teachers to trade their bodies for a single-use pad, but some were trafficked to pay for their school exam fees—fees that donors had already paid for. The same waves of nausea I had felt after my dreams hit anew. Finally, Evelyn, a student who had sat quietly in the corner listening as each reported, spoke up. She said that her sister had been sold from the Centre and sent away, but she still didn't have the proof she needed.

For weeks she had gone to Pastor to report her sister missing, but she was told that no one had seen her sister. She asked Pastor for help finding her. Pastor would simply say, "She just went that way."

Evelyn went from place to place in the overcrowded school calling her sister's name. Since they were orphaned, her sister was all that she had left. Then Pastor started claiming that she never even had a sister; telling visitors that the girl had mentally "slipped" because of tragedies in her life and now walked aimlessly calling for a nonexistent sister. Evelyn saw the looks of pity in the eyes of those who believed Pastor's words just before she became invisible to them and they turned their focus to Pastor and other things.

I closed my eyes for a moment, then touched her arm. She leaned into me. Aggrey, who grew up at the Centre and now taught there, spoke up. He had taken up Evelyn's cause having remembered her sister, and was now convinced Pastor himself had sold her. Aggrey eventually tracked down a small photo of the girl's sister at great risk to himself. Next, the girl's boyfriend spoke soberly of how he too was looking for more clues when Pastor's gang of boys—boys who grew up at the Centre—had cornered him and beaten him so badly that he was hospitalized for several days. He raised his casted arm as proof of the broken bones from the encounter.

Another wave of nausea washed over me. I continued noting their testimonies as fast as I could, having them slow down on occasion, and repeating back to them for confirmation I was capturing the details correctly. As their stories tumbled out, I ached at the thought that I had been helping this man's cause for the past year and a half. I had helped him whenever I came into town. I had intended to help the children, but what I sent clearly benefited this "pastor" as well. As I now looked into the earnest faces of those in front of me, I no longer had to ask what I had gotten myself into. This was the stuff nightmares are made of right in front of me.

Thankfully, our practice had been to fund specific things: stoves, livestock, and exams for which we expected immediate receipts. We had photographic evidence of each purchase. But I was not naïve; I realized now that there was no way to know how much of the support we had so diligently sent had actually been benefiting this man. I took responsibility for asking for support for the school, and I would not turn my back on the children now. However, I knew we had just sent a considerable amount of money for exams. Those funds were for the children and had to be protected and used for their intended purpose.

Luckily, I knew who to call.

Magdalene Wambua, a friend, was the acting Minister of Education at the time. When she heard about the situation, she offered to help ensure that the funding for exam fees for the children would not benefit Pastor. It worked; with the pressure of her position, Pastor paid the fees. However, we soon learned that he had received funds for fees from two other people as well. At more than $90 U.S. for each student, this was a small fortune, and no small feat for everyone to have fundraised. I had stepped into one of the most profitable scams that occur in many low-resource settings throughout the world—orphanage corruption.

By the time the girls all finished testifying at the hotel, it was dark and we couldn't convince any taxi driver to take them back to Dagoretti at night. "It's too dangerous," one said. "My life is worth more," said another. In the end, we had to pay two hundred dollars for two taxis to take the risk of getting them back. I wished they didn't have to go at all.

Don and I called Waithaka and I shared my notes with him. He arranged for us to meet with the chief of Dagoretti in two days' time.

Chapter 24

No Remorse

You can't go back and change
the beginning, but you can start
where you are and change the ending.
—Anonymous

Nairobi, Kenya, November 2, 2008

THE NEXT DAY PASTOR AND MASESE ARRIVED AT THE HOTEL FOR A meeting, not yet knowing we knew of their crimes. When Pastor arrived, the hotel security guards took Don aside and asked, "Is this the man that you said is coming to meet with your wife?" When Don confirmed it, the guards said, "This man is very dangerous."

My meeting with Pastor was short. I told him of the accusations. "These children trust you. Harming them, using them, is inexcusable. You have done much good for thousands of children, but the things you are doing to them will not go unpunished. Exploiting children is not only illegal, it is vile. You call yourself a man of faith, yet these are some of the worst sins you can commit. If you do not stop and move out immediately and put advocates in place that the children can report to, it will be grievous for you."

I thought he would deny he had done anything wrong or at least defend himself, considering that he should be afforded the chance to redeem himself. Instead he became oddly quiet, folded his arms, and stared at the floor for three heartbeats, before returning to his intended subject of budget and support without comment. It was as if the children were negotiable. As if they could simply be set aside.

As he left, I heard him tell Masese, "See, she knows everything and she still supports us." I marveled at his delusion. The guards kept an eye on him as he left.

We spent the evening transcribing notes from the witnesses, preparing for the next day when those who were unwilling to stay silent any longer would get their chance to testify.

Chapter 25

The Chief of Dagoretti

Pay Attention.

Keep Working.

Don't Judge.

Dagoretti, Kenya, November 3, 2008

THE CHIEF OF DAGORETTI COULD MEET WITH US NOW. WITNESSES HAD been waiting on makeshift benches, stretched conveniently beneath shade trees along the road just to the west of the chief's single-story office.

A few minutes later, more than a dozen of us were escorted in. Chief Mary's office was a humble one, but it was neat and tidy. It had a single desk and a few chairs and file cabinets. A Kenyan flag hung near a photo of the president on the wall behind the desk. Because of the size of our group, an extra bench was brought in from outside and placed along the wall under a framed map of Dagoretti. Janine expressed concern when a second bench was placed in front of the doorway. "What if there's a fire?" We all laughed.

Chief Mary greeted us warmly. She looked to be the professional she was, her blue uniform well pressed: a trim dark blue skirt and blue pumps. After we settled in, she asked what brought her the pleasure of the meeting as if Waithaka hadn't already briefed her to get this appointment. Waithaka formally introduced us, giving her the highlights of the matter. I passed her a copy of the notes I had taken the day before. Waithaka was just explaining the nature of the recorded testimony when the fuse box near the office door popped, sparking into flames that fizzled into black smoke that flumed through the office.

Everyone evacuated calmly. Those sitting on the bench blocking the door carried their bench out with them and the rest of us followed.

"I told you so," said Janine.

The flame was short-lived but the metal taste of the smoke lingered. We waited outside while the staff waved file folders, trying to force the smoke and acrid smell from the building. The chief stayed inside. The sun beat hotter than the heat from the sparks of fire. Janine, Susan, and I combined our shillings to order sodas for everyone from a nearby vendor. Sipping our drinks, we chatted about everything except what we had come to disclose, while awaiting the signal to return.

Perhaps forty-five minutes later, we were told the chief could resume our meeting. She seemed just as composed as before. Patiently, she invited each witness to share their stories one by one, including Pastor's wife, who had joined us, testifying that she knew what was going on but there was nothing she could do. She begged the chief to intervene.

The chief listened to it all, leaning forward in her chair, nodding intently at all of the right moments. I was impressed by her present and focused bearing. She did not speak again until the last witness had finished.

Only then she said, "I've also known about this for years. But what would you have me do? Right now, there are two-year-olds whose last parent has just died of AIDS. These children have no way to get water or food, and so they go hungry. Families passing by are struggling to feed their own. Pastor picks those children up and takes them to a place where they have shelter and food, and gives them a quality education. What would you have me do? I have no funding to help them. I have no shelter to give them. For the sake of the many, I must turn my back on the few."

Her passion and sincere caring were painfully evident. I did not want to hear this kind of reasoning, but the reality of bearing such a struggle was clear. After having been admonished for weeks in my dreams—*do not judge*—it was especially raw. In our short time together, I had already seen many signs of her quality leadership. She was a leader with harsh options.

She turned to me and said, "You don't understand. He's one of the good ones. We have some here that are far worse."

The chief explained that many of the orphanages were corrupt. Some of the children were not orphans at all, but taken to generate a profit for a few, in places where it behooves them to have children looking pathetic. They use children, making them endure miserable conditions, at high risk of being trafficked and becoming cogs in the personal money-making machines of a few. Orphanages can be very profitable—corrupt—businesses, even if they do help many.

She sent for Pastor.

Fifteen minutes later Pastor came in smiling, wearing a new hunter-green suit and trendy new shoes I had never seen before. He paused, looking surprised to see us. Then looking around the room, he stared at Waithaka and then back to the chief. He didn't look even once at his wife. The chief told him of the testimony given against him. He didn't deny it. Instead, he said, "What is this? I do so much good for this place."

In the awkward silence that followed, the stark contrast between him and Waithaka was startling. I spoke up. "This man, Waithaka, serves as a leader with the CDDC[6] and is a successful accounting professional who is widely trusted. A man who has given generously to Pastor's cause in the past. He came here with us for one purpose, to make sure that the voices of these witnesses are heard. We commend him for that. Please also take note of his tattered sleeve. I mention it as a badge of honor. This man has access to many funds he could take through corruption but he does not. Instead, he continues to give. But here," I said, pointing to Pastor, "we have this man who claims to be a servant to this community and to the orphans. Everyone gathered here acknowledges that he has done much good but we also must witness that he has become corrupt. This suit, this brand-new suit, these brand-new shoes speak for themselves, but they are not alone in their witness. Those gathered here have come with nothing but courage to stand up for those too afraid to speak." It was perhaps a tad dramatic, but that is the exact phrasing I used. I recall it because the moment held such intense emotion that it is indelibly written in my being. The evidence was in front of us in living linen and stitches.

---

[6] The Community Driven Development Committees was created to allow communities to participate in deciding how to allocate designated government funds, selecting which proposed large building projects they want to see funded and even, in some cases, when funding will be released, which was hoped to reduce corruption where contracts had been paid out without completion as a political favor.

Pastor glared at me coolly and looked back toward the door, which once again had a bench full of witnesses blocking the way. Aggrey was the last to stand. "We all witness that there is corruption and abuse at the Centre." The man who called himself Pastor finally sat down. They each bravely testified and then the chief dismissed Pastor, saying he should expect contact from her, and he left.

"What's next?" I asked.

She looked at me for longer than was comfortable. "I could send him away, but then who would stay with the children? Will you? Will you stay with the children in Dagoretti at night? Will you?" I wished I could answer yes. We both knew I could not.

"For the sake of the many, I must look away from the few," Chief Mary said again, her expression certain, weary, and resolved.

The message of the last few weeks echoed yet again: *Don't judge*. But I didn't need the reminder. The weight of too few resources and crushing obstacles and consequences was evident. It was clear that she was determined to do her best and was thoughtful and dedicated in doing so. Lucky community to have her.

But I could not look away. Not when so many were being abused in a place that I had promised to help. Not when so many risked coming forward against this powerful man. The girls deserved to have someone stand up for them. I believed Chief Mary. I trusted her. I just couldn't quietly step away. Inequity grows in the shade of silence.

Chapter 26

Home Again

Eyes that look are common;
eyes that see are rare.
—J. Oswald Sanders

Lynden, Washington, 2008

SMILES SPEAK NEARLY EVERY LANGUAGE. THE GIRLS' FACES IN THE photo, holding their kits, were undeniably joyful. The good news of how they celebrated their new menstrual kits was easy to report to everyone when I returned. But there was no easy way to tell volunteers about the cost the girls had been paying for lack of period products before we came.

I felt a wave of dismay each time I told of how the girls were being exploited. Volunteers were all as stunned as I had been. We were determined to free girls from their rooms, to end the isolation of sitting on pieces of cardboard during their period, and that seemed big enough. Learning that they were being exploited in exchange for a single disposable pad left most speechless, and then angry. Betty shook her head. "Oh my. I never thought... Oh my."

The stakes were higher than any of us had even imagined. Still, many found it almost impossible to believe that this lack of menstrual products could be happening anywhere else other than this orphanage and school. There were no stories on the internet. I invited everyone to ask organizations they knew to inquire and report back.

Reports of the need started coming in almost daily from all around the world; many people were surprised that it hadn't come up before. The requests for our washable menstrual kits grew in direct proportion. Volunteers redoubled their efforts and talked to anyone who would listen about the need. Word kept spreading. My phone was ringing more frequently every day.

"Time to give this project its own name," I said to my friend Audrey, taking a moment from coordinating the Boys and Girls Club auction we were working on together.

The brainstormed list of names began. "Let's think, what does this project do?" I said, starting the list out loud. "It frees them from their room. It gives them their dignity back. Wings, we could call it Wings. No. It helps them be safe. It's a doorway to vital health knowledge. It gives them back their days . . ."

Audrey said, "That's it! Days for Girls!"

It felt exactly right. I didn't know how much so until I returned to Kenya six months later and asked a group of fifty women being trained as Ambassadors of Women's Health educators (our successful education program for those who distribute kits) what they called their periods. One woman told me, "We say we are on our days." Perfect!

It never ceases to amaze me that after all my searching for keys to reverse cycles of poverty and violence against women, a simple bag of sustainable menstrual care products could serve as both a passport to freedom for days and a doorway to vital health education and conversations that shatter stigma and shame.

Our youngest son, Reed, the only one of our children still living at home by this time, was now a high school student with a mom whose reputation for having a passion about pads was growing. It's not every high school boy's dream, but he and Don became constant champions, repeating the story of what had happened when people questioned whether period poverty could possibly be a real thing. They became two examples of a Days for Girls miracle: they were willing to talk to complete strangers about periods. Let's be honest—most people would rather talk about diarrhea than menstruation, but more and more were braving it. We continued to invite the doubters to inquire of others. Soon groups in Haiti, Uganda, and Sierra Leone called for DfG kits. Within a month of our return, I created our first website so others could easily join us.

By day I encouraged and supported volunteers who had become cherished friends as we worked tirelessly coordinating supplies, communicating, and advocating for why menstruation matters.

At night I worked to stop the exploitation at the Centre, hitting every time zone to keep things moving, checking on news from Kenya in between everything else. I lost my ability to sleep soundly, working eighteen to twenty hours a day sharing the testimony of those at the Centre with anyone who might intervene. From Kenyan Members of Parliament (MPs) to embassies, churches, child welfare organizations, and past supporters. You would think that Chief Mary's admonition to look away for the sake of the many would have been enough to hold me back. But I felt driven to stop the abuse.

Aggrey was too. He spoke up again and again. Pastor had him arrested under false charges of theft. In Kenya, you are guilty until proven innocent. Such retribution can be deadly. Aggrey waited in a crowded jail, lacking bedding or even a chair. Scant food rations and sanitation make the experience truly punitive even while waiting for trial. Supporters and friends sent money to buy food and to bribe guards to give it to him. There was no guarantee those awaiting arraignment will receive the support sent, but we tried. Aggrey waited there four long months before his case was thrown out for lack of evidence. Thankfully, former supporters of the Centre who now knew the truth rallied to do whatever they could to help him. Aggrey was set free. Pastor kept running his Centre.

All the while, feedback from some of the girls was coming in. The pads were helping them stay in class. The design that snapped to attach the pad to panties was most appreciated. They explained that they had tucked their new pads under their mattresses to dry. Why? Plain white menstrual pads showed stains. Who wants to hang a stained menstrual pad in public to dry? Nobody.

I hadn't thought of that, but I did think to ask questions, listen and respond. The feedback kept coming; the few experimental string belt shields we sent were not as successful. The strings didn't stay secure enough. Check. ✓ Check. ✓ And check. ✓ We kept innovating in pursuit of a design that would work best for them.

—

Pastor was arrested three times. Each time he bought his way out. And he did it with the money he made from selling children.

On the third occasion when the police came to get him, we were told that he used the children as a shield between himself and the police. The children obeyed him, happy to protect the man they felt was their only hope. I was warned that he allegedly put a price on my head. I don't know for how much or even if it was true, but Kenya is a big place. I continued my work there, adjusting by keeping my travel dates and destinations private, only revealing details to local organizers whenever traveling to Kenya. Though once, a partner posted news ahead of time that I would be conducting a workshop. Word came that Pastor knew when and where I was coming. Though it broke my heart, we had to shift to another venue for the sake of those we serve with, only revealing the new location to our close contacts to avoid it happening again. Exposing others to the danger was not acceptable.

After Pastor's third arrest, the Centre had been temporarily closed and children were sent to other homes.

For a time, I too tried to help with some of their housing, but that effort was a rock I could barely move. Two tugs forward, one landslide back. Funds I sent were "stolen." Those who had offered to care for the children were feuding. Though we were trying to give their new home sustainable community infrastructure, it could only happen with sufficient local support and the swift shift meant there was no structure yet in this new place. The quality of life we wanted for the children could only happen with strong local leadership. Meanwhile, Days for Girls spread like a sail with its own wind. Girls and teachers who participated in Days for Girls reported returning to classrooms and even standing up to child trafficking and exploitation. Their strength and stories kept us running to match the momentum. Now I woke up early because I couldn't wait to continue the work to grow the movement. As it grew, I realized that I needed to choose. I could continue to be embroiled in trying to address the Centre's problems, a compounding tangle of issues that morphed with each intervention. Or I could lean all in with Days for Girls. One was growing in impact by the day.

One was in continuous chaos no matter how much we tried to assist. Though difficult, the choice was clear. I asked Masese to help find safe homes for the children where infrastructure was already in place. When the challenge you take on lifts you like a sail no matter the weight of it, you have found your purpose. I chose Days for Girls.

Chapter 27

Space

Lynden, 2009

WE NEEDED A BIGGER MAILBOX AT THE ROADSIDE IN FRONT OF OUR farmhouse to hold the packages of kit components coming in from far and wide. It wasn't easy to find one big enough. We found a slightly dented red "shabby chic" one at a local antique shop, where you can bet we told the women at checkout why we needed it. Some people leaned in and wanted to know more; others scurried away under the pressure of a taboo they didn't realize they were facing. We just kept sharing how much it mattered to stand up for menstrual equity.

In short order, the flow of responses from volunteers outgrew our small kitchen table, our porch, and our laundry room. We needed more space.

Don found me scouting out the unfinished basement of our cozy 1927 farmhouse as potential storage. "What are you doing?" he asked.

"Thinking of where we could have more room for Days for Girls."

"Oh no. Celeste. This is the Man Cave," Don said, looking like a man already saying farewell to his last private space.

I gestured to the nearest ten-foot section. "From now on, this part is the *She Castle.*"

Don helped me move shelving into place to separate a third of the space from where the boys had their boxing bag, foosball game, and an old sofa that mostly gathered cobwebs. In the newly defined space, we added bins that kept kit components organized and dry, and an old wood table to work from. The next five thousand Days for Girls kits were assembled by volunteers in that small space. Laughter and hope filled the basement as we squeezed past one another, "Excuse me. Pardon me," on our way to retrieve kit components. The ceilings were low enough that one of our tallest volunteers had to duck his head to avoid hitting the heat ducting. Puddles seeped up through the foundation after a hard rain, but we made it all work, and the joy we felt in doing it was contagious.

—

Soon our mail carrier gave up on using the mailbox and started driving straight to the back porch. She carried piles of parcels past tall flowers in the summer, through snow and rain in the winter. And volunteers kept organizing and packing it all. They were collectively responding to the growing demand for Days for Girls kits from organizations all over the world. Most of the growth came by word of mouth. People were talking about periods.

Soon we needed an even larger space to assemble DfG kits.

This time I turned to the empty barn behind our house. David, Susan, Jacquie, Dave, Jim, Mary, Alex, Tom, and others showed up again and again, remodeling the barn bit by bit with us after everyone's long work days and between DfG kit assemblies. Our new space came together by BYOP (Bring Your Own Pieces), upcycled with the tools and skills each had, with labor paid in cookies and appreciation. Dave brought used insulation from his remodeling sites; David brought beautiful wood pallets he had saved, which we disassembled and repurposed into walls. Amy brought twelve orange chairs. When we were done, our once cow patty–splattered barn shined fresh, bright, and ready for action.

The electrical inspector asked, "What are you going to do here? There are enough electrical outlets to run a battleship." I told him his statement struck truer than he knew; we were battling for menstrual equity. The blank look he gave me was well deserved. I smiled and moved on. The outlets were for sewing machines, irons, and sergers, of course. When the space passed inspection, we added strong shelving and sorted items into new cardboard apple boxes with bright orange labels. Shields. Liners. Panties. Washcloths. Soap. A stenciled sign hung over the coat rack: *Welcome to Our Pad.*

"Amazing." I said, staring at how beautifully it all turned out.

The guys joked that perhaps we should make the barn into their new Man Cave and Days for Girls could have the entire basement instead. Jim gestured toward one wall. "A great big antler rack would look great right between the windows." We all laughed. The next time one of our volunteers and friend Vicky came, she brought a 3D cardboard deer antler set for the wall. We all had a good laugh as we hung it, adding a Maasai necklace to finish off the look in honor of the new space.

My work, between barn raising, speaking, emails, phone calls, and family, was to organize in a way that would allow even more people to easily get involved. I started creating tools as I had for the writers' conference, designing volunteer playbooks, brochures, and expanded content on our website: how to make the kits; how to teach about periods; how to report feedback; and how to decrease the expense and labor of shipping things to us. We also added information to start their own chapter of Days for Girls.

—

In 2011, Carol Olsen was the first person to officially register a Days for Girls chapter. She learned about DfG at our Northwest Washington Fair booth. Families were walking by sharing bags of kettle corn and cotton candy, while Andy and I passed out free pencils with tiny glued-on paper tags that read *Help girls stay in school* on one side, and *DaysforGirls.org* on the other. While glass cleaner products and flavored nuts were being hawked nearby, we talked about how to scale a menstrual movement. Carol volunteered to join the effort on the spot. "Welcome to the team!" I said. I say that a lot.

She likes to say that I "voluntold" her. To hear her tell it, I called several days later to inform her that she was now the first official Days for Girls chapter in the world to be put on our website. She says I completely took her by surprise. Voluntelling is something I get accused of often. But I would offer as proof of her volunteering how she agreed that the best way to scale up would be to help those interested in starting their own chapter where they lived, to source supplies, increase production, and to help more communities in need. She definitely said she wanted to help in any way she could and agreed that being a chapter leader was doable with the right tools. All evidence that she volunteered, right?

Already heavily involved in church and community service, Carol also produced plays at the local theater, hardly the traditional retirement she envisioned after her years of work in banking and finance. Now, she added "first DfG chapter leader" to her list.

Soon our old barn was only the second of many, many Days for Girls spaces that started springing up all over the world: from Washington State to Washington, DC; from New Zealand to Canada; from Australia to the United Kingdom, and beyond—way beyond. Kitchen tables, closets, basements, garages, and entire homes were being taken over by DfG kit supplies, all in an effort to try to meet the growing requests around the globe.

Chapters are a force, and the harder they work the more awareness, momentum, and demand grows. Next, I hoped to see entrepreneur "chapters" start in the places we serve. I pictured that the leaders we heard from in Kenya, Uganda, Zimbabwe, and beyond could become local DfG entrepreneurs, like Avon ladies, only with health knowledge, pads, and sewing machines. I was wrong. It was much more difficult than that.

Part Three

Chapter 28

Zimbabwe or Bust

Everyone has the perfect gift to give the world—
and if each of us is freed up to give the gift
that is uniquely ours to give, the world will
be in total harmony.
—Buckminster Fuller

Zimbabwe, 2010–2011

THE LAST OF A GROUP OF WOMEN LINED UP UNDER THE SHADE OF THE blazing purple blossoms of the jacaranda trees that herald the coming of summer in Bulawayo, Zimbabwe. This place was Linda Guhza's childhood home. Though she now lived temporarily in the United States while her husband fulfilled a postdoctoral associate position in agriculture at the University of Florida, she returned often and brought what the women asked her for—pads. Before she had even zipped up the final empty duffel bag, women were already asking, "When will you come back?" It happened every time.

Linda was only a child when her father went blind, but she remembered how this whole community embraced her family. Her mother had done laundry and other jobs to keep their family together. Now her mother held the prestigious position of office manager for Angelina Masuku, at the time the governor of Lupane, in the Matabeleland North province. And the community turned to Linda's mother to coordinate filling an important need: providing thousands of single-use disposable pads like those that were now in the hands of the hundreds of women leaving from under the community trees of her ancestral home. When in Florida, Linda collected thousands of disposable pads along with the funds to transport them and returned every six months with duffel bags filled with supplies. This time, as she watched the women leaving, she determined she had to find something more long-lasting for them.

Someone referred Linda to Days for Girls. I was the one that picked up the phone when she called and fired questions at me, barely awaiting answers. Yes, these washable pads were comfortable. Yes, they worked well. Yes, we would be happy to serve with her.

Months later she returned to Zimbabwe with her usual duffel bags of disposables along with a single bag of Days for Girls kits to test acceptance. She chose to distribute the DfG kits at the health clinic, quickly running out. The women really liked them. Word got out. For days, women came streaming in, each disappointed to hear there were no more supplies. The media picked up the story. More women arrived.

One girl who stood out to Linda arrived three days later; she was far more distressed than the others to learn there were no more washable pads available. She told Linda that she just wanted to stay in school. She had been using dry corn cobs to stop her flow in an attempt to stay in class, but she had developed chronic infections so painful that scars had literally changed her gait. She kept using what she could find. School meant too much to stop. She was a good student. She couldn't let herself fall behind.

—

Having an option people can count on month after month when resources are scarce matters for many reasons. Dependable products are an important option. The true cost of disposable single-use pads is multifaceted. I have stood on beautiful hillsides in the Philippines where a majestic water buffalo waded through puddles of refuse in the artificial valleys and mounds of plastic and trash that children and adults climbed to comb through for something to sell or eat. Authorities in such places found the idea of less refuse to be one of the most appealing benefits of washable pads. Mountains of refuse are part of the landscape in many parts of the world.

Many single-use pads also contain harmful chemicals, while their expense and disposal issues are universal. According to *Stanford Magazine*, in the United

States alone approximately twelve billion pads and seven billion tampons are discarded each year.[7] For many but not all of us, safe disposal remains an option, though the average woman goes through 250 to 300 pounds of single-use menstrual products in her lifetime,[8] spending an estimated $1,964.33.[9] And incinerators cause their own health and environmental issues.

Usership of washable pads and menstrual cups is on the rise in the global north, which makes sense since they can last for years with no adverse health issues from harmful chemicals. People should have a choice of preference; washable pads are a smart choice for many reasons, and they are growing in popularity. We would learn again and again the many costs paid for lack of dependable menstrual solutions, which stretch far beyond monetary and environmental costs. Linda was determined to help her community in Zimbabwe have long-lasting options. We both were.

—

This time when Linda returned to Florida, it was the girl who "just wanted to stay in school" that had her picking up the phone to call me before she even unpacked.

"Celeste, I have to take back as many of those kits as possible. Let me tell you about what happened . . ."

An hour and a half later, we had a plan. She and I worked together not only to bring DfG kits as gifts from generous DfG volunteers in the United States to Bulawayo, but also to teach Zimbabwean community members to become Ambassadors of Women's Health in their own right. She had experienced how big the need was and wanted to reverse the lost opportunity and shame. On her

---

[7] "Planet-Friendly Periods," *Stanford Magazine*, May/June 2017. https://stanfordmag.org/contents/planet-friendly-periods

[8] Ibid.

[9] Allison Sadlier, "New Research Reveals How Much the Average Woman Spends Per Month on Menstrual Products," SWNS Digital, September 6, 2021. https://swnsdigital.com/2019/11/new-research-reveals-how-much-the-average-woman-spends-per-month-on-menstrual-products/#:~:text=Results%20revealed%20the%20average%20woman,(ages%2012%2D52).

next trip I planned to meet her in Bulawayo. DfG early super volunteers, Mary and another Linda, would join us to help with the training. Everyone would pay their own way.

Don came along to keep an eye on me. Few knew, but a mysterious illness had struck me over a year before.

Chapter 29

Body Wisdom

There are years that ask questions
and years that answer.
—Zora Neale Hurston

Whidbey Island, 2010

TWO MORE PARTY TRAYS WERE ADDED TO THE TABLE BEFORE MY pounding head went full vampire about the light in the room, demanding my immediate withdrawal. A migraine. There's no such thing as a good time for one, but this was especially poor timing. My daughters Ashley and Breanna were both expecting babies in the same month. Ashley's mother-in-law, Julie, was throwing a baby shower, and I would be meeting many new family members within the next two hours. Julie recommended Excedrin Migraine with caffeine, with a Diet Coke as a chaser. "It works like a charm for me," she said.

I don't drink caffeine—truthfully my energy is normally so high that the thought of caffeinating this girl would terrify many. But this was medicinal. I took it and reluctantly retreated to the dark and cozy room she offered in hopes of a quick nap to stave off having to greet everyone with dark glasses and a glazed squint.

It didn't take. I felt dizzy as I rose in response to Ashley's gentle nudging in what felt like seconds later. "It's time. Are you up to joining us?"

More zombie than celebrator, my dark glasses and I joined the party. I tried to smile but my vision seemed to phase in and out in shuttered blocks, like slow-motion movie frames stuck between sprockets. One leg cramped painfully. My head alternated between heavy and floating. Then without thinking about it, my body got up and left the room without explanation. My body knew something I didn't—I was about to have a series of seizures, and since my brain was battling bright bites jolting my skull, my body was polite enough to attempt to leave without taking over the baby shower.

Don followed me out.

The trip to the ER happened in disjointed clips. The dark road. Ashley's voice: "Drive faster." A wheelchair footrest. Bright lights. "Medication isn't working." More sounds, shapes, and shadows and then things started to come into focus. "Welcome back. You're just in time to cancel your ride on Life Flight,[10] but we're admitting you."

The damage to my brain was already grooved in, like a compact disc with a deep scratch in it. If I blinked, I fell to the left. A high-pitched ringing had taken up residence in my ears and I could no longer read well; my eyes had lost interest in working together, one drifting off on its own trajectory at any given moment.

Thousands of dollars in co-pays for scans and doctors' visits later, we still didn't know what caused the seizures, and the side effects from the seizure meds were almost worse. It took three months before I stopped falling to one side, another few months before my eyes started working together. And it was no use fighting the seizures; they would drag me sinking into the bright-sparked darkness at any moment. I'd wake up with our youngest son Reed in the chair by my bed. "You just had another one, but not too bad."

"Reed! Hi. You're home? What day is it?"

"Saturday." He always answered Saturday. I didn't catch that.

Reed would pretend to leave for school before Don went to work and then circle back, skipping school to watch over me. By the time we found out, he had somehow convinced his teachers to grade him on his work, not his absences.

Once, when I was proud of myself for making my way downstairs to do dishes, he and his dad fussed, "Please, go back to bed. You're going to fall. Your speech is slurred."

"It is not!" I answered in complete sincerity because, to my ears, my speech sounded perfectly fine. I woke up on the floor looking up at both of them.

"I told you so," Reed said with his signature twinkle.

---

[10] Emergency medical flight transportation.

It was early enough in Days for Girls growth that the phone number at the bottom of the website was still directed to my cell phone. I answered only when I was feeling best in hopes that any slurred speech would not be apparent. There is a golden tip for phone communications: "Smile and they can hear the smile in your voice." I smiled a lot, only mentioning to close friends that I was answering from bed.

Don or my daughter Breanna showed up to make lunches and check in on me. Then one day, my sister Mercedes unexpectedly arrived from Minnesota. I hadn't seen her in years. "Scoot over," she told me. "You can't hog the bed to yourself." We chatted and laughed for what felt like hours. In between our visits, I slept like a woman making up for a year's lost sleep.

Neurologists were puzzled. Year-end clicked past. More hefty co-pays and a few failed meds later, the mystery wasn't yet solved. My sister stayed for nearly a year in Lynden. My family and many friends volunteered at my side with Days for Girls as I slowly recovered. And Days for Girls kept growing despite my setback.

Then came the day when I felt well enough to feel sorry for myself. What if I never read well again? Before, I could speed-read a book in hours. Now, I was having too many episodes to even be very good at watching TV, let alone corral my vision, organize, and strategize. What if this was my new normal? On the day I started grumbling to myself about it all, I lost my G-force: Gratitude.

The license plate of my car that had sat waiting for me in the carport for over a year reads GRATA2D. For me, gratitude is more than a nicety. The practice of acknowledging blessings is a powerful lens for sorting experience. We magnify the good or the bad in our life by the focus we bring to our journey. Gratitude is a mindset and a great motivator. Gratitude is a team sport. In leadership, it helps "A" players stop to claim their ground and give themselves a cheer before charging off to the next objective. In parenting, it helps keep joy and perspective when the Cheerios are everywhere except in the bowl or the box. I'd seen its effectiveness in my life and applied it at the beginning, middle, and end of every day. But now I wasn't feeling it. I felt useless.

Still feeling sorry for myself, I tried the TV again. The flickering light actually hurt my head, but I hung in there as a marathon of the program *Touched by an Angel* played out in front of me: a family losing their young daughter to disease. I thought, *Gee, at least our children are not dying.* Next, an artist used his last breaths struggling to hold a paintbrush in one trembling hand as he took on the impossible feat of completing a final art installation so his family would have income after he passed. *Well, at least my family doesn't have to depend on income from me.* By the third episode, I got it . . . this could be so much worse. I was surrounded by loving family and friends. I might have to sit on the ground in the garden to weed. But I could still garden. I could fold Days for Girls liners. I could pray for others even when I slurred. And on good days, I could lend my voice to the movement for menstrual equity.

I started to make peace with the fact that my eyes had already read thousands of books in my life, I had experienced many adventures, and maybe my fast-forward life was packed so full because now it would need to shift. I finally started to let go and release the grief of what seemed like a lost future.

That's when healing began. Only after I let go. Trusting it would be okay no matter what. Letting go was once again a powerful transformative step.

That night I had a dream that left me feeling inspired to become a vegetarian. Don't ask. It was gruesome.

No neurologist had suggested giving up meat, and I wasn't eating much of it anyway. But I made the shift, and I increased other healthy options. Within weeks I started to feel, let's say, 60 percent better.

While it took time to learn to listen to the new rhythm of my own body more fully and to start to manage it all better, episodes were now contained to short bursts and tied, ironically, to my hormonal shifts. Now we knew a pattern for when to expect them.

My energy recovered, I no longer risked falling to one side when I blinked, and my ability to read had returned. I began to fulfill speaking engagements again. On the day I tried out for a TEDx talk it was an off day. I could barely rise from my bed, but I prayed my way to the venue and did better in that first tryout than in the final delivery. As I gained back nearly full strength, it was time to pick up the pace again. We would need more resources to do it with.

Chapter 30

The Power of We

Go as far as you can see;
when you get there,
you'll be able to see farther.
—J. P. Morgan

Lynden, July 2010

"WE COULD DO A TEA PARTY FUNDRAISER!" I SAID. "IT WILL BE FUN," I said. A supporter offered to let us use her historic home and gardens for the event.

Fabric isn't free and neither are the other components of Days for Girls kits: panties, a washcloth, a bar of soap, and baggies for pre-rinse as well. Not to mention shipping and luggage costs. We needed more resources to keep making it happen, especially if we were going to support local leaders in Kenya, Uganda, and Zimbabwe. A garden party might just do the trick. After all, the Boys and Girls Club auction that I directed that year brought in nearly $100,000.

Two months later, more than a hundred tickets had been sold. The day before the event we rolled fourteen round tables into position across Andy's back patios. Eight chairs were carefully set in place at each table, and the kitchen was busier still. Volunteers came in and out. More still would arrive in the morning.

The sun was just rising as we started placing the table linens and decorations that had been gathered in the weeks preceding. My daughters were baking tiny lemon tarts and prepping hors d'oeuvres and fillings for delicate sandwiches.

Ashley's newborn baby was sleeping in the carrier next to her as she and my equally gifted daughter-in-law Brandie stood side by side creating delicacies as daylight grew on the horizon. Soon friends and family brought their personal china sets so that each table was set in unique elegance. By the time our friend and staunch volunteer, Susan, added her colorful saucer-sized dahlia blossoms to each table, they rivaled the famed Empress Hotel's formal tea. Cucumbers and strawberries floated in water urns. If there was a breeze, the tablecloths would have fluttered in it. But there was no breeze; the sun was blazing. The ice in the lemonade was melting, and there wasn't much shade.

We had chosen the third week in June because it often had great weather and didn't stomp on many other events. Guests showed up dressed in bright summer dresses and hats. My son Reed and his friends sweated it out in their formal tuxes and tails borrowed from Carol's local community drama production as they parked cars and escorted guests to the party. Volunteers ran to refill the bowls with tasty salads and delicate treats and top the platters with sweet and savory handcrafted goodies made with love by those who had been shopping, chopping, and cooking in the kitchen for days.

Meanwhile, after working to help set up the full day prior, Don offered to take our daughter's children during the event, confessing that he was too nervous to stay. Besides, with all of us busy serving, someone had to entertain the children. He took on four toddlers and two babies, but we all had every confidence in him.

When he returned to us in the late afternoon, happy toddlers ran to their weary moms. We were just bagging the last of the tablecloths to wash later. Slipping off our shoes from aching feet, we each got a plate of leftover goodies and lemonade and sat down. Those minutes of the afternoon before going our separate ways were priceless.

Thanks to the generosity of our guests, we had raised just over $12,000, and that is a whole lot of girls who would now be reached. However, I knew what was possible. I hadn't been able to reach the people in our community who write the biggest checks. At the time, it turned out that most of them were not interested in sitting at any table where periods were the topic.

The annual event became a crowd favorite, but it took its toll on all of us, each year burning out yet another key volunteer. For us, events aren't the best way to raise money. People are. The truth is that individual donors and stakeholders who have the courage to talk about periods are our superpower.

—

A bundle of kit supplies, no matter how small, is celebrated when it reaches a DfG assembly point. They add up to reaching more girls. Volunteers send thank-you notes in response, emphasizing what is well done, and noting any quality recommendations needed. Components are assembled into DfG kits, always delivered with education. Stories of their impact come back. Repeat. It's amazing to know we really can make a difference with our own two hands. But as much as we tried to emphasize the positive, once in a while the phone would ring with a message of frustration.

"Listen. What I sent was perfectly acceptable as is. They don't have anything now. Something is better than nothing."

Yikes. A long conversation was ahead.

A DfG kit truly is a labor of love, requiring a great deal of effort. Many people submitted kit components that were as beautiful as they were practical, looking every bit the gift they are. Others arrived looking pre-worn and misshapen. How could we ever get everyone on the same page even as we grew? We added more templates and procedures. Some didn't like the extra steps.

"Quality shouldn't matter" is a toxic attitude that can entrench rather than shift cycles of poverty. It is easy, in development work, to accidentally portray those served as not just facing poverty, but rather to misconstrue them as the face of poverty. We were determined to emphasize the strength of those we serve and serve with. The harm of an attitude of rescue can cross the line from helping to believing we are the good; when in reality true development is a partnership in meeting need and best gives local leaders voice and ownership anywhere they live.

Different people and cultures all over the world have such strength and wisdom. Facilitating a true global shift in the stigma associated with periods takes all of us. We knew that if we did this right, it would be a global movement that harnessed local leadership and strength everywhere instead of solely promoting the act of giving. We knew it wouldn't be easy, but we needed to make the program as accessible to local communities in resource-scarce areas as it was elsewhere. It was time to become even more sustainable.

In the months of planning that followed, we prepared to travel to the women of Zimbabwe. Many rallied their resources, time, and talents to prepare more than a thousand DfG kits as well as Ambassador of Women's Health training materials and sewing supplies for fifty women in Zimbabwe to learn to lead their own communities to greater menstrual health. We packed and repacked in the *new* She Castle to prioritize what would come with us to support them. We planned to "train the trainers" to teach women of Zimbabwe to instruct others in making their own Days for Girls kits and to become knowledgeable Ambassadors of Health. We trusted that they could master all of it with confidence in just four days.

Women were invited from every province of Zimbabwe: chieftains and local leaders personally selected two representatives from each province to attend. Those chosen were highly respected and trusted to bring back what they learned.

At Days for Girls, a long-standing premise has been that $10 provides a Days for Girls kit for one girl; we consider every donation a sacred trust. Whenever someone suggests a large expenditure, I picture the faces of individual girls, weighing whether an expenditure will help to reach more. To save money and time, we bought a ticket to and from Zimbabwe within my existing itinerary to Uganda. Linda's preexisting ticket also dictated a short time frame for convening local leaders. As a result, we would not even know which local leaders would be joining us for the training until after we arrived. But we trusted the chieftains.

Carol Olsen, our first "voluntold" chapter leader, and I approached every group she thought might invite her to speak about Days for Girls with hopes of asking for support. One such group was Soroptimist International of Anacortes, part of a one-hundred-year-old service group that supports women, girls, and education all over the globe. They first gave Carol a donation, which she used for fabric and supplies to start her new chapter. Shortly after, at her suggestion, they invited me to speak at the next club meeting, and Carol followed up on their recommendation to write a grant proposal, seeking more support.

This welcome opportunity turned out to have unfortunate timing for me. As I arrived to meet them, my ears rang like a swarm of crickets on a hot night. I prayed to speak clearly and to make it through the full event without any neuro episode. I stood up and thanked them for their interest, and the rest flowed easily. Prayers answered, no one ever knew about my predicament and the Soroptimists came on board with $6,000 for Days for Girls International.[11]

We allocated their support for the launch materials and start-up costs for a simple space for Days for Girls in Uganda, as well as money to assist with the costs of Days for Girls Zimbabwe training candidates' transportation, lodgings, and expenses at the Bulawayo YWCA. We had done other fundraising, not only for supplies and training but also for materials. Now, we were headed out to put those resources to work and lay the groundwork with the local leaders.

Who does that? Launching a country program that would support a blooming social enterprise experiment in creating DfG kits and education in one country, and training trainers in another with just over $6,000? We did. Why? To support those who had already proven they were determined to reach their own communities at great personal sacrifice.

—

Uganda had become part of the Days for Girls journey when two different Ugandan women called in the same week asking about DfG. Diana Nampeera, a tall, young Ugandan leader who had her own girls' organization, was one of them. We met over tea at a simple hotel. She took on Days for Girls with full intent and was globally respected for her tireless ongoing work as Country Director of Days for Girls Uganda, later being promoted to DfGI Global Manager of Country Programs.[12] This trip would support the program in Uganda that was just starting to grow, now ready to take the next step in manufacturing DfG kits locally. This was the beginning of the Days for Girls enterprise model to provide jobs while supporting local leadership in making DfG kits available. These beginning training efforts would also be a proving ground for which curriculum components mattered most to them for our DfG Ambassadors of Health program. We knew no part of the trip could be short-changed.

Their sacrifice would be less necessary if we built strategy combined with

---

[11] Soroptimists International and Altrusa, which are both global service organizations focused on helping women and girls thrive, have been important partners of Days for Girls in the years since.
[12] Regretfully, Diana passed away in 2022 and was mourned around the globe.

support. We knew more money would definitely be needed and everything we raised would go straight into support.

Carol kept presenting, coordinating, lugging boxes of supplies back and forth, and cheering all the new DfG Anacortes volunteers on, choosing to later become one of the first official Chapters of Days for Girls. Together with another friend of DfG, Kathy, and some more amazing volunteers, this determined group of champions made more than 7,424 DfG kits for communities around the world, providing days of opportunity while seeding new markets and championing for breaking the stigma and shame around menstruation in our innovative hybrid program. The volunteers were equally committed to creating kits and supporting enterprise growth funding. Thankfully, they were not alone. Between 2011 and 2012, volunteers like Helen Griffin of DfG New Zealand, Gloria Buttsworth of DfG Australia, and Vida Peterson of Canada had each started national organizations of Days for Girls in their own countries beginning with small groups around tables that grew over time to have many chapters and their own country-wide charitable registrations. Their dedication proved the power of people connected with purpose. Sharing the same goals, patterns, feedback, and objectives was now giving days back to even more people all over the world.

Entrusting our patterns and curriculum to thousands of people without limitation was questioned by many. "How do you know they will do it correctly?" But even some of the earliest versions of the kits proved to serve well for years, and we were as tenacious about trusting others as we were in gathering the feedback of those we served.

The experiment in trust was worth it. We had learned, like Linda in Zimbabwe, that there could never be enough suitcases to reach everyone. Yes, the kits were a solution people could count on month after month, and single-use disposables were not only short-term but also created negative environmental impacts that most of the communities we serve did not have the resources to manage. The global efforts of so many people advocating together was building into a wave of awareness and vital dialogues. And we believed that supporting more local leadership was the way to achieve the farthest-reaching results.

Chapter 31

A Bus to Botswana

There is no force more powerful
than a person determined to rise.
—W. E. B. Du Bois

Zimbabwe, November 2010

LOCAL ZIMBABWE VOLUNTEERS DISCOVERED THAT THE CHEAPEST WAY to get quality treadle sewing machines was to travel by bus to buy them in Botswana. They made the trip happen with machines under stowage and balanced on their laps. I can only imagine the heat and crowding, with the additional weight and strain of a hand-crank sewing machine on your lap, yet none of them complained. Their effort made our twenty-two-hour flight seem a small inconvenience. Even after her trip from Botswana, Linda was at the airport when we arrived. Though we were meeting her in person for the first time, it felt like we had known each other for years. Together we went over our plans for the Ambassador of Women's Health and kit construction training. We still needed to purchase more scissors and sewing notions and research more fabrics supply and pricing, as well as get more water, snacks, and food for the next morning, and it was already getting dark.

From our time in Kenya, Don and I knew that it was a bad idea to go out after dark. We had been warned repeatedly that Nairobi streets known to be peaceful in the daytime turned dangerous at night. Surely that applied to Zimbabwe as well. We broke out Don's emergency protein bars and trail mix. We'd be fine until morning. But Linda assured us that in Bulawayo we would be as safe in the dark of evening as we were in daylight. "Mugabe (Robert Mugabe,

Zimbabwe's country leader at the time) would not tolerate violence, especially against tourists. Anyone trying to steal from or harm you would be killed. You are safe. Of course, if you live here and have land or business, he might steal it from you, but that is another matter."

We stepped out in the pleasant temperature of the night and indeed did feel completely safe, though the reason felt nearly equally unsettling. We picked up eggs, digestives (similar to graham crackers), fruit, and large jugs of water. It had been a long day. Our beds and mosquito nets were a welcome sight, both important if you want to get a good night's sleep.

The next morning, we left to pick up "Florida Linda," who was a day behind us after missing a flight. As we traveled, we got a call from the governor of Lupane, Matabeleland North, who would meet with us at noon, right after we left the airport.

A new airport was being built, but the tired metal military barracks–style hangar was still in use. We waited at the nearby sidewalk for her to arrive.

"There he is!" Linda Guhza said with excitement.

"He?"

"Dr. Coltart. That's Dr. Coltart!" Linda said.

Sure enough, a tall, distinguished man approached from the hangar. It was the Minister of Education of Zimbabwe. We had been trying to arrange an appointment with him for months. Each touchpoint proclaimed him to be dedicated and a man of integrity, but unavailable. Dr. Coltart was in demand, and here he was, moving toward us with a purposeful stride.

I eagerly approached him. After months of talking about and researching him, he seemed familiar. "Hello, Dr. Coltart! So nice to meet you. I've heard so much about you."

"And you are?"

"I'm Celeste Mergens with Days for Girls International. This is Linda, Zimbabwe's country representative."

He smiled. "I was just seated next to your colleague on the airplane! I showed her the beauties of Zimbabwe and she was telling me about your program. Here is my card; please call my office. I would like to meet with your team to discuss your program on Friday."

Another Days for Girls miracle. A missed flight and "chance" encounter perfectly positioned us to pitch Days for Girls kits and curriculum in hopes of being officially approved to engage with schools throughout Zimbabwe. A long shot if you don't believe in miracles—but I count on them.

We tucked Florida Linda's suitcases into the back of the car and went directly to the governor's office, who also welcomed our program with strong support, promising to send two delegates to the training. Next stop: setting up for the workshop at the YWCA. We had to make every hour count.

—

The courtyard of the YWCA of Bulawayo was surrounded by cinder block walls, with several large trees for shade. A bulletin board opposite the reception desk held pinned posters for land rights awareness, domestic violence prevention, and one of a drawing of the Zimbabwean bird, a national icon featured on their flag. This one had one wing stretched at the ready to fly, the other clipped close to its side. It read: *Zimbabwe will never soar unless we are all free to prosper. Women's rights are human rights.* That's exactly what we were there for, to break the shame of something they could by all rights be proud of, and to give them the power of their days back. It struck me as equally true that it is not our goal to diminish men, which would just be tucking in the other wing. If we did this right, our work would lift women, girls, and, in turn, their families and communities. We wanted to help communities everywhere rise in equity. Everyone would need to be part of the conversation. If we could create consistent value and market, then local DfG Ambassadors of Health leaders would have the opportunity to do something they believed in and support their families while doing it. This would be the beginning of figuring out how to accomplish these goals, and this place would work perfectly to host the women invited to the training.

Linda Guhza was telling the woman behind the YWCA reception counter, "We will need all twenty-five rooms as agreed."

The donations we had collected and contributed over the past weeks would now pay for fifty women to learn to be Days for Girls Ambassadors of Women's Health as well as supplies for them to make DfG kits. This time, we had not brought duffels filled with single-use pads as Linda had before. Instead, our bags held only a few washable kits; the rest were stuffed with fabric, needles, thread, scissors, and other notions for the women to learn to make the kit components.

More supplies were needed. Linda knew right where to find them—in local streetside sewing shops. Purchasing supplies locally as often as possible remains an important principle of Days for Girls.

Don and Mary returned after dropping off a few items to be printed and picked up markers for the whiteboard and easel. The last of the tables and chairs for the fifty women were arranged. This was it. The moment we had all prepared for.

—

That night we sat on the living room floor of the small house we rented to save hotel costs. The windows were thrown wide open, screening out mosquitos but not the loud screech of locusts outside. Duffels surrounded us as we recounted and arranged the additional supplies we purchased earlier that day.

Linda turned to Don. "We love you, but tomorrow you will not be able to be inside when we speak of women's things. It is difficult for us to speak of such things here. Let alone to have a man in the room. You understand? You have heard already; it is very taboo to speak of these things."

"Trust me," Don said, "I'm completely okay with that. Just say the word and I'll step out at any time." Linda nodded appreciatively and went to make more calls.

Don stood as if ready to proclaim something. "Celeste, you have to promise one thing. Promise me that you won't go too deep when you do the women's talk. We don't know how they will respond. There's a dictator here. It's different. You could end up in jail."

Our packing slowed.

"We'll be fine," I assured him. "We were invited here. We've already met with several authorities and have their blessing. The Ministry of Education is sending a representative tomorrow."

"Exactly my point. You will be scrutinized. I just want you to go easy. I can just see myself looking for a place to live while I work to get you out of jail for talking about periods. You heard it yourself. It's not even permitted to speak of these things to their mother or sister. And you know how you are."

"How am I?"

The packing had now stopped altogether. All eyes were on me. I looked around the room. "We are not doing anything against the law. What we are coming to teach is by invitation and is not shameful, nor dangerous. It is about strength and dignity. And I always teach with sensitivity, you know that."

Don shook his head. "I don't think you are taking the danger seriously enough. You have no fear."

The others nodded.

A ball of frustration formed inside my gut. Not because of what he was saying, but because my own team was asking me to back down. "I know it's sensitive here," I said. "We have Linda and Florence who will be translating for us; they will assist in the balance. We will be fine."

"You don't know that," Don persisted.

The ball turned into a blast. If you ask my adult children, they will tell you that they have only seen me angry a handful of times. But it isn't pretty. "This is not about us!" I said, my voice rising. "This is about them. And I will not back down out of fear. Why do women have to back down because of their basic biology? Why would we have to be silent about our own bodies? If I cannot speak, who can? This is what we came for! You have to trust me."

Don didn't relent. "Celeste, we're all afraid. This is no joke. I'm having nightmares of running behind a prisoner transport, pleading with them to release you. You have to take this seriously."

This was my best friend, the love of my life. I have seen him in almost every mode, and this one, with a tightening in the muscles above his jaw, I seldom saw. He meant business. Unfortunately, so did I, and we had company to witness it. They watched us quietly, heads following us back and forth like a tennis match.

"I can't believe that you don't trust me. You know that you can trust me. But I guess you'll have to wait and see. Or don't come. But I am going."

My don't-tell-me-what-to-do reflex is finely developed. In fact, few want to be told what to do. It is a response so deep in me that even I can see the flare of its extra surge at times. Especially so when someone implies, even by supplication, that I can't or shouldn't do something that my heart sees as spot-on. It's less anger than digging in, like the toes of a track shoe just before a race—ready, set. When fear rules the day, I don't wilt; I prepare to launch.

I marched out of the room into our assigned bedroom. There was none of the "bridging" that I'm known for. There was no finesse. There was only weariness.

We were all tired. But the tiredness I felt was deeper. I was tired of voices that question what is possible for women: *What are you doing in engineering? Who do you think you are? You can't do that!*

Invite me to go with you or to consider something, to see alternatives, I'm all in. Thankfully, most of the time I am inviting others to share their viewpoints and be open to possibilities. Most often, sitting down and letting others speak their truth is the remedy of a moment of fear. That would be my usual go-to, but on that day I had chosen another way. It's taken me many years to realize that having sufficient sleep helps one stay in the zone, and none of us were well rested. That night it left us in brittle zones.

—

Breakfast was less than jovial the next morning. The trust I had always seen in my friends' eyes was missing. It was clear that sides had been taken, and I had lost a contest I did not mean to enter in the first place. What should have been a celebration was muted. For me, anger has seldom, if ever, resulted in positive forward movement, not even when it seems justified, with carefully accounted proof. It shatters trust. Sprinkle fear on top and the mix is explosive. These were all dear friends who mattered to me. I prayed that somehow we would mend the gap over the course of the day. As we lifted the duffels, and shifted the load in the SUV, the fog of fear and disagreement slowly dissipated in enthusiasm for the work ahead. In the light of day our sense of purpose, turning periods into pathways of opportunity where there had been taboo and stigma, now united us again.

When we pulled in at the YWCA, Andrew, a blind man who occupied the sidewalk at the curb near the entrance the day before, greeted Don by name as we approached.

"How did you know it was me?" Don asked.

While we made arrangements the day before, Don had sat with him several times, bringing water and food that they enjoyed together as they chatted.

"I recognized your voice," Andrew said.

Andrew was again sitting on a tattered blanket, his metal cup ready for people to drop in coins. "It's a big day for us," Don said. "Hoping it's a big day for you as well. I'll be back to check your work," he joked.

Andrew laughed. "See you."

Don and Andrew were soon sharing breakfast on the sidewalk as the line to registration grew. We were expecting fifty people. Well over one hundred were already in line, and there was still a half hour left before registration was to officially start.

Chapter 32

I Never Knew

Let us be bold.
Let us be brave.
Let us be together.
—Brad Henry

Zimbabwe, November 2010

"YOU MAY NOT ENTER. YOU ARE A MAN." LINDA GUHZA SAID TO THE thin man who had made his way to the front of the registration line growing quickly in front of her.

The man, who introduced himself as Lumeik, stood taller. "I have been sent by the governor."

"You are a man." Linda said, as if that were explanation enough, waving him away, to continue registration for others.

"But I have been sent by the governor to attend today."

"Do you see these people?" Linda said, pointing to what was now well over two hundred people in line for the training of trainers. "I have no time for this. I have to sort through all of these people to find those who were truly sent, and you are a man. You may not enter."

In Zimbabwe, public perception is improving, but at the time the taboo of menstruation meant that most didn't speak of it to anyone, not even sisters, daughters, or aunts. In fact, for some, it was believed that speaking of it could bring drought. It was courageous for them to have convened to discuss and learn about menstrual health and solutions, let alone having a man in the room while they did it. I wanted him to be able to stay, but this was not my decision. This was Linda's community. I trusted her to know what was best. I thanked him for coming.

"There are only supposed to be fifty of them. Who are they all?" I asked.

"Word is spreading," Linda said and invited the next person to the registration table. Ten confirmed as officially invited, forty more to go. Mary stayed at her side. We had no idea how Linda would sort them but she was managing her way through it. I brought her more water, then went to find Florence.

Linda had selected Florence, who was fluent in several Zimbabwean languages, to translate. As we reviewed the material of the day, wrote the agenda on the white board, and answered her questions, I explained to Florence that Days for Girls is neutral—Switzerland. We are people of all nations, beliefs, and backgrounds, and for the sake of those we are reaching, we are not of any one nation, people, religious belief, nor nonbelief. It has been an important distinction. We are tenaciously focused on the importance of turning periods into pathways, and we have been clear that our focus is not on anything that divides us. For the sake of those we serve, we are focused on ensuring that anyone who menstruates has access to quality menstrual care they can count on month after month, as well as menstrual health education that brings greater dignity, health, and opportunity to all. Any other choice would be out of our ethos and hold us back from reaching everywhere. Period.

Florence agreed and studied the presentation materials so that she could feel confident in translating them. We didn't have an official flipchart yet, though everyone was given a copy of our manual, which covered the facts about menstruation, how babies happen, hygiene, and how much their wellness and days matter. Important conversations would come up as we went through the dialogue, such as whether rape was sex or violence. Or whose "fault" it was if the wife only birthed daughters. We took notes, adding the facts they were requesting and seeking expert review as we advanced the education to suit their needs. Eventually, more than seventy iterations were brought back to medical experts for consultation of accuracy and wording, a process that eventually resulted in our flipcharts now translated into more than thirty languages.

Linda was talking with a group of five women when I returned to the registration table. "I'm sorry," she said to them. "We called for only two representatives from each province. We regret that we do not have accommo-dation, nor supplies for more." The women stepped away to decide which two would stay.

But the line was still growing. Heat radiated off the stone walls of the YWCA courtyard as the team stood at Linda's side for the next three hours figuring out who had been officially invited.

Lumeik was back at the front of the line. Linda looked him up and down. "I have told you already. You may not enter." He left, but unbeknownst to us, simply went to the back of the line once more. Linda continued her sorting process and soon he was in front of her a third time.

"I have been *sent* by the governor," he said, this time more emphatically. "She sent me because I am a tailor by trade. I can get her on the mobile if you would like."

Standing nearby, I could see his sincerity. "Linda, what if we let him attend the sewing and education portions, and then you all decide about the women's health components? Would that work?" I asked.

Linda agreed. It wasn't until early afternoon that we confirmed all who were actually invited and settled everyone into their rooms. Sessions could start in earnest.

Just before we began official welcomes and orientation, a tall and imposing Zimbabwean official walked up. He announced himself as a representative of the Ministry of Education. This time Linda did not hesitate. "You may enter."

—

Introductions took a while, but it was clear that the chieftains and communities had sent a strong group. Only three puzzled me. One young woman looked to be about fifteen years of age, with a baby swaddle-wrapped to her back. Another was so shy that she focused on the floor when people addressed her, answering, if at all, in a barely audible whisper. How would she instruct others in what she learned? The third was an elder woman who seemed to have difficulty staying awake even for introductions. I wondered if she had been sent for a vacation, but all three were admitted. Their communities had selected them. I had long ago learned to trust that.

Soon we were well into the day, reviewing our purpose and intentions, sharing the history of Days for Girls, introducing Days for Girls kits and explaining their care and usage. One woman asked me almost suspiciously, "Do *you* use these pads?"

I pointed to the yellow cloth bag at the front of the room near my backpack. "That's my Days for Girls kit. You may have noticed that I took it with me at each break. That's because I am using it right now. I have used every version we have made. I would not ask someone else to use something I would not use myself." A murmur of response spread through the room.

Florence translated in two languages that our next topic was "Periods and Women's Health." Every woman in the room started shifting in their seats and looking back toward the two men. Charles with the Ministry of Education rose and asked if he could speak, as he made his way to the front.

A formidable man in both appearance and role, he paused, looking around the room earnestly before beginning. "I am an educated man. Even I am with the Ministry of Education, and I never knew what you women go through. I didn't know until a young woman's case came before me. She is one of our finest runners, but she refused to run for an important race. Her coach told her that she must run or he would beat her. She did not run. He beat her. He told her if she did not run he would kick her out of school. She still refused to run, and so her case came to me. I asked why she did not run. Her representative explained it was because of her days. I asked, 'Her what?'

'Her menstruation.'

'Her what?'

'Her period, bleeding.'

"This is how I learned what menstruation is. I have a wife. I have a mother. But no one had ever told me. Now I know that there are girls that use rags, feathers, and even inserting rocks and the tips of bull horns. We must speak of these things or it will not change. It is time for us to speak of these things." Everyone looked at me. "It is not up to me. You are the leaders here in Zimbabwe," I told them. "Will you vote to allow these men to stay and learn with us? Or should they leave the room?" Every single hand went up in support of having them stay.

Including men, everyone in the health conversation has gone on to be an important part of the work of Days for Girls. To truly shift stigma, it takes education for all of us, not just some of us. Menstruation connects us all. None of us got here without it. Even test tube babies were originally part of the cycle. All of us are.

Chapter 33

The Facts

Education is the most powerful
weapon which you can use
to change the world.
—Nelson Mandela

Zimbabwe, November 2010

"THIS IS THE UTERUS" ECHOED FROM ENGLISH TO SHONA AND NDEBELE
dialects as I pointed to the illustration. No one flinched as they had when they
first heard what we would be talking about. I held up my hand, fingers curled
into a fist: "Your amazing uterus is only the size of your fist and is right here in
your body. It is strong enough to stretch to hold a growing baby for nine months,
and then push that baby through the vaginal canal and into the world, and still
go back down to the size of your fist. That's an amazing muscle!"

Layers of languages filled the room with knowledge of anatomy, health, cycles, and the somehow missing truth that frees people all over the world—menstruation is natural, healthy, and important. I glanced at the back of the room
where Charles, our official government representative, sat. There were no lines of
concern in his face, only earnest interest. I held nothing back, and those in the
room leaned in.

When Florence finished translating about what a period is, I added mischie-
vously, "So the next time you are menstruating, know you have something you
can rely on to manage it (pointing to their new Days for Girls kits); you can walk
with your head high and say to yourself: 'Without what I am doing now, none of
you would even exist!'" I laughed. They didn't. Instead, a sigh spread throughout

the room, some even closed their eyes as they nodded their heads. That collective sigh is one of the most memorable Days for Girls moments for me. It felt like I was watching the weight fall from their shoulders. They were right. It was no laughing matter. It was important. And a great privilege to share that moment with them.

After dinner, the evening included sewing Days for Girls shields by hand, preparing for the next day when we would use sewing machines. There would be another surprise for them, thanks to the funding of Soroptimists International of Anacortes. The treadle machines brought from Botswana would be given to each group to take back with them.

We walked around the room assisting and checking handwork for understanding and quality. I stopped by our two men in the room. Predictably, Lumeik's work was outstanding. Though normally handwork is not as durable, nor as well finished as machine work, his was exceptional.

Charles, who had said he would have to head back to the Ministry of Education at the first break, had opted to stay all day and was busy making his shield. "Wait until you see how many women I teach this to," he said with emphasis.

Though others were struggling, Grace, our shy participant, was stitching tiny impeccable stitches, as sure as a sewing machine's straight line. I didn't know which language she spoke, but I admired her work aloud anyway. "That is the best hand sewing I have ever seen."

To my surprise, she replied in clear English as she peeked up at me. "This is going to change our lives."

We finished the long day happy and feeling like a solid team. Both Lindas thanked the group for their attention. Participant homework would be to drill each other on the women's health they had learned that day. We would review it first thing in the morning. I added that there would be prizes for correct answers in a "fun" verbal practice quiz the next morning. They looked concerned. "No really, fun. I promise."

—

Silence isn't golden when not a single woman has a thing to say about what they learned the day before. A teacher is supposed to allow silence for time to respond. There was a lot of silence. Linda waited. Florence waited. I waited. I reminded them that we had prizes, including scissors, sewing kits, and solar lights. Nothing.

Okay, no problem. We would just go over the education again. But then, the young woman with the baby stood up. Everyone in the room turned their attention to her. She started repeating, in English, every word I said the day before, rapid-fire and verbatim (I couldn't even do that). For what felt like at least three minutes, she didn't pause. As she sped on, it appeared that she may very well be able to repeat the entire day. Finally, between her hurried phrases, she paused for a breath. I found opportunity to commend her remarkable feat. "Well done! You win the first prize!" Everyone clapped. She smiled, chose a solar lightbulb, and as a bonus for being first to answer, a pair of scissors, and sat down. Her community had sent their phenomenal human recorder. Once again, I was reminded of the wisdom of community. Her courage to speak broke the ice, and the rest of the women followed suit.

In the end they had all taken in the lessons and our four days together were well spent. Our quiet new friends really came to life when it was time to be awarded their certificates. They sashayed, danced, cheered, and photo-opted their way up to receive them.

Figuring out who would carry home treadle machines and their return transport fare was much faster than registration. We had learned the hard way that not everyone is good at sewing. It is a skill, not an instinct. As with any skill, some are more naturally adept than others. Many around the world who first came to DfG would not believe us when we shared that giving a sewing machine does not automatically equate to a successful pad business as surely as giving someone a car does not equate to a successful taxi service. Successful ventures take many skills.

And the elder woman in the room? She would be the one that would bring us to Kgotsu.

Chapter 34

Getting to Kgotsu

I am no longer an orphan,
I am a leader of women.
—Kgotsu, age twelve

Midlands province, Zimbabwe, 2010

THE ELDER WOMAN WHOSE HEAD TIPPED AND STARTLED AS SHE SLEPT through lessons on periods, puberty, and sewing was, it turned out, the wife of a historical iconic Zimbabwean. All along, her attendance had represented community endorsement. Yet another proof to trust the wisdom of those we serve even when it is puzzling. As we finished our goodbyes, she extended an invitation from her chief to come to their community as soon as possible. The community would provide several more treadle machines as well as arranging for two hundred schoolgirls to receive the education and learn to make DfG kits. This inaugural program was important if it was to gain a strong start in the region. But we would only have one day to do it. The elder woman assured us that would be sufficient.

We left at 3:30 AM, with the moon still bright in the sky. We cleared the asphalt roads right at daybreak, then continued on treacherous and slow-going roads by the earliest light. We were unexpectedly diverted to another school as protocol, a delightful excuse to stretch our legs, but the sun was now climbing in the sky. Next we were informed that meeting the students we planned to teach could only happen after first meeting with the chief.

Plumes of powder dusted the air from a large asbestos mining plant rattling its chalky fibrous load up a large metal conveyor belt. We wondered aloud whether the community knew of the health risks as we turned off the asphalt road leading to the plant and bounced our way up the dirt road to the chief's compound.

There was no mistaking him. He stood with the confidence of a chief, though different than I expected. He wore a white shirt and jeans, with a large rodeo-style belt buckle. He and the elders offered us each a short, traditionally carved three-legged stool to sit on. We thanked him for his time and for granting us an audience. I smiled at his four wives who looked on curiously from afar but did not approach. He nodded appreciatively at our explanations of the Days for Girls kits.

Next, he led us to a small community room where he explained his goals for his community. Returning to the stools, we answered more questions about our program, kits, and education until he stood abruptly, and granted us permission to go to the waiting schoolgirls of the village. But first he would like each of his wives to receive a Days for Girls kit. A bit embarrassed not to have offered them to begin with, we happily agreed, thanking him for the honor of both the meeting and his permission. As we met with each of his wives, we could already feel the afternoon sun moving past midday.

At last, we drove down the dirt road to the school where we were expected several hours before. Every moment seemed to tick loudly, reminding us how much time had passed. We pulled up to the school, where the headmistress quickly greeted us. There were hundreds of girls waiting. Although we had brought enough materials to teach two hundred girls, due to the various delays we only had time to teach one group of seventy-five how to make the kits on treadle machines, while simultaneously teaching the education. There was no way the outcome could be anywhere near what we hoped.

The teachers divided the girls into three groups. Girls lined up at treadle machines. Other girls stood near the chalkboard to hear the basics of health education. A third group learned how to use and care for their kits before rotating to another station. Still other girls, whom we could not possibly teach this time, leaned in the windows and doorway and pointed to themselves, indicating, *Me. Choose me.* It was heartbreaking. We had no choice. There was nowhere for us to stay, and there was no way we could miss the meeting with Dr. Coltart the following day. We finished what we could and promised that Linda and others would return as soon as possible, leaving the remaining fabric as a token of our promise.

It took Linda four months to make the long journey back, and when she arrived, the headmistress said the fabric was gone. Linda was devastated. "Why?"

"The fabric was made into those kits you taught us."

"Really? Who was able to do that?"

I was as shocked as Linda when she told me that someone in that group had managed to absorb enough in that short time to be able to construct DfG kits for all the remaining two hundred girls! We wondered who could remember every single step after seeing the entire process once.

It was twelve-year-old Kgotsu.

The photo Linda sent shows her standing in a pink striped shirt, with a big smile on her face. She had not only remembered the instructions but had also helped every girl to make a kit. She had also used the small scraps of moisture-barrier fabric (polyurethane laminate, or PUL) to make little pouches for the girls to put their soiled liners in. A true DfG champion and an innovator, too.

When asked what she felt about it all, she said, "I am no longer an orphan. I am a leader of women."

Four years later, two DfG volunteers returned to Zimbabwe to visit Kgotsu with Linda. Kgotsu was still using the same Days for Girls kit she had made for herself. The volunteers gave her a new one, just in case. Today we know that while most DfG kits are reported to last an average of two to three years, many women report their kits lasting four to five years. A few as long as six. And education and confidence? Timeless.

—

Our driver was the only one who stayed awake on the drive back, getting us safely to Dr. Coltart just in time. We took just the briefest drive-by stop to freshen up and change into appropriate attire. Dr. Coltart was as engaging and present as reputed; we left his office with the promise of an official letter of approval for Days for Girls to offer our curriculum in any classroom in the country.

Chapter 35

What Woman Would You Have Me Say No To?

*This is more than work. When you understand
it's part of your purpose, you constantly dream
of ways of improving and going beyond
the normal call of duty.*
—Chipo Zoe Chikomo
(Days for Girls Zimbabwe Leader)

Victoria Falls, Zimbabwe, 2010

THE OWNER OF THE BULAWAYO FABRIC WHOLESALE COMPANY DIRECTED his entire family to assist us. They scoured half-emptied shelves and sturdy tables to retrieve all the PUL and flannel fabric they could find among the colorful, carefully folded stacks. While we approved suitable supplies, he filled out a receipt ledger in tidy rows of blue ink.

As he wrote up our purchases, he said, "I don't know how much longer we can hold out. Most of the others have gone. We are liquidating just in case we have to flee the country for safety reasons. My family is more important than business."

We took all the PUL fabric and flannel he had. He would not be ordering any more fabric. Businesses, factories, and the jobs that went with them were emptying like sand from torn sandbags. Zimbabwe's famous blanket factory still remained, but many of the manufacturers were now gone, and the fabric district in Zimbabwe was barely hanging by a thread. Local businesses had been "reassigned" to friends of President Mugabe, leaving the businesses without the expertise of those who had founded and managed them.

The fabric wholesaler's shop closed completely within months.

The Zimbabwean leaders distributed all the supplies to the new Ambassadors of Health who were as dedicated to making pads as they were to the health and safety education. They took Days for Girls to women in prisons, to girls in schools, and to women in community centers. They taught and shared everywhere they could. They were so eager to get started that they were doing what I had been told was impossible—volunteering.

Nyasha, a thin woman with a shy smile, reported that she was going to schools to teach what she had learned to others. When asked how she was making it happen, she shared that she was skipping meals to be able to buy a bus ticket to reach them. Nyasha had HIV. Skipping meals meant her antiretroviral meds would not work as well. She was risking her life to reach women in her country.

We were sending all of the support we could, but they were ready and eager to go bigger. It became clear that forming DfG business enterprises would help women like Nyasha do what they were doing for free but now with resources to support their families. But the market for washables wasn't even established yet. People needed to know what quality washable pads were and how well they worked. Chapter and team volunteers were sending thousands of free kits delivered with education, seeding local markets around the globe by proving the quality and demand. Locally made DfG kits and Ambassador education delivery were elements that could scale and create important local benefits, including jobs for people like Nyasha. But we had to make a business plan.

Lumeik, who wouldn't take no for an answer when it came to attending the Ambassador of Health training in Bulawayo, now wouldn't stop until his community had the menstrual care and knowledge they needed. He knew that if he gave the kits out, he could reach only about fifty women. So he adapted the standard DfG kit components from our DfG Supreme Kit (two shields, eight liners, two panties, two baggies, two waterproof bags for transport,[13] and a bar of soap contained in a drawstring bag) down to only one shield and four liners per kit so

---

[13] Back then we used plastic baggies; today we use PUL reusable bags.

they were more affordable for local community members to purchase—in a place with some of the fewest purchasing resources in the world.

"How do the pads work if they don't have panties?" I asked. Linda reached out to ask him, telling me his response later: "The women and girls may not be able to move as freely as they did with panties, but at least they could manage. Then later, when they sold extra tomatoes or a goat, they could buy panties or more liners at cost." Lumeik said, "Some of the women ask me to give them for free but I tell them, if I give you for free then I must tell two women that I do not have anything for them to buy at cost. Which woman would you have me say 'no' to?"

At first women had refused to talk to a man about periods, but Lumeik reminded them that they would talk to their son-in-law to plan a funeral when they got HIV! They would talk to their doctor when they got an infection. Why not talk about how to not have either? He became their most requested Ambassador of Women's Health. With the support of the governor of Matabeleland North, Lumeik and his team went on to reach a reported 13,624 women and girls in Lupane in one year.

Today, Days for Girls has hundreds of social entrepreneurs and enterprise leaders around the world working on the frontlines manufacturing DfG kit components and serving as local leaders to their communities while providing vital local jobs. Their work and their stories are powerful, and it was time to bring more awareness to both their plights and their progress while proving what was working and what wasn't. I was focused on that endeavor when life threw me a curveball.

Chapter 36

Movement

I have found the paradox,

that if you love until it hurts,

there can be no more hurt,

only more love.

—Mother Teresa

Lynden, 2010

OUR TWO-YEAR-OLD GRANDSON WESLEY PULLED OUT A FEW BLUE LARK-spur flowers along with the weeds we were in pursuit of in our garden. This was his first day of being a brand-new brother, and while his mom was at the hospital I was his official helper. He ran off laughing. I ran after him. Suddenly a sharp and warbling cry arose from him, louder than seemed capable of his little body. It was as if a swarm of invisible bees had attacked him. I caught up with him and searched his stiffened left leg for any stinger. No stinger. As suddenly as it started, the pain passed. He ran off playing as if nothing happened. A few hours later, while he ate his triangle of grilled cheese sandwich, it happened again. Something was wrong. I called my daughter Brea, who was at the hospital with her newborn son. "Maybe you should take him to the doctor," she advised.

Within hours, Wesley was tugging on the doctor's stethoscope while his kneecap was tapped with a tiny triangular mallet. Ears. Check. ✓ Nose. Check. ✓ The doctor patted his head and declared him in perfect shape. "Sometimes big brothers with new babies are looking for ways to get attention."

This pattern repeated itself for six months as the frequency of painful twisting of his body increased, striking him again and again and then passing as quickly as it came. Wes was bright, energetic, and adorable when doctors met him. Not the boy in pain that we were reporting. They looked at us like we were the ones in pursuit of attention, but his intermittent symptoms were getting worse, and the boy who only slept a few hours a day his whole life was sleeping even less and no longer eating well.

His new pediatrician said, "Toddlers do this. Ignore it. Eventually he will get hungry enough to eat."

The shine in his eyes was gone, and though he had previously been able to count to twenty, he was no longer speaking at all. When a particularly vicious episode hit, we drove directly to Children's Hospital emergency room two hours away. Maybe they could help. But by the time we arrived, his symptoms had passed. When we insisted something was seriously wrong, they called to consult Wesley's pediatrician. The ER nurse hung up, quietly suggesting that we find yet another pediatrician. "We have no choice but to discharge him." The two-hour drive home was quiet.

Days for Girls headquarters was, at the time, still based on my laptop and cell phone, and conveniently moved to Brea's house. Before, during, and after Days for Girls calls and emails, I helped Brea juggle a newborn and two toddlers, one of whom was mysteriously and gravely ill. My divided attention only further overwhelmed his frustrated and exhausted mother. We were all adrift in the puzzle and pain of what was happening to Wesley.

Don and I were scheduled to leave again soon. We worried about leaving Brea and her boys, but our airline tickets to return to our work in Kenya were purchased long before and only a few days remained. We debated as the day of departure crept closer. Our mutual friend and Days for Girls supporter Cathy Habing offered to stay and help while we were gone. We would be gone for ten days. If the trip didn't have such a demanding schedule, and others weren't already booked to go with us, I would have stayed. I felt torn and anxious.

Hours before Don and I left for the airport another call came in; my father was in the hospital in San Diego. His liver was failing.

When Aunt Brenda handed him the phone, he chuckled. "I was perfectly fine until Argentina forced me to go in for a checkup. And what happens? I came out of the visit with hepatitis C. Don't ever go in for checkups."

It was so like him to still be in good humor despite the seriousness of the situation. His new liver transplant was not as strong as he was. I offered to give him a piece of mine, but I have an overachieving liver filled with cavernous hemangiomas, which is medical-speak for tangled blood vessels, completely benign unless they are eager to set growth records, which mine were. In any case, it left my liver out of the running.

Dad was fighting for his life. Not because of the checkup as he suggested, but rather because of a blood infusion after a construction site accident decades earlier. As a contractor, he had fallen from a rooftop while assisting a roofing crew on one of his builds. A blood transfusion had saved his life, and was now taking it back.

"I'll be fine. Don't worry," he said.

I offered to cancel my trip to Kenya and fly down to him.

"No. I'll be here when you get back. Please, I want you to go. I'm really proud of you. Go." He sounded weak.

I talked to my aunt Brenda again. "What do you think?"

She said, "You heard him. Go. It's what he wants. We'll keep in touch." I left on the plane to Kenya concerned on two home fronts.

—

It takes twenty hours of flying to get to Nairobi, followed by the long wait for luggage. It took the whole team to drop the duffels at the guest house storage space before we trudged to our rooms weary and ready to lay flat. But jet lag had both Don and me up long before dawn, so I picked up the call from Aunt Brenda on the first ring. Her voice was hushed and somber when she told me the news: my father had just lost his fight. He was gone.

I had meant to visit more. I had meant to call more. I thought we had more time. A thousand could-haves/should-haves collapsed inside me. A thousand might-haves sunk away. I dropped to the edge of the full-sized metal bed in the room.

"What is it?" Don asked.

"It's my dad. He's gone."

Even saying it out loud didn't make it feel more possible. "Aunt Brenda, I'm still close to the airport. I can just get back on the plane and head to San Diego now."

My aunt said no. He wanted me to stay. My coming to them would not change anything. I hung up, feeling like I had been ejected into a submarine wake without oxygen. Don held me.

—

As agreed the night before, we met our travel group at breakfast. Hearing the news of my father, friends that were new to me circled around. At that moment it felt like we had known each other all our lives. Shortly afterward, Paul arrived to take us to Kisii.

"Are you sure you'll be okay?" Don asked. He was scheduled to head out to check on the Clay International School.

"Today, I either turn around and leave, or manage to feel my feelings and walk my walk at the same time. Today I will walk for my dad."

We'd meet back up in a few days.

Kisii would be a good distraction, an important one. Along the way I was able to shift to excitement for moments at a time between grief and concern for what was happening back home.

We went over the checklist as we drove through the traffic of Nairobi, stopping at the surprisingly big Chandarana supermarket to get water and food supplies. You would think you were in Walmart or Target except for the exotic fruits and the enormous storks in the treetops as you exit.

We would spend a few days working on the community development projects we had fundraised and prepared for, then on to meet with a member of parliament to discuss the importance of menstrual health and products. A stop at the Maasai Mara National Reserve, and we would be back to Washington within nine more days.

Paul dodged most of the potholes successfully on the way to the green hills of Kisii, updating us on his family and local news. Volunteers chatted and napped for most of the five hours it took to get there.

Chapter 37

Cutting

I cut the trees without knowing
what the shade means to us.
—Linti ene Sampue,
former circumciser

Kisii, Kenya, 2010

THE WALLS OF OUR HOTEL WERE WEEPING WHEN WE ARRIVED IN KISII. Kenya's rainy season was in full force and unbeknownst to us, the hotel that came so highly recommended had removed the roof to add a third floor. The only thing between us and the driving rain was the promise of an additional story to come! There were no other places immediately available. A pleasant young man, dressed in a white shirt and black pants, greeted us with enthusiasm as he pushed water out of our way with a long squeegee—using it like a magician's wand. It was as if to say, *You do not see the flooded walkway.* But he only said a bashful, "Careful not to slip." The first floor seemed relatively dry and night was falling, so we had no choice but to register as planned.

The next day we chose to divide and conquer: one vehicle went to purchase local shoes for an orphanage, and the other traveled to serve a deaf school where the girls, still unaware of why we were there, shyly signed "Hello" in response to the culturally common, lengthy introductions of each visitor. But when the translator told them that the duffels lined at the side of the room were full of Days for Girls washable menstrual pads, eyebrows raised, and the girls waved their arms high over their heads with dancing fingers, the sign for a cheer.

It was the greatest cheer I never heard.

After ensuring each girl received both a DfG kit and the accompanying education, we narrowly outran the afternoon rains as a swollen waterway threatened to overtake the narrow concrete bridge we crossed on our return. We entered the hotel grateful for any roof at all and were immediately greeted by the cheerful boy with the squeegee.

—

Weeks earlier, when I was still home, Masese, whom I had met at the Centre in Dagoretti, had invited me to meet with the cutters. He had explained that the next rite of passage was happening in just a few months.

"Masese, I appreciate your trust in me," I said, "but I have no say when it comes to their traditions."

He disagreed. "You are known and trusted here," he insisted.

I wasn't convinced. How could anything I said matter or be relevant in any way? Masese added that 92 percent of the community participated in the cut. I told him I would think about it.

Now I needed to understand more about the cutters and the practice. In the days that followed, I researched more about the tradition and about what it meant to those involved. I read what I could online.

The ancient tradition convinces some that their daughters will be more valuable wives because the families know there will be no pleasure in sexual relations. The reality is far more extreme: it can be painful to have any physical relations, so women are unlikely to have extramarital affairs; thus, husbands can be assured any offspring are theirs. Those participating are considered true members of the tribe. And though some may consider not cutting, they don't want to face the ill will of family and friends. Any conversation to the contrary is limited to the very immediate family—if it takes place at all. Their silence perpetuates the practice, as those who decide against it are left feeling isolated in their decision.

I asked Kenyan friends about cutting. They said that female genital cutting (FGC) was against the law and that it was unlikely that more than 13 percent of the population took part. Masese reassured me that he had inquired and it was more like 92 percent of the population.

I believe in saying yes whenever I can; but in this case my yes was only to a conversation. My intention was to listen and respond if invited. Not to lecture or give advice. Conversations can be powerful.

Just days before I left home, I was working out with my friend Andy and told her about Masese's invitation to meet with the cutters. "I know what I have to do," I told her. "I have to find ways to make them right. Things about what they are doing that are good."

She stopped midstride. "That is the stupidest thing I have ever heard you say," she retorted. Which was alarming, considering that she is almost always right and one of the smartest people I know. "It's dangerous. Why would you want to make anything so wrong seem as if it is right?" she continued, getting back into motion, shaking her head.

"I hear you. It's just that development so often makes people wrong. And no one wants to be wrong. When we tell people they are wrong, they tend to put up their guard, but in truth we are all constantly learning new things and new ways of doing things."

I reminded her that in the 1940s doctors in the United States told expectant mothers that they should smoke to minimize "hysteria" and keep the baby calm and healthy. "We know better now. I'm sure there are things we do now that we will later change our minds about. So why should we shame people instead of having a conversation? Reasons change. Minds can change if we don't make people wrong. What if we found ways to make them right?"

Now here I was in Kisii, a green place of banana trees, peanuts, and tea crops located to the southeast of Lake Victoria, headed to a meeting with the cutters— and about to test my theory.

The day before I was to meet with the cutters, a group of volunteers had just settled at the dining room table making purple awareness pins. Rosemary Obarra walked in confidently and obviously in charge. She was then Gusii Water District's superintendent, an important role. She also specialized in sustainable water and sanitation innovations, which is what had brought us together. Despite many email exchanges, we were meeting for the first time.

"What are you doing?" she asked.

"We are cutting small lengths of purple ribbon and looping them into awareness pins," I explained. I told her about my upcoming meeting with female genital cutters the next day, and how the purple ribbons would symbolize that women are naturally beautiful and powerful. Instantly, tears welled up in Rosemary's eyes. Scissors stopped mid-snip. No one moved until my friend Jacquie offered her a bottle of water and whispered, "What happened?" At first, we couldn't make out Rosemary's reply.

Rosemary told us tearfully that she was seven when she asked her grandmother to help her become a woman. She didn't know what the rite of passage was, but she knew she wanted to be a "real Gusii woman." She arranged to travel from the house of her mother and father to her grandmother for what her parents thought was just a visit. Her grandmother happily took her to the cutter.

Her parents had decided against cutting her, a tradition which includes cutting away the most tender part of a girl's anatomy. The practice removes parts or all of female genitalia. The initial trauma is only the beginning as women often experience chronic pain, chronic pelvic infections, scar tissue, infection of the reproductive system, and post-traumatic syndrome. Urinary and menstrual problems are common as well.

A multi-country study by World Health Organization (WHO) in six African countries[14, 15] showed that women who had undergone FGC had significantly increased risk in childbirth, and that genital mutilation in mothers also has negative effects on their newborn babies. According to the study, an additional one to two babies per one hundred deliveries die as a result of FGC. But women in these communities do not see those studies, and their tradition says the opposite. So the practice goes on.

Unaware of what it entailed, seven-year-old Rosemary was now with the cutters.

For days she was instructed in the ways of the women of her tribe, how to be a wife, a mother, an official woman of the community. Then came the day of the cut.

---

[14] Kiros Gebremicheal, Fisehaye Alemseged, Haimanot Ewunetu, et al., "Sequela of Female Genital Mutilation on Birth Outcomes in Jijiga Town, Ethiopian Somali Region: A Prospective Cohort Study," *BMC Pregnancy and Childbirth*, BioMed Central (2018): https://doi.org/10.1186/s12884-018-1937-4.

World Health Organization: WHO, "Female Genital Mutilation," January 31, 2023, https://www.who.int/news-room/fact-sheets/detail/female-genital-mutilation.

[15] Some communities in Africa, Asia, and the Middle East engage in FGM/FGC.

She and two other girls were shown their small huts and then taken to the river where they were asked to disrobe and step into the cool water, sitting in it up to their waists. Three woven reed mats were placed along the shore. The girls were told that they would be held down and cut, but if they made any sound they would not be real Gusii women.

Rosemary lowered her voice. "Women I trusted, and even my own grandmother, held me down on the mat and used a sharpened can to cut away my most tender body parts."

They placed the pieces in a traditional woven basket with goats' hide on the bottom, as proof to show the elders that she had been cut. Girls are often stitched closed, so tightly that it can be difficult to urinate or even pass menses.

She continued, "Afterward we were taken to three small huts and told to stay there. We were told we must stay awake and keep a small fire burning for three days, and if the fire went out, we would not have healthy children. I had prepared a few leaves and twigs ahead of time. I was to keep the fire going around the clock and use cooled ashes along the edge of the fire to dust onto my wounds. Three days later, we were instructed to bathe in the creek and dress. The chief came to a clearing not far from the huts and sprinkled ashes over us in celebration, declaring us women. We went on to a community celebration. My grandmother had invited my parents. They were not pleased, but they celebrated with us. If I saw the woman that cut me again, I would kill her for all the pain and suffering and the huge price I have paid since that day."

We were speechless as Rosemary reached out to pick up a pair of scissors and said, "How long do you want these ribbons?"

Deeply moved, we gave our sympathy, and acknowledged her strength while we returned to the work of preparing for the next day when she would serve as our translator. She did not again speak of her cutting.

—

It was agreed that the next day most of us would focus on distributing kits and providing education at the school we came to work with. Only a couple of us, along with a few Kenyan friends, would go to the meeting with the cutters, especially since we only expected a few women to come to the meeting. After all, we reasoned, how many cutters could there be in one community? The meeting would be held in the house Masese's aunt was donating as a clinic.

We got there early. The room started filling with women, far more than the six or so that I expected. I asked who they all were, reminding them that we were to be meeting with the cutters, and was surprised to hear that these were the cutters, approximately fifty by Rosemary's count. I was shocked. We found ourselves backed up nearly against the wall to make room for them all.

The sun beamed in from the windows as we started with short introductions. There were so many faces staring back at us, waiting. I took a deep breath. My friend Beth earnestly gave me the "all stop"—gesturing one hand across her throat. I nodded in assurance, then dove into the heart of our conversation.

"Thank you for coming. You were invited here because you are leaders in your community who are trusted and respected. We understand that you are all cutters. Can you please tell us about what happens before your rite of passage?" Rosemary translated. No one answered. This might be a short meeting.

I had arrived ready to listen. I was eager to find common ground before ever making any invitation to consider new behaviors and ways of thinking. First connect, then invite. But it was looking like there would be no conversation, until one woman near the back raised her hand. "We gather the girls to teach them about being a wife and a mother."

Ready for that answer, I could sincerely respond that I loved the intention and wished we celebrated the transition to womanhood in more intentional ways where I lived, too.

"What happens after the rite of passage?" I asked, taking care not to imply judgment by referring to it as the clinical term, female genital mutilation, nor cutting. Calling it the rite of passage was just as accurate as the cut, or mutilation. We needed to connect, not shame these women for their traditions. Again we waited, our backs to the wall in the crowded room.

Finally, another woman raised her hand. "We celebrate that she is a woman now. The community gathers with traditional gifts, food, and dancing."

To that I could answer sincerely—everyone knows people can feel when you are not being authentic; it's important to create and comment on things you can be honest about—"I love that. I wish we did more of that where I live. I will tell others of your celebration."

"Now let's talk about the cut," I said.

Every one of the women crossed their arms with Venus-flytrap speed.

"The law has not been able to stop you," I said.

The women jutted their chins. "Uhmm."

"The new Constitution will not be able to stop you."

Again they agreed. "Uhmm."

"And we are not here to stop you."

"Hmm?"

"You are leaders who are looked up to in your community. Who are we to tell you what to do? Kenyan women are beautiful and powerful naturally. You have Wangari Maathai, a powerful Kenyan woman, even a Nobel Peace Prize winner who the whole world looks up to. And you have Magdalene Wambua, the acting Minister of Education [at the time]. They are beautiful and powerful Kenyan women, naturally. And you are beautiful, powerful Kenyan women, leaders in your whole community. Who are we to tell you what to do?"

There were murmurs of agreement.

"What if you kept your rich tradition and simply cut out the cut? What if you made a new decision?" I picked up one of the ribbons we brought and pinned it to myself.

"These purple ribbons symbolize that we believe that women are beautiful and powerful naturally." I held a basket of ribbons up and added, "We have some for you, if you too agree."

The room was still. Time hovered motionless in the silence that stretched on. Silence that was suddenly broken by ululating trills rising as the women leapt up and down. I turned to Beth, raising my voice over the trill of celebration. "I think that's a yes!"

———

Clusters of cutters still lingered in conversation. A few were already giving out purple ribbons to others. But we couldn't linger. Rosemary had a surprise in store. It was her intention to take us to share the purple ribbon message with even more people.

We climbed into our vehicle after Rosemary as she explained that the event we were headed to was a festival and field day in one: Mashujaa Day, Swahili for

"Heroes." But today dignitaries would also speak, and she intended to use her own allotted time to introduce the purple ribbon. Our vehicle bumped its way along the road as we prepared purple crepe paper from a wrapping paper multipack, taping it into one large representative ribbon before folding it in a scroll for an official ribbon cutting after she invited her community to naturally honor their women and tradition. The van had hardly stopped when Rosemary jumped out and rushed off, calling to us.

"We must hurry," she said. "The celebration has already begun."

Bleachers full of community members and dignitaries gathered around a broad sports field. Parades of students in brightly colored school uniforms marched down the field. The crowd of what seemed like thousands cheered.

"Follow me," she said, taking my hand as she hurried toward the center stands. Five of us climbed straight up the colorfully draped center bleachers. Most of the occupants of the stands were dignitaries in full uniform or academic regalia, too focused on the singers, traditional dancers, and school sports events to notice us. With Rosemary at our side, those who did notice us seemed not to question our arrival. Rosemary found us a few seats. "Stay here. I will tell you when it is time, Celeste. Join me when I signal."

"Rosemary, this is your day, your leadership. Not mine."

She shook her head. "I will signal you," she said, hurrying toward her place in the front center rows.

The celebration took place in many parts of Kenya that day but, thanks to Rosemary, included a special surprise theme in Kisii. She signaled as promised. I hesitated. She waved me forward again with insistence. I stood just behind her as she acknowledged everyone, announcing what the purple ribbon represented. She asked me to step to the microphone. For the first time I noticed the news cameras at the edge of the stand. I took a deep breath before repeating the list of powerful women I had named earlier that day, and my invitation to consider a new decision that could include all of their rich tradition but simply cut out the cut. They, the strong people of Kisii, could make a new decision. The choice was theirs to make. A cheer went up. Rosemary and the chief dignitary, a woman in full regalia, continued the speech from there, before using the scissors we brought to symbolically cut the ribbon. Another cheer rose up.

With that, Rosemary signaled again and we hurried after her from the covered area down onto the path, reporters following along beside us asking questions. I seldom tell people of the bleachers and the ribbon and the press. Who would believe it? Fortunately, there are news clips somewhere. Anyway, it is what happened next that matters most.

—

"There are some women here who want to talk with you," Julie Ndinda said two days later, gesturing to the women standing just behind her. Thanks to generous supporters, we were conducting a bit of microlending for community members associated with supporting a few of the children who had come from Dagoretti.

The six Kenyan women standing near Julie included one I recognized from the clinic two days before; her smile stood out in all the crowd. It turned out that she was one of the lead cutters; her name was Francine. Her purple ribbon was still pinned on her lapel. All the women were wearing them. We sat on the ground together.

Rosemary translated for us. "She is saying, 'We have decided to lay down our knives. Our daughters' husbands have gone to others who could be real wives and have brought home AIDS to our daughters. So, we're laying down our knives.'" Rosemary and Francine fell into each other's arms and wept.

The fact that some husbands looked outside of their marriages to others who could respond in a way that their wives' mutilated bodies no longer could and brought illness into their families was something I didn't know about nor had I considered. But the women knew. They knew the real price of cutting all along, but no one had ever invited them to make a new decision that honored their strengths, traditions, or their ability to decide.

Rosemary, Francine, and the other five now former cutters continued to rally the community long after we left. They were even featured on the radio. They shared purple ribbons and reported that "even men were wearing purple ribbons."

Two months later, Rosemary called with news that cutting had dropped by 30 percent. Would that have happened if we came with the intention of shaming? I don't believe it would have. Shame is a common tactic in development and in responses ranging from politics to boardrooms to negotiations with teenagers. Making people wrong is perhaps the least effective way to create a real shift.

Real change happens when we come together with new perspectives and truly connect. People support what they help to create, not what is forced upon them.

Female genital cutting continues to be one of the issues that comes up during Days for Girls health discussions offered with Days for Girls Kits. Unfortunately, Kisii has since had several aggressive FGM shaming campaigns, resulting in some rallying to return to cutting. When we followed up four years later, the women who laid down their knives were still advocating to *cut out the cut*.

To invite others to consider new possibilities holds far more power than telling somebody what to do. Few people like being told what to do. People know their own needs, and an invitation to consider a new path may be all that it takes for a complete paradigm shift. But only if it is done with sincerity, respect, and without shame.

Invitation to inclusive conversations creates new possibilities. "What if?" "I invite you." Those phrases have power when they are sincere. In my experience they are equally effective for everyday, practical connections, from getting teens to do chores to bridging far more difficult conversations. Trauma is a dangerous adversary to connection and healing. Connection is a great healer, especially if you can bridge the gap between trauma and possibility. Days for Girls has done that again and again. The call for our unique combination of product, education, and an invitation to crucial conversations has helped DfG grow around the world.

Chapter 38

The Secret Hidden in Our DNA

DNA is a "thing"—a chemical
that sticks to your fingers.
—Sam Kean

Lynden, Washington, 2010

THE DRIVE HOME AFTER THE LONG FLIGHT FROM KENYA WAS FILLED with calls to check in with each of our children. Everyone said they were doing well, including Breanna, who technically only answered she was hanging in there. Home again, Don went to rest, having driven straight from the airport while I slept. Concerned, I drove to Brea's home, adding another twenty minutes of driving time directly after our twenty-hour flight. Two-year-old Wesley was limp on the sofa. He normally ran to me when I entered the house, but this time his pale face tipped only a tiny nod toward me as I entered.

"How long has he been like this?" I asked, touching his cheek.

"A few days now. I took him to the pediatrician. They said he might have the flu."

She didn't look too good herself.

"Flu? This is no flu," I said.

I called my friend Dr. Elise Mullen. "I know you don't do pediatric care, but we can't get the pediatricians to listen to us." I described Wesley's weakness, how he was intermittently dragging one leg, his eyes flickering, his face sagging slightly on one side. "Something is really wrong, and they are not listening to us. You know me. We do not rush to doctors. I do not overreact."

She promised to call a friend of hers in pediatric neurology and get right back to us. A few minutes later, her instructions were short. "Take him to the nearest ER. Mary Bridge Children's Hospital is sending a Life Flight for him."

"They won't even run a test on him, let alone put him on a Life Flight!" She insisted.

Don and a friend came to watch the babies while Brea and I headed to the ER with Wesley. As I sat next to him in his car seat, his eyes seemed to look past me, his parched lips quivered slightly. I tried giving him a small sip of water. He sputtered and gagged.

"Go faster, Breanna."

The ER doctor looked unimpressed. "He may be a little dehydrated. Maybe a slight bit asymmetric around the mouth, but I can't imagine anyone Life-Flighting him."

He was paged and answered the call just outside of the room, so we got the pleasure of overhearing his stammered response to the call from Mary Bridge's head of pediatric neurology. "Yes? He's here. Maybe a little, but he's . . . No. Yes. Okay."

He walked back in looking somehow more defeated than puzzled. "Mary Bridge Life Flight is on its way for him," he said, then turned and left us in the room alone together.

Wesley's eyelids started fluttering again after the doctor left. His leg stiffened and turned. We didn't bother calling the doctor back. We just prayed the flight would hurry.

In what felt like impossibly quick timing, a matching set of Amazon-esque women in flight suits walked in, cheerfully soothing Wesley as they strapped his limp body to a gurney, assuring us that he would be okay. We followed them out and watched the helicopter lift off from its pad, the *thump thump* of its blades still echoing as we ran to the car to start our three-hour drive.

—

By the time Wesley arrived at Mary Bridge Children's Hospital, he was vacillating between being unresponsive and atonic, unable to hold himself up.

"I don't know how he got this bad for this long without a single test," the neurologist that greeted us said. "But we're on it. He won't leave here without an answer."

Even in the pediatric hospital bed, Wesley looked so small. He wore a yellow hospital gown. His head was dotted with dozens of electrodes encased in a white mesh cap. The camera overhead was recording the painful episodes happening to his little body, but they were not showing up as seizures on the EEG. Still puzzled and concerned, the doctors transferred him to Seattle Children's Hospital a few days later. Neurologist Dr. Nigel Banford was on duty. One of the world's specialists for rare movement disorders, he was able to confirm the reason for Wesley's torment, paroxysmal nonkinesigenic dyskinesia (PNKD), a dystonia movement disorder.[16] Few people in the world have the disorder; fewer doctors understand it. When Wesley's little brother started showing symptoms, writhing in pain, doctors thought he was copying his brother. "To have two siblings with this disorder would be like winning a slot machine two pulls in a row," they said. "Nearly impossible."

Apparently, we had hit the DNA jackpot for this one; unfortunately, and seemingly impossibly, his brother had it as well. The doctors shared that they did not know of any other family who had this kind of disorder density. We were told that researching their DNA could help shed light on understanding more about dystonia and migraines. But, they explained, there had to be someone else in the family that had it. There was no way it showed up in all of the boys without precedence. It was like a spotlight lit up my own medical mystery, different but similar.

Standing next to my daughter in the geneticists' office, I almost raised my hand. It was me. I was the carrier of this rare recessive genetic disorder. Ironically, considering what my life focus had become, women carry the gene but only exhibit symptoms during hormonal transitions: puberty, periods, and perimenopause. It explained the cyclical nature of my episodes. Of all of the things I hoped to share with my beloved grandchildren, this was not one.

---

[16] A rare and painful intermittent movement disorder in the family of Huntington's and Parkinson's.

The road ahead for Brea and her small boys with a serious movement disorder would not be easy. I balanced helping them as much as possible while supporting the global movement of women's equity and Days for Girls. A balance that, as for so many women in the world, often left me feeling torn.

Chapter 39
When the Stakes Are High

On any given day, more than 300 million
women worldwide are menstruating. In total,
an estimated 500 million lack access to menstrual
products and adequate facilities for menstrual
hygiene management (MHM).
—World Health Organization[17]

Washington, 2010

WOMEN. PROFESSIONAL, STRONG, EDUCATED WOMEN WHO I HAD COME
to admire, who I knew had balanced many things to shatter glass ceilings, were
suddenly squeamish about being associated with periods. Mallory, a friend and
early DfG supporter, had recommended Days for Girls to her women's investment
philanthropy group. What if their next dividend profits went to help strengthen
the days and wellness of more women and girls? After weeks of deliberation
between several organizations, they chose Days for Girls! We were overjoyed as

---

[17] According to *The World Bank*, each day, 300 million people menstruate across the world. A
conservative estimate suggests that at least 500 million women and girls "lack access to menstrual
products and adequate facilities for menstrual hygiene management."

"Menstrual Health and Hygiene," *The World Bank*, May 12, 2022. www.worldbank.org/en
/topic/water/brief/menstrual-health-and-hygiene.

"Periods Don't Stop for Pandemics—Neither Will Our Efforts to Bring Safe Menstrual Hygiene to Women and Girls," *The World Bank*, May 28, 2020. www.worldbank.org/en/news/feature
/2020/05/28/menstrual-hygiene-day-2020#:~:text=Every%20day%2C%20some%20800%20
million,development%20and%20overall%20gender%20equality.

we rang our supporter "school bell" to celebrate the big leap forward in greater dignity and health for more girls. The group's $10,000 commitment represented not only the success of their group but also a huge impact with DfG. That's a lot of people we could reach! The next day we got totally unexpected news: they had changed their minds. Mallory sounded as sad and deflated as I was. "They feel concerned about being so closely associated with periods as a group as we just start out. Especially after they fought so hard to break through the glass ceiling as women in finance. Maybe later."

Everyone was stunned.

Their group was not the only one. A service group in New Orleans had, only weeks earlier, canceled my "highly recommended" speaking engagement after learning what I "talk about."

I thanked Mallory[18] and took a deep breath as I hung up the phone. Find the lesson and the opportunity in every experience. I grabbed a notebook and pen to channel my frustration into ways to make a shift. The Shift Key ring on my finger came into focus. Crafted and gifted to me by a volunteer from the iconic shift key of a manual typewriter, it symbolized the change I knew we could make in the world. I whispered, "Come on, Celeste. Be brilliant." And with that I dove into a storm of scribbled possibilities, unfiltered. From wildly impractical to practical ways to shatter stigma and help people get over period phobia and get comfortable talking about a natural function that connects us all. The top of the page had large block letters: *What are we afraid of?!*

My brainstormed ideas were admittedly more doodle than brilliant, but I was feeling better. I crossed out most of the list and left only "Host a Protest," "Famous Band Writes a Hit Song about Periods," and "Win a Guinness World Record." I circled "World Record" but also contacted a friend who knew the lead singer in the band formerly known as the Grateful Dead, by then known as the Dead. Couldn't hurt, I reasoned. But it was a no-go. A dead-end lead.[19]

---

[18] In 2022 Mallory's new team, Alterra, would make an almost equivalent contribution to DfG. She made it happen after all!

[19] Years later, actress and singer Chrissie Fit would accomplish my idea with her song, co-written by DfG team member Nicole Gupte, "All About Them Days," based on Meghan Trainor's song, "All About That Bass," raising awareness about Days for Girls.

What would it take to make a world record?

We had already held several "Sewathons," sewing DfG kits around the clock worldwide while posting photos on social media every hour. It was fun, productive, and engaging, but exhausting. We had trended on Twitter with the hashtag #5MoreDays, a campaign focused on asking, *What would you do with five more days? You can help girls get their days back with Days for Girls.* That success was a credit to our many passionate volunteers. But a world record?

I Googled the possibilities. What matched our mission? World's biggest pad? *A lot of material waste.* World's biggest pad fight? *Maybe, but the record-winning pillow fight had over 5,000 people. Hmm. Maybe not.* Biggest pair of panties? *Waste again.* Most people sewing at once? *That would be a lot of extension cords.* Most pairs of underwear worn at once? *Bingo!*

I called Janine, a Days for Girls supporter from the very first distribution. As a former Ford model, she was familiar with modeling underwear. Would she like to break a world record with me? At first, her laughter made it hard to tell whether she said yes or no. I explained that a man from Japan held the record. In the video footage on YouTube he looked like a giant bottom-heavy ant as he neared his record of 231 pairs of underwear. One thing was clear: we would not only need 270 or more pairs, we would also need them in graduating sizes, ensuring that they could stretch to include the very big ball of underwear it would take to beat the record.

Setting a world record takes preparation and practice. We would need to apply and invite accountants to serve as adjudicators and tally keepers to save the cost of bringing in an official Guinness judge. We would need an uninterrupted video record of it all. And we would need to buy a whole lot of underwear. We chose Valentine's Day weekend for our event.

—

People don't often invite other people in to see their underwear, but we invited friends, acquaintances, and the media in to see ours. Janine's friend Grace offered her downtown Seattle meeting space for the event; open with a modern loft, it would allow for plenty of people to gather with us. The radio featured our upcoming event, emphasizing the importance of ending period poverty, which is aggravated by three Ss: silence, stigma, and shame. *Evening Magazine TV* sent in a camera crew. This was going to work. We had just finished setting up tables and *Love Wins* signs in honor of our mission and Valentine's Day, as people started to arrive. The upstairs balcony area featured a laundry line strewn with panties as our banner decoration. About 150 people in attendance cheered as Janine and friends, including my daughter Ashley, all wearing *Love Wins* T-shirts, came down the stairs carrying orange bins full of carefully stacked bundles of twenty-five sets of underwear in graduating sizes.

To win the title of World Record Holder, Janine had to pull up every pair herself, but the team passed her stacks in strategic order and held them in place for her to step into. By the time she hit 114 pairs, she was a little out of breath and stopped for a drink of water. There was spontaneous cheering. Michael King of King5 News asked, "Are your legs numb?"

"Not yet!" Janine shouted over the excitement of the crowd, and kept going. Number 200 was a purple sparkly pair.

A giant ball of underwear had formed as she raced past the former record, 231. The crowd cheered at 250 . . . 251 . . . The final count: 252 pairs![20]

This wasn't just a stunt. It was another attempt to bring/spread/generate awareness of something much sillier than a giant ball of underwear: fear of periods.

Days for Girls now holds two Guinness World Records. The second was made on September 8, 2017, when volunteers at the dōTERRA International Convention packed 5,110 kits in 36 minutes. It took DfG volunteers six months of steady effort to prepare for the record. Volunteers at the event packed the huge volume of materials into DfG kits long before we ran out of time for the record. Confetti showered the room in cheers that would be matched by those of the girls receiving them around the world.

---

[20] It should be noted that someone walked in front of our video camera obscuring the view for several of the panties, so though the crowd counted with each, and the accountant record showed 252, we were credited with 249.

Chapter 40

Men Who Know

No matter what has happened in the past, we should always
treat people with respect and value. As a Men Who Know
health ambassador, I am someone who always respects and
values girls and women. To me I personally love all the girls in
my life, like my sisters, and I respect women like my mother.
How about you?
—Ang of DfG Project G

Zimbabwe, November 2011

"DO YOU KNOW WHAT THEY ARE TALKING ABOUT IN THERE?" DON ASKED
the dozens of young men and their teachers who surrounded him outside under two msasa trees. He gestured to the classroom full of young women whose
laughter came in waves as they attended a Days for Girls distribution. Once, in
Kenya, some boys risked standing outside enduring the whipping rains of an
actual monsoon to peek in windows to see what the girls were talking about with
us.

Don was teaching the boys to build a simple Tippy Tap handwashing station. They lashed a single stick to the broad "Y" of the branches of a low tree to
hold a water container. The boys were almost done. "Pass me the string, please,"
Don said. A string attached from the container to a stick served as the simple
foot lever (think "gas pedal") to tip the jug to start the flow of handwashing
water without the need to touch it or risk cross-contamination. Don continued,
"They're talking about menstruation . . . Pass me the soap and nail, please. You
see, menstruation is . . ."

The young men were eager to talk about it. It was the beginning of a long conversation that led to what strength means and the significance of having respect for one another. Don asked, "How do you feel when your father beats your mother?" Spousal abuse was commonly accepted. A boy answered, "I don't like it."

"What if when you are a husband you chose not to?" Don asked.

The boy answered, "Then she would not respect me."

Don replied, "Hmm. In our family no one hits anyone and we respect each other very much. Let's watch Celeste when she comes out and test how she acts toward me even though I have never hit her. You may find it interesting."

I didn't know why they were staring at me when I walked up later and put my arm through Don's, greeting them all. "How's it going, guys? Good-looking Tippy Tap!"

Don laughed and said, "See?"

Years later, we now have a full flipchart that facilitates discussions among men to define strength. Is it only physical? Or can it also be the leadership and actions we take in family and community? The flipchart includes invitations to lead the way for better health and, yes, period equity. The program and the flipchart are called *Men Who Know*. Data shows that when boys and men know about menstruation, they are less likely to shame or mock people with periods and are more likely to make providing menstrual resources a priority for their family. All of which can help break stigma and create commitment to stand up for menstrual equity.

Days for Girls success stories often focus on the women and girls we reach. But our goal is to impact the entire community so that periods are no longer a problem for anyone, which means including everyone in the conversation.

Isaac Areba is just one example of how DfG transforms lives. My friend Kayla-Leah and I met him in the Days for Girls Uganda office. Isaac cut fabric at the Uganda production center. He was cutting out shields as he shared his story. He told us that DfG was his family now and he felt that his life's mission was working in the cutting room in production at DfG Uganda.

His father and sister had died on the same day in the Rwandan genocide of 1994, and his widowed mother succumbed to breast cancer soon after. This left Isaac and his younger brother to live with their aging and disabled grandmother, who died a few years later. At the age of seven, Isaac had no other option than to live on the streets. With little food, shelter, or clothing, his life was reduced to surviving day to day. He lived this way for nearly three years until a couple working in his community invited him to their church. They clothed him and found an orphanage for him and his brother.

As Isaac grew older, he wanted to work to support his brother and so he moved to Kampala hoping to find a job. This is where he found Days for Girls. The DfG Uganda team welcomed him with open arms. When asked why he cared so much about Days for Girls, he recalled his best friend at the orphanage. She was his chore partner, and one day while cleaning the kitchen he noticed she was dripping blood on the floor. He was very concerned about her and urged her to get medical help. He knew nothing about menstruation and thought something terrible was happening to his best friend. But she didn't explain. He was so relieved to learn through DfG that what he saw was not due to illness but rather a healthy and natural process.

Men like him, advocating for menstrual wellness and working to normalize it from a place of fact and celebration without shame, have a powerful role in creating menstrual equity. After finding DfG, Isaac frequently led community discussions, serving as a menstrual health advocate to encourage men and boys to support girls in menstruation. He is not alone; there are many who serve around the globe. Boys and men who know the facts are less likely to shame menstruators and more likely to support those in their communities to make sure that they have what they need. Men like Isaac invite important healthy conversations—and it matters.

Stigma against menstruation is still far-reaching, and it can't be just half the population trying to shift it. All community members coming together can make lasting change by engaging in authentic conversations. Meaningful conversations change lives. Uniting with purpose changes everything.

Chapter 41

Every Girl. Everywhere. Period.

Everything is impossible, until it is done.
—Pliny the Elder

Whidbey Island, 2011–2012

COLORED MARKERS AND BLANK POSTER BOARDS LINED THE LONG AN-
tique table under the copper-lined cove windows of the Clay family's Whidbey
Island home. Each Days for Girls International board member and champion
in the room had a set of markers in front of them. It was 2011, our first board
retreat. Their assignment? To chart out a timeline of their life, including how
they found Days for Girls and what it meant to them. We laughed and cried as
we shared the scribbles that traced each life.

Andy's friendship and foundation had brought me to Kenya in the first place.
She is a woman with a master's degree for every season: one in nursing, one in
creative writing, one in global sustainable development (the one I audited with
her), and now a new professional certificate in nonprofit and board management.
Andy volunteered to be our strategic plan consultant.

"What measurable and achievable goals have you set?" she asked.

"Every girl. Everywhere," I answered sincerely.

She gave me *the look*. She can do that; she's one of my best friends. She replied, "No, I mean something you can *measure and achieve*."

"Every girl *is* achievable and measurable. It will just take correct solutions,
clear calls to action, partners, coalitions, and scale," I answered with surety. I
could already see it.

She looked to the other members for some backup. "Okay, what's another objective that is perhaps a little more immediate?"

Silence.

"Twenty chapters of Days for Girls!" I answered.

"That's more like it. How many do you have now?"

"One," I replied.

The idea of DfG chapters was just starting to catch on around the globe, but there was a reason for my optimism. By July 2010, a volunteer in Tanzania reached out, and of course, Zimbabwe as well. A volunteer in New Zealand came on board in August 2011. Quebec, Canada, and the UK followed in September, all joining in with Carol Olsen who had joined in earlier that year. It was October now, and there was no sign of slowing.

We had already begun the long road of scaling up to demand. Chapters would be an important part of both awareness and growth.

Andy took a long, shallow breath. "Let's go back to defining measurable and achievable," she said. "What are our challenges?"

Despite our efforts for improving quality control, we still faced a wide spectrum of component quality. Some of the components were made of beautiful, stain-busting fabrics and expertly crafted. The makers of these products knew that each Days for Girls kit was a gift that needed to last. Jan, one of our first official sewing specialists, told everyone, "What would you want it to look like if it was for your daughter, sister, or friend?" We once received a set of pad liners that were sewn perfectly but were constructed of flannel sheeting so worn as to be shredded along one side like a pantyhose run. A sad waste of the talent and time for something that could never be counted on month after month, never mind for years.

Quality matters. It matters so it will last. It matters because it can make a statement about periods. Not a last-use rag, but a quality solution that is as beautiful as it is practical.

Quality matters because girls have said it is the softest thing they have ever held. Young girls have told us that they couldn't wait to have their period after seeing one. I have seen girls hug their kits, dance with their kits, and walk home from school wearing them as a backpack. Many girls report carrying their schoolbooks with them every day tucked inside their Days for Girls drawstring bag so they are ready for school and for their periods at any time. Their kits serve for years. We have spotted shields and liners on clotheslines in Peru; we have seen them on desks in India and carried by students in Nigeria long after they were received. To those who are counting on these kits, quality matters.

So, we added the need to create more tools for standardizing our patterns and programs, incorporating videos and more detailed instructions, and we planned to add a quality assurance campaign on our leadership Facebook page: Chapter Chat.

We also set the goal of having a new logo. It would be simpler but the same color: we had chosen orange. Pink was not as strong as we wanted. Red felt too *in your face* for a world that could barely say the word period. Whereas orange, the color of creativity and creation, felt alive and confident. Orange and school bus yellow. Perfect. Soon the orange flower of DfG had five petals, representing the average days of flow, a red period at the center. Its shape was slightly asymmetric, like a girl doing a cartwheel, stitches lacing its edge to represent how stitches were adding up to a strong rope pulling women out of poverty and isolation.

Our successful retreat paved the way for even greater success over the next year and beyond.

We reached our twentieth chapter one year to the day after the retreat. And Days for Girls went on to reach 297,331 girls and women in 31 countries by the end of 2012.

Our tagline became *Every Girl. Everywhere. Period.*

—

The next year we gathered again at Andy's place. Twelve women and one man sat poised with markers in hand around the table. This time there was a new assignment. "It's ten years from now and we have reached every girl. What has happened as a result? How did we do it?" I asked.

Blank stares.

I tried again, "Let's say we leapt forward in time and we reached our goals. We're looking back now. What did we do to get there? What has happened as a result?"

Ideas flew rapid-fire.

"Girls have their days back!"

"They have what they need."

"Confidence."

"No more shame!"

"Everyone is talking periods." (At the time, that one was laughable.)

"Our pads are so good they are patented."[21]

"Volunteers all over the world. Local ownership, too!"

"Sustainable DfG social entrepreneurs."

Large white presentation sheets of paper quickly filled up. I peeled the first one off and hung it with blue tape on the window behind us. I switched marker colors. "Great! Now, who did we partner with? Who joined us to make it happen?" My pen squeaked as I rapidly recorded their words into blossoming bubble maps of our shared vision:

"Corporations."

"Foundations!"

"Clubs."

"Schools."

"More organizations!"

"Large multilaterals."

"Ohhh . . . Designers design custom fabrics for us!"

"Celebrities."

"We won global awards!"

"Oprah!"

We used an orange marker for the next vision-planning process: how to reach every girl. Our curriculum and templates needed to be printed. Videos would help tell our stories. We would need to develop better monitoring and evaluation skills.

By lunch there were almost a dozen colorful word clouds taped on the windows, cabinets, and walls around the room.

Two days after the retreat, Janine got a call from the organizer of a personal

---

[21] At that time we were on version twelve of our Days for Girls pads and were only just registering as our own nonprofit. Today we hold two patents reflecting the genius of those we serve and serve with all over the world.

trip she was about to take with a friend. Would she mind having an unplanned celebrity on the trip with her? It would mean signing a nondisclosure agreement as well as extra security. Janine would have to agree to potentially being included in video footage.

Oprah Winfrey would be on her trip.

Chapter 42

A Single Page

Nothing is impossible. The word itself says "I'm possible!"
—Audrey Hepburn

Lynden, Washington, 2014

A YEAR AND A HALF LATER, WE WERE SWORN TO SECRECY OR RISK THE death of our article. Oprah's iconic *O* magazine was set to do a feature on Days for Girls. As long as no one let the word out until it was published.

It wasn't, as you might think, due to Janine's meeting Oprah; we have Linzee Kull McCray to thank for the article. Like so many of us, Linzee had no idea that girls and women paid such steep prices for lack of the simple basic need of menstrual care products until her neighbor told her, "There's an organization called Days for Girls . . . I'm hoping to help." Linzee, a successful craft magazine freelance writer, wanted to help, too. A few weeks later Linzee was visiting her sister and saw a copy of *O* on the coffee table. She was not yet familiar with the magazine when she flipped through its pages—her focus was crafting and quilting magazines—but she thought it looked like a good option for Days for Girls.

Her timing was perfect. *O* had just launched a new segment and responded quickly to Linzee's query. Her article would be a good fit. That was huge to us! But we didn't realize how thorough *O* magazine was. They followed Linzee's expert interviews with several of their own, looking for expanded specifics. They researched and vetted us. They needed written permissions and verification on every point. Linzee went over and over her article with them, for what would become a 323-word piece. And thank goodness she did. It was all I could do to keep this exciting news to myself! But we needed to prepare. Being featured in *O* would expand awareness of Days for Girls exponentially.

Days for Girls had been managed exclusively by our phenomenal network of volunteers who took on commitments with determination, complete with playbooks of deliverables, accountability, and procedures. They even updated them with current best practices as they went. In the future when newcomers came on board, my offer to connect them to volunteer support teams would be met with, "Oh no, volunteers don't have the same level of dedication." They weren't able to imagine the truth: we had the opposite problem—our volunteers didn't stop. I wasn't worried that they wouldn't follow through. I was worried they would take on too much.

Our chapters director at the time, Shannon, was an engineering firm manager by day and international chapters director by night. She often put in as many hours after her paid work as she did during the day, for years. Everyone from myself to our distribution coordinator, social media, and sewing specialists all volunteered, determined to set goals and outcomes that rivaled any professional team. The point wasn't pay; it was excellence at a level money alone cannot buy. It is my experience that true "A players" don't do what they do for money. Though pay is one lovely reward for their accomplishments, it is not their primary objective. Remarkably, our volunteer strategies worked and were scaling to the point that we had large teams within teams. Entire volunteer country programs would grow from them, some thriving to this day. Though I didn't ask anyone to do anything I wouldn't do, the wear and tear on many of us was starting to show. People were balancing impossible hours. Because I didn't want to be responsible for working everyday heroes to exhaustion, we needed to hire a development officer to help us get help.

Leah was the first Days for Girls unicorn staff member to join us, the kind of impossible wonder everyone wishes they could hire: as passionate as our volunteer power, and uniquely gifted in taking on almost any challenge at hand. Together we worked on even more systemization. Every time we built a new system to manage growth, we would quickly outgrow it.

"What does the Red Cross use to manage their systems? We need to build something Red Cross big but on a Days for Girls thin dime budget," I said. "With *O* magazine coming, we will need it."

Leah agreed. "We need to build a better surfboard so that we can catch the wave when it hits."

We worked with our amazing volunteers to get it done. Since we love what we do, most of the time it is hard for any of us to consider it work, an intoxicating mix of passion, puzzle, challenge, and accomplishment for volunteers and new team members alike. The more we worked, the more we got results, and the more proof through the girls' stories came in. That impact fueled passion and pace. Repeat. A cycle of influence that continues today.

As the release of the O magazine article neared, Leah and I worked on not only the day to day but also the transference of the website to a platform that would be less likely to crash if a lot of people tried to log in at once. We prepped press releases and worked on strategy with global teams while writing several grants from my dining room table overlooking the field and barn. It was a blistering NYC-style pace at the edge of our pasture. Dividing and conquering the tasks, keyboards ablaze, we met one deadline after another.

One late afternoon, only days before we expected O to hit mailboxes and newsstands, we both finished separate deadlines in the nick of time.

"What next?"

We looked at each other, dropping spontaneously to the floor at the same moment, then spent the next minute laughing.

"Aww! I'm done! You broke my brain," Leah said.

"That might be the limit," I answered. "Thirteen things at once is our max."

"Yup," Leah said in her typical, cheerful, understated way. Just like that, we were back up and at work.

Building a better surfboard while surfing world-class, thirty-foot waves became one of my new taglines.

———

As we prepared for the release of the magazine article, I had visions of explosive growth in true Oprah fashion: "You get a pad! And *you* get a pad!"

The article was published on page 23 of the January 2014 issue of O magazine.[22] I flipped through its scented glossy pages for the first time in aisle 8 of

———

[22] Linzee Kull McCray, "Period Drama: Helping Girls Around the World Navigate 'That Time of the Month,'" Oprah.com, accessed February 15, 2023. www.oprah.com/health/celeste-mergens-days-for-girls.

my local grocery store, eager to find the article. The cover featured Oprah in a gold gown, surrounded by orange, Days for Girls' signature color. I wanted to stop everyone at checkout to show them. Instead, I just smiled ear to ear all day, sending out social media notices and dialing every friend I knew. "Days for Girls is in *O* magazine!"

When I called my mother, she said, "Hmm. I wonder where you would find a magazine like that?" I answered, "Anywhere. Your grocery store, gas station, Walmart, bookstores. You name it."

The website didn't crash. But the uptick in applications to join or create Days for Girls chapters increased dramatically. Better, *O* magazine copies have staying power. People hold onto it, share it, pass it on. To this day in many of my travels and speaking engagements, at least a few people will say that they found out about Days for Girls in *O* magazine, often tucking the clipping away until the day they could act on it. I send an annual thank-you email to the editor responsible for the article. The article was a small footer segment that would expand the reach of Days for Girls around the world.

A single question. A single connection. A sliver of a page can change lives around the world.

Days for Girls Outreach back in 2014

340 chapters; 82 countries; 447,120 individuals reached.

Part Four

Chapter 43
The Wisdom of Those We Serve

To be beyond yourself
Is the gate to wisdom.
—Sorin Cerin

Mozambique, 2015

VEGAS HAS NOTHING ON THE DRUMMERS OF KUWANGISANA, SENA, MO-
zambique. They pound their mallets in rhythmic, muscled, full-swing strikes,
switching drummers mid-stroke. Perpetual-motion drumming. With dancing
so vigorous that after five minutes I had to downshift to a clap and a sway.

For a time after the civil war of the late twentieth century, not even the train
made it all the way to Sena. But it was Perpetua Marcos Alfazema's story that
brought our group to Sena.

My shirt began to stick to my skin the moment we left the plane. Perpetua
picked us up from the airport in Beira, a day's trip from our destination. Although it was already dark, the heat clung to the calm streets as we neared our
basic bed-and-sink lodgings, which felt luxuriously welcoming after the twenty-hour flight. It was good to see Perpetua again. The last time I met her was at
the Days for Girls Ambassador of Women's Health (AWH) training in Alberta,
Canada. Her homeland was a very different place. Here we could hear the waves
of the beach nearby as we stood on the porch. We all sprayed our legs and arms
with insect repellent as we briefly talked about the day ahead. There would be
meetings with the Ministry of Gender, and we would be researching the supply
chain. Then the jarring eleven-hour trip to Sena, where Perpetua's work focused.

Perpetua explained that she had become a refugee from Sena as a child during the war. She was taken into Kenya, then Canada, eventually becoming a citizen there. She had returned as an adult and started a successful health clinic—a sign of her dedication to her home community. Once, just before a trip from Canada, someone suggested that she bring Days for Girls kits with her. "I didn't think anyone would need them. I had pads growing up in Canada. I didn't know to ask," she said. After being repeatedly assured by a local volunteer, Cathy Habing, who had now moved from Lynden and taken Days for Girls with her to her new location in Canada, that the kits would be needed, she agreed to take only one large duffel bag containing seventy-five kits.

It was the end of the trip before she remembered she needed to "deal with them." Not wanting to lug them home, nor abandon them, she asked local area leaders if they knew anyone who would want them. Several said yes, asking if they could have one to give their wives. The same happened when she talked to the traditional midwives and the local clinic doctor. She now had seventy kits left. Each of the leaders agreed to spread the word that she would be at the open community market for the AWH education she had trained for, and each participant would receive one of the Days for Girls kits.

This was her last day. She hoped someone would show up.

She arrived to a crowd of what seemed like more than one thousand people in a place where such a crowd is relatively unheard of. Where did they all come from? Now what?

On the day she told me about it, she said, "I was so nervous I felt like I had to go to the bathroom, but I couldn't leave. These things are like *gold*!" She and the midwives huddled to brainstorm ideas. One of the women suggested they teach all of the people and then challenge them to answer questions based on what they learned. Correct answers would win the prize of a DfG kit. Several people drove off to hurriedly retrieve a loudspeaker from a local government office. Cultural norms of flexibility with time worked in favor of the day. This community didn't cancel or postpone; they waited together talking, dancing, and drumming until the sound system arrived. They listened intently as Perpetua shared the AWH education she had learned. Afterward Perpetua and the midwives, dressed in their traditional colorful kitenge wraps, took turns asking questions. Shouted replies came from the crowd. "Please, raise your hand and we will call on you," Perpetua said. It became a festival of learning, with the community determining the winners: "No! Not good enough!" they shouted. Or "Yes! That is correct!" Afterward, they divided into three groups to discuss how these solutions could come to their whole community. That had brought Perpetua's request for us to join her in Sena, to help answer the call.

The town of Sena lies to the east of the Zambezi River where many of the community goes to bathe in its murky waters, despite the risk. "Once in a while a crocodile or hippo takes someone away, but it is a price we pay." It was not the first time I heard such a statement, and each time it stopped me cold.

I had heard of it in Malawi, too, where a community described women waiting in a designated hut outside of the reach of their community during menstruation. They explained that the odor of biological matter breaking down attracts wild animals, and, as one person told me, "once in a while a woman [was] dragged away." Viewing the deaths as "a price we pay" left me feeling a mixture of sadness, anger, and frustration knowing that women faced danger simply because of lack of what they needed and the stigma, which endures in global silence and misunderstanding about menstruation. It sharpened my resolution that education and resources should be made available to all communities. This time I heard the comment with added insight.

The night before, after we had gone to bed at our host's home, the drumming continued well into the predawn, leaving me hovering at the edge of dreams and the sounds of drumming. The next morning, over tea, I laughed, declaring Sena the "drummingest" community I had ever seen. Perpetua explained that people were drumming to protect friends and family who had fallen ill. "To chase away what is hurting them," she said.

They drummed for each other, with such determination that developing a mid-strike mallet-pass had made it possible to go on even after they were exhausted. And many were doing it on just one meal a day. It remains one of the most tangible gifts of community I have ever witnessed. In this place, with the moringa trees, red pathways, and large round mud-and-thatch huts, I had an *aha* moment. Perhaps, if you have to face the daily mortality of loved ones, your "thermostat of trauma" would have to move down a bit to survive emotionally. Some things would become an accepted price, not because you thought them justified, but because there are so many things beyond your control. The sound of drums reverberated each night under bright stars, and now I heard in them a mixture of celebration of community and a harbinger of loss. Once again I was grateful that small things can make a big difference.

—

Breakfast was moringa tea and a small, sweet banana. The soft voices of the surrounding families started to rise up outside while we ate. As we walked to the town center to prepare for the training, Perpetua called out to friends and neighbors, "*Bon Dia!*" She took us on a tour of the clinic—a simple horseshoe-shaped building where staff continued to work without pay after a large USAID grant had run out, a burden she shouldered. She desperately wanted to keep her team employed.

Even as the day started, lunch was already being prepared for those outside the white wooden church where we were given permission to conduct the day's training. Dozens of women were already chatting on the broad steps and veranda as Perpetua's team prepared registration. At the community's insistence, we waited an extra hour to make sure everyone had arrived. This time instead of a printed educational flipchart, we would use a tool developed with the feedback of many individuals and medical specialists all over the world: a portable projector to shine the pages onto the wall so more women could see the images and we could respond to their feedback in real time between sessions.

Perpetua and I conducted the first training; she led the instruction in Sena, the local language, as well as Portuguese. This first group would then lead the education for the next, each taking a page to present, the women giving feedback as they practiced each page. I sat on the floor nearby, next to Mighty. As strong and capable as her name implies, and equally as beautiful, Mighty served as the clinic's impact manager. She translated for me as I observed the training. Both of us took notes of any questions or comments and where the newly trained Ambassadors added or skipped things. In between sessions, Mighty worked on translating the written material as well.

I could hear the women applying newfound handwashing techniques—"Like doctors do"—as we washed up to eat lunch, one important activity-based page of the flipchart complete with singing to time the length of washing. The lilt of their Portuguese-African accents rose from outside as they washed while singing, "Happy birthday, clean hands!"

They returned and queued up to receive large portions from each of the pots on the table. Masamba vegetables, goat meat stew, a fried bread called Pao, and the main staple, nzima (pronounced shee-ma), a starch basic that has a texture somewhere between Cream of Wheat, mashed potatoes, and sticky rice. I loaded up on vegetables and nzima. When some women noticed, I explained that I am vegetarian. "More for you" usually works, though they seemed completely puzzled that I would skip the meat. Being vegetarian can be tricky; once a beloved team in Uganda had worked for two days gathering grasshoppers and carefully removing the wings and legs before deep frying them in honor of my arrival. I am able to report that they tasted like cold french fries.

We sat, spread out on their colorful wraps in a circle, visiting as we ate before returning to our work. What did they think was most important? Did anything feel unnecessary? Did they have other questions? Were there any sections they wanted to know more about? Less? There we sat talking about things usually left unsaid. They asked many questions such as, "How can we have more sons so our husbands will not leave us if we fail to have one?" Chalk in hand, I leapt up to illustrate that whether an ovum (or egg) becomes a male or female is based on which sperm gets to the egg first. The man cannot blame the gender of a baby on the woman. Neither is it under the man's control.

"That makes every one of us a winner from the first moment of conception—the product of the Egg of the Month meeting up with the Fastest Sperm."

When Mighty translated to share that fact in Portuguese, the women broke into chatter. Mighty leaned over to translate. "This is very important to know," she said.

An illustration was added to the flipchart projection in real time. Small things adversely affect women's lives and equity in a big way. This one fact turned out to have global significance in nearly every place the education reached.

In the next round of practice, the women took the education to the next level.

We repeated this technique throughout the trip as we visited six countries in five weeks for follow-up and evaluation and then compared the responses to the results of previously collected feedback on our curriculum from several other countries.

This process of teach/listen/respond/repeat had become key to Days for Girls. The focus groups this time included Bangladesh and Nigeria, where my friend from the United Nations, Dr. Ugochi Ohajuruka (Dr. Ugo for short) hosted an Ambassador of Women's Health educator training. Afterward, thanks to her efforts and DfG supporters, refugees from the Kuchigoro Internally Displaced Persons (IDP) camp in Abuja welcomed us and engaged in DfG health education before receiving their DfG kits. In Ghana a lovely family assisted. By the time we got to the Dominican Republic training, no further changes were recommended. In fact, one doctor in the room said, "I have been to many health curriculum training sessions, and this is the best I have ever attended."

Walking with partners in cities, through poverty-stricken areas, in communities seasonally displaced from swollen rivers, near the rolling Jordanian desert, or in the rainforests, everyone who participated echoed common themes and needs, and, of course, we always stuck to the facts. Our bodies are amazing. And everyone's health matters. Comprehensive health education, covering the facts of puberty, periods, pregnancy, self-defense, handwashing, and preventing human trafficking, is vital and must be factual and relevant to what is needed and wanted. Powerful interactive engagement and knowledge imparted and gained in as little as ninety minutes. All the result of listening to the wisdom of those we serve and serve with.

Now I had to face the dilemma of how to fund ongoing programming for these phenomenal self-driven local leaders. This problem was in my thoughts and prayers on each leg of the journey home. Sitting in the airport answering a backlog of emails, I envisioned the faces of the women when they had shared what they needed and why it mattered so much. I sent their recommended changes to DfG's expert volunteer medical consultants. The consultants would give their confirmation, support, or sometimes alternative recommendations.

At the time, we were on version seventeen of the flipchart. Today, we are well over seventy versions! And we still remain responsive to updates from the field, global health organizations, and other experts. We're still listening, and

I still find myself drawn out in prayer for the leaders engaged in this vital work all over the world. When I first visited Perpetua's homeland, we didn't have a lot of resources to help them expand their efforts. Their voices, faces, and determination captivated me anew as I filled my notebook on the flight home with all I had learned and the proof of their immense potential in reaching more people.

Chapter 44

Then Get Up

Fear leads to more fear, and
Trust leads to more trust.
—Dean Ornish

Lynden, 2015

ON THE EVENING I RETURNED HOME FROM THE LONGEST GLOBAL PUSH
I had ever made, my eyes closed but my mind couldn't stop. We had to find a way
to support the amazing leaders I had just worked with. But how? It would need
to be a really big leap in support.

Despite very little sleep, I still woke up at my usual 4 AM. My natural rhythm
worked against me that day. Don't misunderstand—I don't leap into action at
4 AM. It is my routine to lie there and sigh into stretches and prayerful gratitude,
although putting it into those words makes it feel more formal than it is. I really
just hover in the space between wakefulness and sleep, feeling the blessings in
my life, and allowing visions of how the day could unfold. No expectations from
anyone, just me and the joy of all the possibilities of the day. I listen for sometimes surprising inspiration before I rise from bed and do a double-knee touchdown for a more "official" prayer. By 4:30 AM, I'm ready to actively start my day.

On the morning after my return, however, the edge of wakefulness was
filled with pleading: *Please. Please. Please tell me how to find support for the amazing
leaders to reach large parts of their countries and communities. Please.*

Then get up! was the immediate impression that came clearly to mind. I was,
if I'm going to be completely honest, a bit insulted. I threw off the covers and
marched off to the computer thinking, "Like 4:30 AM isn't early enough?"

Opening the computer, I found an email from Rob Young of dōTERRA Essential Oils, asking me to call him. Rob and his wife, Debbie, had given a generous donation to Days for Girls months earlier. It was in large part their support that had just made the entire training and research trip possible. They had given us the biggest single donation we had received to that point, $75,000. I wondered if perhaps we had not given them enough reporting. I wasn't sure how much gratitude was expected for such a game-changing contribution. I had wanted to throw a parade for them, actually calling the local high school to ask if we could video them marching with signs of acknowledgement, but students had exams. Sighing, I proceeded to answer the usual email load of more than one hundred emails per day, while I waited for a more reasonable hour to call Rob.

He answered on the second ring. "Celeste! How are things?" I told him about the trip and how much their support mattered and how much it was making possible—travel expenses and important training and materials for local programs and leaders.

"How much support can you manage, Celeste?" His wife had just returned from Guatemala with the dōTERRA Healing Hands Foundation team. "This work is too important to wait. We want to help make more happen faster in a big way. Can you come meet with us to talk about it?"

I managed to remain calm and grateful until I hung up, after which I cheered, laughed, and cried tears of joy almost all at the same time.

Get up, indeed.

The answer had already arrived.

—

Don and I flew to dōTERRA headquarters in Utah to meet the team before experiencing Rob's trademark rapid-fire inquiry in their conference room. As we talked, he drew bubble charts of notes on the whiteboard based on my answers, underscoring his astute key strategic questions. After what felt like two hours, he walked to the head of the table and stood staring at us. I waited. We were startled when he slammed his long arms on both sides of the large mahogany conference table. "I'm in. I'll talk to the partners," he said. Shortly afterward the other owners generously joined in. dōTERRA became and remained our biggest corporate sponsor and champion. Their ongoing support has vastly multiplied our reach all over the globe.

Women Know This?

Polochic Valley, Guatemala, 2015

Here are details Debbie Young shared about the Healing Hands Foundation service initiative she had just returned from in a mountainous region of Guatemala from which the company sources botanical materials for their pure essential oils.

The girls had been waiting in the classroom in their finest hand-embroidered, traditional blouses and full woven skirts. Soon their mothers filed into the back of the classroom to join them. Debbie was waiting in the room with Vilma, the local midwife who had coordinated the students for this Ambassador of Women's Health event. One girl brushed the end of her shiny black braids as she stared intently at the stack of duffels next to Vilma. "What is in the bags?" she wanted to know. The girls were all surprised to see the little cloth bags they were about to be given: washable DfG menstrual care kits.

Debbie helped Vilma conduct the health training and distribution of more than 250 Days for Girls kits. Vilma translated the education from Spanish into the K'iche'[23] language, smiling as the women responded. She told Debbie, "They didn't expect anyone to think of their needs."

The second presentation that week was for the mothers. Debbie told me, "We were in the middle of teaching about the menstrual cycle when one woman who was about four feet tall [common for the area] stood up, shaking her fist as she gave what appeared to be a passionate speech in K'iche'. I looked over at Vilma wondering, *Was this woman mad at us?*

[23] Pronounced "Ketchy."

Vilma translated, "She is saying, 'Women know this? Why haven't we known about this before? This has been so hard on us to cook and make fires and work in the fields and feed and take care of our children, and try to find ways to collect our blood. She pointed at the diagram of the menstrual and fertility cycle. Where were you eight babies ago?'"

Debbie decided right then that she was all in with Days for Girls, as the women in front of her pleaded their case for wanting all women to know how their bodies worked. She spoke to Rob, who sent his email to me soon after that.

"Later, the schoolmaster took us aside to show us the school attendance rolls, explaining that they had 135 boys and only 26 girls registered. He told us that the girls give up because they are missing school when they don't have what they need for periods. He thanked us profusely for providing what they needed," Debbie said.

"We were talking with the women and girls about their responsibility to take care of their bodies and their ability to make life. We explained that saying no to boys now is saying yes to a stronger future. During the conversation a girl near the front asked, 'I can say no?' This simple washable menstrual kit system had opened the door to an honest fact-filled conversation she and her friends, teacher, and mother were eager to have."

Debbie continued, "dōTERRA Healing Hands did many service projects that week. At the end, when the leaders of several communities in which they served came together, the leaders expressed specific gratitude and enthusiasm for the Days for Girls training and what it meant to the future of their community. While they were in the room together, all of these questions came up that led to mothers and daughters talking more. That interchange made a profound generational connection."

Several years after Debbie's trip to Guatemala, Jen and Colin Kelly and their family, who had long lived and worked in Guatemala, went on to support Days for Girls local leadership there. Thus began a countrywide initiative that reached more people in Guatemala while supporting women to lead Days for Girls enterprises there and in other parts of Latin America.

The Ambassador of Women's Health curriculum has now been translated into thirty-one languages[24] and counting. Rob says that one of his tips for getting Days for Girls kits through customs smoothly is to put the education flipchart open to the menstrual page in every duffel. "It works every time. They move right on," he says with a laugh. Rob is more than a supporter; he is a champion of global menstrual equity. He is one of many exceptional men who have become some of our finest Ambassadors of Health. We are all important on the path to ending menstrual inequity. Menstruation truly connects us all. After all, without periods there would be no people.

---

[24] As of May 26, 2022.

Chapter 45

Failing Forward

Real change, enduring change, happens one step at a time.
—Ruth Bader Ginsburg

Lynden, 2015

THE BRIGHT ORANGE ACCENT WALL OF THE DAYS FOR GIRL'S HEAD-
quarters was the perfect color for the level of activity that day in Lynden, Washington. The phone was ringing on both lines. Three volunteers were helping
manage the determined Girl Scouts who had only just arrived but were already
carrying bins of supplies to the large central office table to start packing Days
for Girls kits. Lora and Emily reviewed how each component had its designated
place in the kit, making it easy to quality check and be efficiently compact for
shipping. We had learned the wisdom of both details the hard way. Something
we call "Failing Forward."

At Days for Girls, we meet failure as an opportunity to do better. Failure is
feedback. Information about what is not going well is as important as what is,
because you can't improve without understanding what is needed for improve-
ment. And it's harder to stick with it if you don't celebrate the good that is in
your learning and progress. After all, you paid a price for everything that goes
"wrong." Why not gain the gift? And celebrate it. My response to a problem often sounds like a celebration. I shift to, "You spotted an opportunity! What can
we gain from this?" It can be puzzling to people the first time they witness it. Jan
had just spotted another "opportunity."

"Celeste, I know we prefer the latest rounded shield pattern, and they are nice . . ." Jan said. I could hear the "but" coming. Sure enough, ". . . but too many are coming in like this." The shield she held in front of her looked more like Gumby[25] than a shield. I'd noticed the trend, too, but was hoping they would get more consistent in quality with time.

I nodded. The enterprises were having the same issue.

"Honestly, we aren't getting any feedback that rounded is more comfortable, are we?"

I had to admit we were not.

"It's a lot of waste for just a softer appearance. The squared end style is more consistent, and I have an idea for trimming it that will soften the ends," Jan added. Quality was her passion and the look of determination on her face was built from years of equal part retired executive, expert sewist, and dedication to the girls.

When done well, the version she held in her hands was far more polished in appearance than previous versions, but this poorly made shield was the final evidence we needed to confirm the need for a change after seeing it again and again around the world.

"You're right, Jan," I told her.

Kris, who volunteered with us full-time, was watching out of the corner of her eye as she snapped a tall stack of shields. She was clearly waiting for an answer as well.

"Kris, will you grab the bell?" I asked.

We ring a bell when something happens that will help us reach more girls: a large donation, special media coverage, and identifying a place to do better, or a fail forward. Kris chose the small silver bell, a gift given to us when I spoke at a recent university service event.

"Celebration time! Ring away," I said. Kris grinned and set off the celebrating chime. Jan had just found a way to make DfG pads even better. We all clapped. Jan looked relieved.

Next came the work of testing, pattern revisions, and preparing communications before we could announce the transition. You can't announce a problem without a clear pathway to a solution. We had learned that lesson the

---

[25] Gumby is an asymmetrical cartoon character that is flexible: www.gumbyworld.com.

hard way, too. The more people who joined us, the slower we had to take on changes.

—

People who sew well have a very particular set of skills, and a common thread (pun intended) is their attention to detail. That strength can come with a hazard: when you are meticulous, shifts can be stressful. Our volunteer leaders painstakingly informed and retrained their volunteers every time a pattern change took place. They reprinted new instructions and made new templates by hand, a set for every change forward. We knew it was a lot of work for them, and we wanted to make sure we had an appropriate and complete change before we let them know.

There was the original ribbon style: girls reported that the pads crept forward, and "they looked like a man." Pockets, we decided; we needed pockets.

We tried a thick, plush padded version. It took too much water to wash and too much time to dry, both important factors for those we serve.

One moisture-proof material that we tried, now affectionately referred to as "go-go boot vinyl" was dismissed in a matter of hours—it crinkled when you walked.

The Diamond version was designed to make shields easier to cut out and easier to sew on a treadle machine. Plus, they tessellated well, fitting together like puzzle pieces, not wasting a scrap of fabric. But straight pockets with consistent depth proved nearly impossible for most sewers to master. Then field feedback taught us they were harder for those with disabilities to hold in place while snapping. We moved on to the next version.

The list went on and on. Each version held a significant reason for change—a carefully raised and answered concern. But change fatigue is real, and getting everyone updated on a new style was, there is no way around it, a pain. But once they heard the reason, almost every volunteer stuck with us and miraculously made the changes—twenty-nine times. Our willingness to be what I call "tenaciously flexible" in listening to the wisdom of those we served and served with resulted in genius design. Genius that has now been awarded two patents.

Genius is also in simplicity. Making things more complicated is easy. Keeping the best ideas and distilling to focus on them and stay on point—that is a determined decision that is the key to scale.

We are often asked about menstrual cups. They are a great solution, lasting reportedly up to ten years. They use little water and are ideal if you have a heavier flow. We love the idea of cups, but only about 3 percent of those we serve are open to using them for personal or cultural reasons. That number is rising, but it is still a barrier. We do offer menstrual cups where we are permitted to (some communities forbid it), but the truth is that the uptake has not been huge so far. For example, one partnership group brought two thousand menstrual cups to Uganda in 2016 and could not get a single student to try it. Education can help. Since then, uptake has increased, and maybe someday cups will be completely accepted. But the reality is everyone has their own preferences, and they should have a choice. We are providing both options, but washable pads are still more versatile and readily accepted.

The bell ringing that day in our office was the welcoming of the beginning of one of those shifts. But for now, everyone got back to packing the kits on hand, setting any Gumby shapes aside.

During all of the buzz, Gina was busy answering accounting questions for Days for Girls Ghana; she tapped on my open office door. "Celeste?"

"You're knocking? This must be serious," I said.

"We are an *international* organization," Gina said with a serious expression. She had only been with us three weeks.

"Yes . . ."

"I mean, I knew that, but it's hitting me just how big what we do really is. It's huge!" Much to my relief, she laughed. "Good thing I like a challenge."

Gina is still with us more than five years later and has taken every opportunity to carefully and deliberately learn to keep up with our growth and become the phenomenal CFO that we are so fortunate to have with us today. It is a rare individual who is both brilliant and humble enough to take on such a challenge.

—

A short time later I had two meetings, one a phone call. The other in person. The first was a return call to a man who ran a group of CPAs who volunteered their time and services to help nonprofits. Gina and I agreed that more help would be useful while she migrated our records to a new platform. He was answering my email applying to be considered for the services of their team.

"Where does most of your funding come from?" the CPA asked.

"Donations are mostly individual donors and family foundations. For example, we just got an unsolicited $50,000 check in the mail today. That's unusually high for us, but it happens all of the time," I answered.

"You're telling me that you get unsolicited foundation donations regularly?" he said incredulously. "That doesn't happen. If you can't be honest, this isn't going to work." The phone went dead. He hung up on me. I stared at the phone.

My next appointment, let's call him Bill, arrived just as I hung up. He stood in front of the large colorful map of the world dotted with hundreds of pins marking the locations of chapters, enterprises, and DfG offices, which now included Uganda, Nepal, Ghana, and Guatemala. I waved him in. "Welcome back! It's busy out here; let's go into my office. What can I do for you?"

"I told a friend about our last meeting. He has a lot of fundraising background. I was telling him about how this ragtag bunch of housewives with people running around everywhere is somehow reaching countries all over the world. He wanted me to find out how you are doing it."

Deep breath. He probably didn't mean it the way it sounded.

He paused. "So how do you do it?"

"It's an inspired program and we have phenomenal volunteers and area leaders who are as gifted and generous as they are dedicated. And we work together in respect, trusting each other's wisdom," I answered.

"Uh-huh. So how do you do it?"

"We systemize functions, stay connected to learn best practices, and partner with people all over the world."

"Yeah, but how do you do it? It makes no sense. I think my fundraising friend should come meet you in person, don't you? He may be able to help." He offered me his card. "Call me and I'll set up a time for him to come."

People are welcome at Days for Girls, and we give them our time and attention equally. We love meeting them, hearing their stories, and sharing resources. Visitors traveling from all over the world—Canada, Australia, New Zealand, Sweden, Guatemala, Zimbabwe, and beyond—join us for photos in front of the three round chalkboards marked with our audacious goal and inspiration: *Every Girl. Everywhere. Period.* It was only in coming together in a shared purpose that we were reaching so many and shifting the stigma so fast.

I thanked "Bill" for his interest but never reached back out. He couldn't hear me, let alone acknowledge or respect the beauty of what he was witnessing. Nothing about any of this was ragtag. Everything about this is built of determined action focused enough to create miracles.

Chapter 46

Speaking Up for Periods

It's time for change. It's time to raise
awareness for an issue that affects 50 percent
of the population . . . I'm not ovary acting.
—Rachael Haberman

Edmonds, Washington, 2014–2021

"I DON'T THINK HE'S RIGHT," RACHAEL SAID. HER JUNIOR HIGH SCHOOL
teacher had assigned a persuasive essay and speech. She had chosen the subject
of menstruation. He felt that the topic was too narrow to make it a good speech,
and he wasn't sure the boys would be interested.

She was disappointed. Her mom, April, was quick to respond. "I don't think
he's right either. You should do your speech on what you want."

A few days later Rachael walked to the front of the classroom determined to
do periods proud. When she finished, her teacher came up to her desk, told her
how good the speech was, and invited her to join the speech team.

Rachael and April discovered period poverty years earlier while returning
from attending Julie Metzger's acclaimed educational puberty celebration held
regularly at Seattle Children's Hospital. Rachael, still too young to ride in the
front seat, sat in the back, enamored with the period supply kit given out at the
end of the class. She asked, "Mom, what do homeless people do for pads?"

They researched to see what organizations were providing supplies and,
finding nothing, they finally asked Julie. Her reply? "Hmm, nobody that I know.
Nobody is doing it."

Rachael really wanted to help. April contacted the homeless liaison at the local school district and the answer was the same. "Nothing. I never thought about that before." That's when the liaison realized that there were 200 girls of menstruating age in the district whose families were registered as homeless; 180 of them needed pads. Proof that period poverty is everywhere. The truth remains that anywhere a family or individual has to choose between food and pads, food wins, and assistance vouchers do not cover menstrual products.

April's first thought, like mine, was to collect disposable products. She posted the call for donations on her Facebook page. Someone responded, "Talk to my friend Celeste. They are making washable pads." April took DfG kits to the school district liaison along with the education for how to properly care for them. She helped Days for Girls coordinate distribution of quality single-use products donated by Honest Company as well so girls had a choice, and formed a Days for Girls chapter in Edmonds, Washington.

Over the years we have learned that in places where girls feel "everyone has a pad but me," a washable solution can seem like "a poor girl's choice." But when we offer both a single-use and a colorful product that lasts month after month, then the washable product is often seen as a smart choice that not only saves money but is also comfortable, durable, chemical-free, and better for the environment. The smart choice is reusable, though circumstances can make different solutions optimal. Part of why personal product choice is so important.

As a result of Rachael and April's efforts, thousands of people have received menstrual care products. Rachael and April have also both met many new friends who came to volunteer at their chapter. It's been a multigenerational effort, from ninety-six-year-old Merilyn, who was a whiz at making shields, to Rachael's teen and preteen friends who joined in to cut the ribbons for drawstring bags and help assemble kits. The women also coordinated many fundraisers like Mother's Day teas where the girls did all of the serving, raising thousands of dollars for more girls to have what they need.

When Rachael started her period, she was already a certified Days for Girls Ambassador of Health and quickly became the confidant for her young friends to lean on. Her home was a safe place to talk about periods, their bodies, and their health. Then in junior high, Rachael wanted to go to Africa to see their kits distributed for herself. She and April followed another chapter leader, Carol Hendricks, whose chapter had helped form the first DfG social enterprise in

Eswatini, Africa. Since then, they returned again with friends to bring further support to the enterprise and to do distributions at a women's prison.

For ten years, April and Rachael have been all in for periods. Their golden retriever is, too. She greets volunteers who drop off and pick up supplies on their front porch rocking chair. April says, "It doesn't feel like something I do. It is part of who I am. The volunteers and those in Eswatini are an expansion of our family. And I see the world with greater depth than I did before." April became part of Days for Girls' development team, helping to invite corporate sponsors like Starbucks who have become important champions with us as well.

Rachael and eighteen other girls also formed a Days for Girls club as part of their chapter, meeting once a month to do service projects.

"It just keeps on growing," April says.

Last year, for her oratory competitive topic, Rachael once again took on menstruation. She won third place at state level and went on to nationals. For Rachael, talking about menstruation is not only natural but vital. On one visit to Eswatini with her mom, she hadn't been expecting her period, but it started after they had passed out all of their washable DfG kits and components. They had nothing left for Rachael. It took a half-day of looking to find anything available for purchase anywhere.

"I was glad it happened there. It was only half a day and it was miserable. Imagine not having any access at all."

Rachael and other young DfG leaders, who form Days for Girls Clubs at their schools and serve as mentors for others, are fearless voices for menstrual equity wherever they go around the globe. As are all of the now more than seventy thousand people around the world who have volunteered with Days for Girls. They, like Rachael and April, are exceptional. Extraordinary champions who are all in for girls, women, and people with periods everywhere.

When you reveal that you volunteer to help more pets have shelter, or people have water, or artists have canvas, people understand your impact. It takes an extraordinary person to take on something others don't even want to talk about. Ironically, other causes can seem far more "sexy."

When Days for Girls volunteers explain why they have a cart full of flannel and cheerful cotton, "I'm making washable pads and helping others have access to menstrual care and health education" is not the answer most expect. Some wince and look away; others light up and go from "What?" to "Wow!" Either way, these volunteers keep diving all in, for the girls, giving at a level that is not only inspirational but arguably unparalleled. They receive calls for Days for Girls kits needed all over the world and work to fulfill the requests within their communities: holding events, constructing kits, fundraising, speaking, and connecting, all while advocating to end period poverty and penalties within their own governments. Many talents and skills are needed in Days for Girls efforts.

Photos of chapter leaders distributing kits in the field and discovering outstanding potential local leaders are inspiring. Some of these leaders expanded their efforts to include supporting DfG enterprises whenever they could. We know it is going to take all of us, wherever we live in the world, to reach all of those losing days to lack of menstrual care supply, but doing it consciously and sustainably matters. A global puzzle that kept me up at night, inspiring me to rise early each morning to start again.

Chapter 47

The Power of a Crowd

I come as one, but stand as ten thousand.

—Maya Angelou

Washington, 2014–2016

IT WAS GOING TO TAKE A MIRACLE FOR US TO WIN.

Singer, songwriter, actor, and producer John Legend had partnered up with entrepreneur Ron Burkle of CrowdRise[26] to support girls' initiatives; they called it Operation Girl, and they wanted the power of a crowd to select the winners of their support. Every donation would count as a vote for the winners. The stakes were $50,000 high. That's a lot of girls. We were all in.

Days for Girls was already proof of the power of a crowd.

When you walk into a DfG community service event, you can feel the hum of people and sewing machines. Ironing boards, boxes of soft and colorful materials, and rows of tables are surrounded by everyday people willing to spend their entire day helping create menstrual kits for people they will probably never meet.

One example of a very big event was in Rocklin, California, where a thousand people from diverse communities and faith groups gathered. It had taken a year to prepare. Over two thousand DfG kits were created in one day. There were at least that many smiles and moments of laughter in the room as well. All over the world, events like this happen. Some are small events or even individuals working from their own homes. Many take on the efforts almost full-time. Others, like sixty-three-year-old Ron, a committed volunteer from the Rocklin

---

[26] Burkle Global Initiative, ROYT, and CrowdRise.

chapter, do what they can. He painstakingly threads ribbon into twenty draw-string bags for DfG kits every single week. His hands tremble and his body strains in directions he cannot predict, due to cerebral palsy. Each bag takes him twenty minutes to complete, but he stays at it. His sister shared a video of his determined success. His pure dedication left us speechless. He is not alone.

There is the woman whose friend brought her to an event in hopes of get-ting her out of the house after the devastating loss of one arm. "I can't help," the woman told the DfG volunteers, pointing to the pinned-up sleeve where once her arm had been. Candice, a DfG leader, sat her down at a serger sewing ma-chine with a nine-inch-long strip of fabric. "Just try." It worked. A few minutes later Candice left to get more material for the new volunteer to sew and returned to find the woman in tears. "I am not useless after all," she told the volunteer.

There is the woman who lost her husband and said after starting with Days for Girls, "For the first time in seven months, I have a reason to get up in the morning." Thousands and thousands of others also find joy in making a differ-ence because they care. Because they can. Because they choose to stand up for equity, health, and dignity. Karen Wilkes, the team director who delivers sup-plies and receives Ron's bags weekly, says, "I love being a team leader of DfG. I'm so lucky to interact with so many who dedicate their time to helping in whatever small way they can. It all adds up to so much good."

Everyone is in this together. Enterprises, volunteers, community leaders. All over the world. Each person doing what they can becomes a movement big enough to reach over 2.8 million women and girls in communities around the globe—so far. This is the Power of We.

This time, for the John Legend event, we were being asked to come together in another way.

As usual, we kicked into high gear. The overall amount donated to our crowdfunding campaign would determine the winners and included weekly bo-nus challenges. Our chapters, teams, and supporters rallied, each fundraising to benefit their local efforts, the tally of funds raised by everyone adding up to the possibility of winning the $50,000 award for DfG efforts worldwide. We tackled each weekly challenge strategically.

Week 1: The first organization with ten donations of $100 or more would be put into a drawing for $5,000. We doubled down and got twenty individuals to commit to setting an alarm to donate as soon as the new challenge started. We won.

Week 2: The organization that raised the most in one week would win $5,000. We planned ahead, asking people to save their planned contributions for that week. We won![27]

The top four organizations' totals were pulling ahead of the crowd, and we toggled between the top rankings on the leaderboard daily. Ahead, behind, behind.

Week 3: Our network leaned in and kept pushing forward. I was attached to the phone, calling anyone I could speak to or make an announcement with; everyone got a personal contact from me or the others on our team that week. We were all determined to win the challenge.

Even with the strength of our many volunteers and supporters, the other organizations were far more financially endowed than ours. The leaderboard teetered back and forth all month.

With just days left we were behind.

We kept at it.

But life was about to put my personal efforts on hold.

—

I answered on the first ring. It was one of my daughters calling. She and the boys had moved to Idaho to live closer to her husband's family, and we were missing them all. "Hi, Brea!"

"Mom, it's Gibson. He's in the hospital. We can't wake him up."

Gibson was tall for his two years, and strong. He hadn't shown any signs

---

[27] One of DfG's volunteer leaders, Ann Lewis, won a prize to talk with John Legend in person. She gave our team the privilege of meeting him instead. He took the video call in his living room and paced as he chatted, apologizing for his late arrival to the conference call. "Sorry, it was a late night last night, but I'm happy to meet with you." He mentioned that he was grateful to support Days for Girls and the other benefiting organizations, and that his mother sews, but did not once mention that the late night had been the Grammy Awards. Impressive.

of the disorder his brothers had. Could this new development be the rare PNKD dystonia disorder that his brothers had? The only good news is that though his brothers had trouble going to sleep, they did not have difficulty waking up. But like his brothers, the writhing movement in his legs had happened just as he lost the ability to talk, and now this. I flew to Idaho, arriving within hours to stay with the boys while Brea held her vigil at St. Luke's Children's Hospital.

Two days later Gibson was released with new meds and the diagnosis she dreaded, dystonia. Brea was both stunned and exhausted, but her duties still called.

While she met in Wesley's parent-teacher conference to discuss workarounds needed to help him succeed in the classroom, I was pacing the brick-lined halls, cradling her youngest son in one arm until he fell asleep and pushing their triple stroller with the other to soothe his brother. Soon they were both asleep.

I tucked the baby into the stroller next to his brother, and checked in on the campaign. There were forty-five minutes left in the Operation Girl competition, and the first-place team had just pulled ahead by nearly $20,000.

Rolling the stroller back down the hallway, I made two more calls. "Ann? Good news! We are in the top two, and there are just minutes to go. Thanks for all of your effort. Any more ideas? Anything you can do in these last few minutes would be brilliant!" The last calls symbolized the last of my options for the Operation Girl campaign. It didn't look hopeful. I did what was left: I prayed harder, turning the stroller to pace the other length of the long school hallway, past the library and the drinking fountain, where I had stopped repeatedly to give the children sips.

The phone rang. It was Leah on our DfG team. "A dentist from Tennessee wants to take Days for Girls to Cambodia and noticed how close we are to winning. She hasn't donated before, but she says she will fund ten thousand dollars if we get someone else to make a ten-thousand-dollar match for the win!" In fifteen minutes, the campaign would be over.

"That's amazing. Seriously? And . . . ten thousand dollars in fifteen minutes. Does she seem sincere?"

"Absolutely."

We had already done all that we could. But I promised to try. I hung up, stopped the stroller again, and, grandson on my hip, called the one person I had left, Don.

Our family not only contributes to Days for Girls, but Don had always cheerfully helped out and understood that most of my time and attention went to the organization without any financial compensation. And now I had this really big ask of him. I gave him the pitch that he had overheard a thousand times: "We could reach so many more when we win."

"Are you suggesting that *we* donate ten thousand dollars to Days for Girls, in the next fifteen minutes?"

"Yes. That's exactly what I'm asking."

"You've got to be kidding me . . ." He continued on exactly the argument that I expected. How much more could I ask?

"Don, if we win, we will have more support for the girls, and I'll let the board start paying me a little bit like they have been asking."

The board had been saying that not paying an executive director of an organization at our level was unsustainable. "We will give it as a donation, but it will come back to us," I said. "The girls will be the ones who win."

"What if we don't win?" Don said.

Only eight minutes remained.

"We'll be strategic. We will only donate if we are within striking distance. We will have all of the payment information preloaded and poised to go and click at exactly three minutes to the hour. Enough time that if the payment process fails we can try again, but a short enough time that others will not see it coming."

Don started entering the card information on the donation site, ready for go time.

Leah called the dentist, who assured us she would do the same.

—

The CrowdRise team said they had been watching closely as more donations poured in for all of the organizations. Days for Girls was creeping closer to first place. Then, moments before the deadline, their team saw the first $10,000 come in for us. Seconds later, another $10,000 along with hundreds of other donations. We got a call from CrowdRise. "You won first place! What a win! We couldn't believe it! We were cheering when we watched you pull ahead."

I was still jumping up and down when Brea came out of her meeting. "What happened?" she asked.

—

About a year later, a call came in from Rolls, the same woman who organized Operation Girl, to invite us to Revlon's "Love Is On" crowdfunding challenge, focused on women's health. Were we interested? Absolutely!

Revlon needed some convincing. By "women's health" they meant diabetes, heart disease, and breast cancer, not periods. Rolls campaigned for us, assuring them that menstrual equity is indeed a women's health issue. The stakes this time were $1,400,000 strong: $1 million for first place, $250,000 for second place, and $150,000 for third, while inspiring what would end up resulting in $6 million total support and advancement for the organizations participating.

The large donors and donor base of the organizations with strong historic reputations and rich funding trusts that Revlon had already selected would be a force to keep up with. We didn't have the highly resourced supporters and decades-old endowments that several of the other orgs did; this would take another miracle. I met with the board of directors of Days for Girls and explained the opportunity. Would they be willing to allow us to divert every pending donation for the next month to our challenge? Our bottom line would look really skinny for a month, but in the end, with good strategy and targeted timing, the reward could be huge for Days for Girls. Either way, we would keep everything we fundraised. They agreed. With that, we were at the starting line to go toe to toe with some of the biggest nonprofits in the United States.

Our small, mostly volunteer team planned the communications and strategy, then contacted all of our chapters and teams, major donors, and friends with the update. We were going for the big time with the *Power of We*.

Each of the selected organizations was assigned a web page to share with supporters. At go, the big organizations started pulling ahead. But the campaign page for Days for Girls started stacking up with the square icons of new Team Champion pages started by chapters, teams, and supporters, like dozens of blank canvases suddenly filled with images worthy of our *ooh*s and *aah*s. Their local support started pouring in. Once again, we witnessed the power of a crowd.

Meanwhile, I kept calling supporters and reaching out to every potential option. The dōTERRA Healing Hands Foundation had agreed to hold their committed contribution until the competition and send their contributions in strategic measure over the weeks.

Calls started coming in. "How does this work again?"

"Your donations right now all count as votes for us to win up to one million dollars and we'll gain high-profile recognition for the importance of menstrual health. Imagine the game changer that would be for communities all over this planet!"

We won weekly challenges. We kept reaching out. Personal calls worked better than emails. It was a lot of phone time, speaking, and meetings, and it was working. We were bobbing between sixth and third place for weeks.

When we got within striking distance, Rob and Debbie Young came in to increase their support to an amount they asked me not to share, but it was huge. Every effort. Every dollar. Every donation, together. We finished in an impossible fourth place, up against influential organizations such as the American Heart Association, and we raised significant support, as well as growing awareness. Winning one of the top ranks was, for the uber-sized organizations, a small part of their budget. For us, an organization for whom the smallest donation makes a tremendous difference, it was truly a huge leap forward in impact and results.

The next year Revlon invited us again, and they upped the ante for their million-dollar challenge. This time the competition was even steeper. Three weeks after it started, our team was exhausted with the effort of contacting, promoting, brainstorming, and stretching with amazing champions of Days for Girls. But we still didn't have a legacy endowment with major donors five layers deep like some of those who were in the game. With days left, my prayers for inspiration got slightly desperate and increasingly determined. *You know the needs; please help me to know who to reach out to. Let the right people show up at the right time. Or at least let my heart be settled in acceptance of what is. But I'm not giving up if you aren't.*

Soon a return call came in from Julie Cook, a long-time friend of Days for Girls. I explained the stakes. She said, "Let me talk to Greg and see what we can do." Minutes later she called back. "Greg and I are coming in," she told me, offering a contribution that quadrupled what I could ever have dared hope. I was speechless, wept in gratitude, followed by a spontaneous squeal of delight that

I'm sure hurt her ears. The volunteers in the office came running when I said, through tears of joy, "This is going to happen!" Every person in our office did an actual happy dance while ringing both bells in the office, celebrating the girls whose lives would be changed.

Third place! Cancer Research Institute, Penn Medicine's Basser Center, Days for Girls International, and Beyond Type 1 Diabetes Foundation, in that order. The surprising (to them) third-place win brought home a giant check (literally) for $75,000 from Revlon, and raised $757,850 in donations for Days for Girls. Not only did all of the support add up to the tremendous ability to reach more women, girls, and communities, but the awareness raised was phenomenal. We were invited to New York City to attend the awards ceremony and meet the Revlon team in person.

—

Rockefeller Center was dressed up for the holidays. Ice skaters were twirling at the famous outdoor skating rink as we arrived. Our team, including my daughter Ashley who had just borrowed the skates of a stranger to experience doing "one loop around" the open rink (dressed in her formal black dress, no less), now piled into the elevator. It traveled so fast up to the sixty-fifth floor that our ears actually popped. We chattered about how special this place, this moment, and this time was. The famous Rainbow Room stopped us mid-sentence, sparkling with crystal chandeliers and dazzling lights. The press was there, not for us, but for celebrities like Olivia Wilde and Halle Berry. At the awards ceremony we met and congratulated other winning teams and thanked the leaders who made the opportunity possible. Then our team stepped onto the platform to receive the gigantic check signed *Love Is On*. Halle Berry, who is even more beautiful in person than on the screen, smiled when she said, "I love Days for Girls. What you do really is important."

Days for Girls' reach went from 270,367 girls the year prior with the boost of the last campaign to 321,660 in the next year alone. All thanks to the power of a crowd.

Chapter 48
The Earthquake that Shook Up Periods

We walk on the crust of an unfinished planet.
—Charles Kuralt

Nepal, 2015

THE ELEPHANTS KNEW FIRST. JUST BEFORE THE 2015 EARTHQUAKE struck Nepal, the elephants made crazy sounds. Their feet shifted beneath their riders, but they didn't run. Everything else seemed to move; even the water splashed in an odd way in the river. Birds flew erratically overhead. Maya, who is Days for Girls Nepal's Country Director today, was assisting with a National Trust for Conservation trip in Chitwan when the earthquake hit. She pulled her phone out of her jacket pocket to call and check on her aunt at home. It rang once and went dead. Maya's supervisor gave her permission to leave immediately, assuring her that he would get the fifteen students safely home. The trip to Bhaktapur usually took her seven hours, but landslides and fallen houses now blocked the roads, stretching her journey to nearly twice that. By the time she got to Bhaktapur, the smell of dead bodies beneath the rubble rose in the air.

Two floors of her aunt's stone home had collapsed, and Maya herself nearly collapsed with relief when she found her aunt alive and well. Neither of them imagined that a second earthquake would hit less than a month later while they were still trying to pick up the pieces of their lives. The second earthquake was 7.3 magnitude and almost as devastating as the first.

Maya had thought that it was a made-up story when her grandfather used to tell her about the 1934 earthquake. How all was dust after the ground cracked and growled. But when it happened this time, she said, "Okay, my grandfather, I see now."

Two days after the earthquake, thieves arrived, stealing things from people too busy lifting stones from survivors to stop them from emptying what was left in the cracks. When exhaustion forced people to stop their rescue efforts, there was no chatter; only the sound of crows filled the lost spaces. But Maya and the others rose back up again and again to help. With little help from the government, the people helped each other. Fallen houses and debris still blocked roads. Someone's scooter became the aid vehicle. Others carried their own sack of noodles, sharing what they had.

—

While Maya and her community helped each other, Mercy Corps, a leading global organization with a primary focus on disaster relief, called for five things most needed to give aid after the earthquake: tarps, blankets/towels, clean water, cooking utensils, and hygiene supplies—specifically soap and washable sanitary pads. For the first time in emergency response, washable menstrual care products were in the top five of the list of needs. Why? No one said it then, but in time we would learn it was in large part due to *chhaupadi*.

Chhaupadi means "menstruating woman," but in Nepal and in India as well it is also the term for the exile of women during their periods. Women are considered untouchable during those days and even seven to twenty-one days after giving birth to a newborn. It is isolation born of the myth that menstruating women could cause ill fortune, sickness, or even death. They were exiled to cattle lean-tos, underneath the crawlspaces of homes, in caves, or to elevated stick platforms, forests, or sheds made specifically for the practice. Anywhere but near those they loved. While secluded they are at risk of snakebites, animal attacks, and exposure to the weather.

The Supreme Court of Nepal had outlawed the practice of chhaupadi in 2005, but the tradition continued nonetheless. When the earthquake happened, there was nowhere to hide the gap between law and actual practice. Temporary tents did not have any "away" to send women to, and menstruation went from a silent untouchable taboo to an urgent crisis in need of being addressed.

Mercy Corps called for washable pads when the earthquake hit because not only did the women need supplies they could count on month after month, but also disposable single-use products added to the existing refuse problem in makeshift emergency camps. Washables save resources and funding, a smart choice almost anywhere. Thousands of Days for Girls volunteers from Australia, Canada, New Zealand, the United Kingdom, and the United States, as well as other organizations, started responding to meet the need.

That earthquake shook up the silence around menstruation within the development sector in a big way, but the movement had already been growing around the globe. The day after the first Nepalese earthquake in April, London-based artist and activist Kiran Gandhi ran the London Marathon without menstrual care products, choosing to let the shock of the stain advocate for breaking the stigma of menstruation. Most people wouldn't go "full marathon" to heighten the conversation. She did. In August of that same year, a U.S. presidential candidate tried using a slighting reference to menstruation as a slam to a newscaster. Instead of backing away from the insult, people responded with the resilient insistence that it was time to break the taboo: #PeriodsAreNotAnInsult.

National Public Radio (NPR) would go on to declare 2015 the Year of the Period,[28] and they didn't mean punctuation! Periods were finally having their day. Their year. But the stigma and shame associated with it were far from disappearing. Days for Girls Nepal kept working, determined to change that.

In March 2017 I got the gift of returning to serve with the DfG Nepal team again, this time as they prepared to travel to address the issue of chhaupadi.

I had been on the road to understanding the puzzle of period poverty for years and had learned long before that shifts in cultural norms require more than a program. People support what they create. Real change comes from within individuals and communities themselves. It is neither shame nor punishment that creates shifts. Conversations, education, and invitations to new considerations can.

—

[28] Malaka Gharib, "Why 2015 Was the Year of the Period, and We Don't Mean Punctuation," NPR, December 31, 2015. www.npr.org/sections/health-shots/2015/12/31/460726461/why-2015 -was-the-year-of-the-period-and-we-dont-mean-punctuation.

You have to depend on the kindness of strangers when you arrive at Days for Girls Nepal, based in Kathmandu. Not the team's kindness; that is a given. They feel like family from the first namaste. The challenge is rather the pulsing traffic pushing when there is neither pull-over nor parking possible on the narrow roadway adjacent to the tall stucco sliver of a structure so generously made available for the work of Days for Girls in Nepal. This is a drop-and-go zone.

Our driver slowed to a stop just long enough for us to grab our luggage and run to the first step of the narrow stairs that lead to a small terrace above. A team member beckoned us up. Before we even removed our shoes we were welcomed with namastes, smiles, and bright orange traditional kata greeting scarves draped around our necks, tokens of well wishes for happiness and prosperity. We placed our shoes along the step's edge before exchanging heartfelt namastes with the others who had just learned of our arrival.

We followed them through the doorway, lower than customary in other places. Later, much to the delight of my husband, who is 5 foot, 10½ inches (he always mentions the half-inch), he hit his head on one of the doorjambs and smiled, saying, "I have met my people." Most people feel that way when they meet the team in Kathmandu. Part of the floor has been sloped since the earthquake, and it's not located where other such offices would be. But it is part of the miracle of Days for Girls. The stucco building was the family home of Dr. Usha, cofounder of DfG Nepal, and her siblings, Sam, Luxmi, and Tara. After the earthquake there were a few cracks in it, but it was structurally sound. They generously donated its usage for a few months as the office and work area for Days for Girls Nepal until our need for more space grew, and funding from projects was sufficient to cover rent. Even then, for a time, Dr. Usha used the rent to repair the home until they felt it suitable enough to charge real rent.

For the women and men in the office, this is not a job. Rather, it is a chance to help those who are losing their days due to a lack of suitable menstrual care that they can count on. It's a chance to break the cycles of stigma and shame. No one has to tell them to focus on quality, nor to go faster. They have that part in their hearts. And their sewing specialist Makama Luxmi is ever ready to encourage excellence. New sewists start on bags and not until they have proven their proficiency do they get to graduate to the next kit components, liners and then shields. Each advancement is treated as an opportunity and an honor. You can feel it even when you work side by side with them. Draped in beautiful colorful saris, they are a force to be reckoned with.

On that trip, we gathered in the front room of the house, reviewing Days for Girls' cultural bridging tradition, honoring the wisdom of communities and individuals, and seeking to understand instead of shaming. If there was ever a time that we would need to bridge a gap of understanding, the issue of chhaupadi was one.

Lila, a woman whose slight frame and quiet nature belies her strength, was the DfG Nepal team member willing to leave the comfort of her home in Kathmandu to return to the home of her childhood, Kalikot, a place where the practice of chhaupadi was still prominent. Lila had asked to take on bringing the education and pads to an estimated 20,000 women there. She unfolded a sheet of paper where she had written a song about menstruation to help in her quest to break the stigma and shame. It was catchy and moving. The team loved it. I asked if she would reconsider one line that said chhaupadi was backward, in hopes that another phrase might support action without making the community wrong. She agreed and changed the phrase on the spot.

We finalized our agenda; Maya, Lila, and the entire Days for Girls Nepal team decided who would do what, how we would get there, where we would stay, and how many kits we would need. DfGI program manager Sarah Webb had been working with them in the weeks before my arrival and now took notes of their expanding plan. Just before leaving to work in the countryside, we had a meeting with a representative from Splash, the esteemed water organization. The plan was to do a special event on Menstrual Hygiene Day on May 28. As we talked, I suggested that perhaps with enough volunteers and funding we could reach twenty-eight schools on that day. Normally, when I come up with a "Celeste idea" there are one of two responses: terror or excitement. Sometimes both. Celeste ideas are usually big and sometimes need some discussion to get pared down to a panic-free scale. I waited to see which way this would tip. They were excited.

The team brainstormed further. Splash would communicate with twenty-eight of their schools in preparation. Days for Girls Nepal would provide the PODs. A POD is the smallest unit of a Days for Girls kit, a Portable Object of Dignity, and includes one shield and two liners. Days for Girls International would also provide the funding as well as the majority of the volunteers and trainers, who would teach the Splash team how to do the DfG education. They would also coordinate poetry and poster competitions about menstruation. Splash would design activities at each location and manage the Monitoring, Learning, and Evaluation (MLE).

Soon our friends Rob and Debbie Young of dōTERRA arrived on their way to a dōTERRA Healing Hands expedition. I shared the vision of what the team had just been creating. Before we got to the third room of their DfG Nepal tour, they had enthusiastically agreed to fund the special event, with dōTERRA Healing Hands Foundation joining us. With that, the door was opened for Days for Girls Nepal and Splash to accomplish the improbable: reaching five thousand girls and five thousand boys with vital health education and, in the case of the girls, washable menstrual care products they could count on month after month, all in just one day.

The teams celebrated together, already envisioning the outcome of colorful celebrations of poetry, dance, games, and the declaration that periods are healthy and natural. That result would not come about for several months, but on that afternoon in Kathmandu, with the cars honking below, we felt excited as we climbed down the stairs to the van that would soon whisk up in time for us to jump in before we moved back into traffic and back to our hotel. Our final mission of the day was to rest. In the morning we would leave for Kalikot.

Chapter 49
Untouchable

I may not have gone where I intended
to go, but I think I have ended up where
I intended to be.
—Douglas Adams

Nepal, 2016

THE TWELVE-PASSENGER PLANE SKIMMED BELLY CLOSE TO THE SPIKE of the mountaintop before tipping sharply down toward the airstrip at Nepalganj, three hundred miles west of Kathmandu in the Terai plains. We swooped past the edge of the mountainside below, a steep-winged approach that left us grateful for our seatbelts. Then almost before we leveled out—touchdown.

Romeo, the friendly Nepalese driver who greeted us, warned us that the next part of our journey was the most challenging. He helped us load up the vehicle with the heavy duffels we'd brought along. They were filled with the hundreds of DfG kits created by, and purchased from, the team at Days for Girls Nepal. The team was still busy working to make more kits that would arrive by bus later. Next stop, Kalikot, and the launch of DfG Nepal's menstrual health campaign there.

The road to Kalikot started out innocent enough. Lush and colorful mountains and valleys unfolded. The driver repeated that this part of the journey would take us to one of the most dangerous roads of Nepal. I had been on a lot of roads in a lot of places. How bad could it be in comparison to the steeply precarious roads on the way to the cloud forests of Costa Rica or the rutted roads of southwestern Zimbabwe? I smiled. We would be fine. Almost on cue the road worsened. Landslides of silted slate spilled across the road and over the cliffside. I held my breath as Romeo nudged the vehicle along the shifting bare edge of the slope. Ahead were steep gully-washed turns that traversed a thousand-foot drop-off without the benefit of a side rail. Buses came nose to nose on the seemingly single-lane road. One somehow backed up enough to do a side-by-side shuffle on an only slightly less narrow bit of road nearby. This was a stew of all the dangerous roads I ever traveled. I prayed that if our vehicle joined the others at the bottom of the cliffs that my family would forgive me. Then I shifted to more positive thoughts.

The going was slow and, though we had hoped to get through in one day, darkness was soon falling on a road that is impossible to travel by night. Trucks and cars stopped at the barricade that wisely blocked passage. "Well, that's it for today," said Dr. Usha, climbing out of the car with our driver. "We'll go find a place for us to stay for the night." As beautiful and elegant as she is tall, Usha walked away in sure strides, quickly disappearing between the rows of trucks and vehicles, returning a short time later. They had found a place to stay in a local woman's guest house. There was a warm meal and a shared room with electricity, water, and a plank bed for each of us, an extra blanket to serve as a mattress. We were grateful. Sleep came quickly. Tomorrow it would all be worth it. We would reach some of the women we came to be with.

—

By afternoon the next day, the village we were aiming for appeared perched along the slope at the top of the hill above us. Romeo skillfully navigated the last of the serpentine roadway that led to it. Over a lunch of spicy curry potatoes, vegetables, and delicious fresh roti flatbread, Lila spoke again of chhaupadi.

Women consigned to chhaupadi are not only considered untouchable but are not usually permitted traditional milk, honey, or ghee. At mealtimes they are often limited to a plate of breadcrumbs or rice. The risk to others is considered so great that their plate is pushed to them over the ground from a distance so as not to risk the contamination of touching the plate at the same time.

Chhaupadi is an exile that doesn't exempt you from work. Except for cooking. You're not allowed to cook. And you can't eat normal food, or be with your family, or sleep inside where you are safe, warm, and dry. As a young woman,

Lila hid in the forest and in caves during her period. "I didn't understand what it was. I was afraid of the dark at night, and I didn't have enough clothes to shelter from the cold. I could not be in the warmth with my family." The last girl reported to have died during the isolation of chhaupadi suffered a snakebite while waiting alone. Her shed was a clay structure just big enough for her to sit in at the edge of her family's plot on a steep mountainside where she waited out the days before ritually cleansing.

For days every month menstruators become untouchable. How untouchable? Untouchable enough that families, women, girls, and communities feel compelled to risk lives for something basic to our biology, for something that connects us all: menstruation. Knowing the dangers, why would families risk the lives of their daughters, mothers, and friends? Despite being outlawed, and later made a fineable offense at the end of 2018, why does the practice go on?

Consider that almost everything we associate with blood is illness or injury. If you truly believed that being in your home could potentially cause ill fortune or even death to your family, could any law or fine be able to convince you to risk their lives? If you didn't know what menstruation was, and your tradition held firmly to defining it as a curse, it would be easy to believe you are untouchable. These women and families are willing to do anything to protect each other. Wouldn't you? That's why shaming and punishment isn't stopping them. I'm betting that you, like me, would go to the shed to protect them if you thought you were saving them. Sure, we likely would add on to the shed and make it more comfortable, but I believe that we would still go to the shed.

Chapter 50

These Are Not Mountains

The real voyage of discovery consists not in seeking
new lands but in seeing with new eyes.
—Marcel Proust

Kalikot, 2016

THE PATH NARROWED AS WE CLIMBED. THE GRACEFUL NEPALESE woman in front of me led the way. We were walking back to our lodgings after having participated in the first Days for Girls women's health circle in Kalikot. Gray and beige mountainsides created an accordion-pleated terrain before us. The small pathway we walked was a thin thread on a mountain's edge, along a sheer drop of likely one thousand feet or more. "These mountains are beautiful," I said, attempting to keep my eyes focused on the mountaintops where the receding daylight now changed the tinge of the mountainsides from beige to purple and blue, and away from the cliffside.

My new friend answered, "Oh, these are not mountains; these are hills."

I held back a laugh, answering instead, "Where I come from, these are definitely mountains."

The woman replied with quiet assurance, "No. These are hills."

Trust me when I tell you these were steep mountains by any standard I had ever seen, and I live within view of Mount Rainier, which clocks in at 14,417 feet. A fellow team member later added, "Even by Colorado standards, these are mountains." But I knew better than to disagree. I learned long ago that when someone shares a perspective different from your own, it is wise to ask questions and listen before assuming your own perception is correct. Even if it feels so far off that it is hard not to laugh in response.

Good thing! Because only a few days later, as we flew out from Nepalganj I looked out the airplane window and recognized those same "hills" below in comparison to the mountainous peaks—the sisters of Everest—that towered far above the cloud line in front of us. When you live in the neighborhood of Everest, clearly you see mountains in a whole different way.

We all see different kinds of "mountains" based on our experience. In my life and work in the world, I had to learn to stay open to finding understanding across great voids of difference. The wisdom of those we meet isn't always shared unless we ask, and truly listen. It's listening and intently observing that allows us to start to see pathways where we once saw mountains. Once in a while we come face to face with this truth and sometimes it surprises us. One example went viral a few years back; maybe you saw it. The striped dress.

Chapter 51

What Color Is This Dress?

Culture is the song, not the instrument;
and we're all in this symphony together.
—Bjorn Maes

Lynden, Washington, 2018

"WHAT COLOR IS THIS DRESS?"

A few years ago, the photo of the striped dress came in on my family's text storm. "White and gold," I answered.

A flurry of texts followed unanimously. "Blue and black."

"Are you kidding me?!" I asked.

My youngest son, Reed, responded by texting a photo of a white and beige puppy. "Mom, can we keep the blue and black puppy, please?" We laughed.

But it was no joke; some people really did see blue and black and I was absolutely seeing white and gold.[29] Scientists say that only 30 percent see the dress for what it is: blue and black. How is it possible that we can look at the exact same photo and see it so differently? Scientists say the culprit is the photo's background. The same part of your brain that interprets color in the varying light of dawn, noon, or dusk adjusts your sensory response based on the surrounding pattern—it is all about perspective.

Perspectives and experiences shape how we see everything and we often don't even realize it. Here's another example: What is cold? Certainly people

---

[29] The so-called "dress-gate debate" began on a Tumblr page where someone asked for help in deciding the true color of the dress.

acclimated to Rio have a different answer than those who live in Finland. Cold tap water feels hot when running over hands chilled from playing in the snow. Dim light can seem blinding if you just stepped out of a darkened theater. And of course, we cannot know what light is if we have never experienced the dark.

Scales of perception vary for almost everything we are familiar with. Time, ownership, leadership, communication, wealth. You may think of a calendar or a clock and say, not time; that's linear. Time is time. Or is it?

Does time really fly when you're having fun? Of course. Time is a variable stream. How slow were the days before the holidays when you were a child? Or the last moments when you are waiting for the arrival of a loved one? How fast are the last hours to cram for study before a difficult test? There are cultures who see time as a place. Some cultures see time as circular. And they are *right*. We all are right. Time, like energy and space, is a flexible expression of relativity.

Physicists even debate whether time is real.

My husband is the Swiss watch of humanity. If we are ten minutes early for a function, to him we are already late. I am more flexible with time, seeing it as a helpful reference for shared planning. I have to set alarms to show up on time for meetings, squeezing too much in before my next one, while Don makes sure that he is where he needs to be when he needs to be there with no alarm required. I trust I am always where I need to be when I need to be there. For decades now, we have taught each other new ways to navigate time.

We all see different hills and mountains. We all see different colors in the dress. And that is a very good thing. Without our differences we couldn't build all the possibilities that can change our world and fill it with brilliant new potential. We all have different strengths and weaknesses. And often our greatest strengths are hidden in our weaknesses, and vice versa.

What if we celebrated our differences? What if we asked more often about the colors others see? Did you know that the Maasai helped in the invention of mobile banking? Known for their red robes, colorful beads, and warrior spears, they might not typically be consulted about a new form of currency and banking, yet I am told they played a pivotal part in the inspiration for mobile banking, a service giving millions of people access to the formal financial system in otherwise largely cash-based societies. While walking aside their livestock, they innovated using mobile minutes for currency and were observed doing so, which became one of the sparks for mobile currency. Wisdom does not live in one place or one viewpoint. Imagine if we entered every encounter with curiosity and eagerness to learn from each other.

I learned how to navigate difficult situations by trying to see the viewpoints of others, communicating from the viewpoint of what matters to others, and seeking connection where we have common ground. When I enter a situation, I am not just standing in it; I am watching with the finely tuned senses that my upbringing developed well. I am watching for responses, listening for subtext, asking questions with curiosity and interest, and then reflecting on what I have learned through as many lenses of consideration as I can manage, a prism of potential based on listening and connection.

At Days for Girls, we call this technique "cultural bridging." We listen with interest. We don't shame. We don't talk down to anyone, nor assume we know more. We don't demand change. We invite new considerations. We have conversations. And conversations are a powerful thing.

When the team reaches communities practicing chhaupadi in Nepal, their invitation to leaders is shared by women from their country, in their language. Holding up a colorful Days for Girls flipchart, they turn the pages and hit the highlights. They hold up a soft folded pad and then smile and confidently await questions. It is only then that they ask permission to hold women's circles in the community, hiring and training local women to teach beside Lila. An invitation to make a new decision that sounds something like this: "The law has not and cannot stop you. What if you as leaders honored your rich tradition in new ways? What if you ritually cleansed the washable pad and chose not to risk the health of your young women?"

Once, when I was present, one Hindi pundit spent almost thirty minutes talking afterward about how the time had come to practice in a new way. Invitation and acknowledgement are powerful.

So far, leaders in every community have agreed. They approve of women and girls practicing chhaupadi in new ways and honoring family tradition while still being free to go to school and be in their community. Not so long after that first visit to Kalikot, Days for Girls leaders in Nepal were providing education and DfG kits throughout the region. As of this writing, they have reached more than

21,000 women and girls in Kalikot alone. Communities report shifting attitudes and improved conditions for girls in attending school.

In November 2020 and February 2021, Days for Girls partnered with the Monitoring and Evaluation (M&E) firm Rural Senses to speak to girls and women in the Kalikot region in rural Nepal. Here are their key conclusions.[30]

In communities that engaged in Days for Girls' services, 60 percent fewer women say they practiced chhaupadi compared to non-DfG participating women, which demonstrates success in destigmatizing menstruation and overall shifts in community attitudes surrounding this harmful practice.

Eighty percent shared they feel safer during menstruation now than they did before, crediting DfG programming as playing an important role in this.

It is evident from the evaluation that the women have benefited significantly from DfG's interventions. From the DfG training, they most valued their introduction to menstrual hygiene and the use of reusable sanitary pads and panties. Seventy percent of them still use their DfG kit today (several years since receiving it), and value this as it provides privacy, cleanliness and enables girls to go to school during menstruation.

The women showed the highest sense of self-worth and gender equality and the most accurate understanding of the purpose of menstruation. They showed the least shame in discussing menstruation in their home and community (when compared to the baseline control group).

And the result that I had seen again and again in my interactions with those going through our program was shown in one significant conclusion.

Days for Girls program intervention increases women's self-esteem and empowers them to be decision-makers in their families and communities. Supporting Findings: DfG women show higher self-worth and understanding of the value of women and menstruation. In response to the statement, "yes, women are as valuable as men in society," there was a sixteen-point differential between those women who had not

---

[30] Find more report details at "Menstrual Stigma in Nepal: Key Insights (Part 2)," Days for Girls blogspot, July 26, 2022. www.daysforgirls.org/blog/menstrual-stigma-in-nepal-key-insights-part-2/.

received DfG education and those who had: only 56 percent of the former affirmed the
statement, compared to 70 percent of the latter.

Would it have worked so well if we came to shame? I don't believe so. Is it perfectly solved? No. That's the point.

Shifts of cultural significance are a dance of culture and knowledge, born of conversations that live on when they are owned and held by those who are within the prisms of the culture itself. Priceless shifts worth sacrificing for.

Chapter 52

The Longest Layover

BE S.A.F.E ... E is for EXIT with friends.

It's safer to walk with others than alone.

—Segment from Self-Defense in the DfG Ambassador of Health
Education

Lynden, Washington, 2016

THE LAST SERIOUS SEIZURE I HAD WAS A BONE RATTLER. IT STARTED with fireworks, electric snakes biting the inside of my skull, lightning in the darkness. I wanted to call out to Don, but I kept falling backward into the abyss.

Don woke up to my voice raspy and shallow. "Snake. Snake."

Moments later my body vacillated between jolting and stillness in a way he had never seen. I wouldn't know. I was lost in the abyss. I opened my eyes to Don holding a damp cloth on my forehead.

"That was a bad one," he said. "You okay now?"

It had now been almost a year since I had that seizure, and I was doing much better and back to regularly traveling again. I was giving about fifty speaking engagements a year, along with training Ambassadors of Health and regional office check-ins. Don and I had made the agreement long ago that I would no longer travel alone. But the reality of budget limitations and timelines felt reasonable enough to justify bending the rules this once, for a rigorous agenda that I assured him could make all the difference in the world. I had strong team members meeting me in Bangladesh for the training of Ambassadors of Health; in Hong

Kong for the Asian Women's Conference Keynote; and in NYC for speaking at the United Nations' Commission on the Status of Women. "Friends will be meeting me at every stop," I assured Don. "I've been seizure-free for a long time now. I'll be fine."

On the first leg of the trip, Don FaceTimed from home. "Celeste, the doctor called; you were right. You have an infection. Your second culture came back positive, but it's an unusual strain. Your travel antibiotic won't work." He sounded anxious. "Can you get specialized antibiotics in Bangladesh?" He spelled out the name of the medication.

I turned my cell phone screen and Don's worried expression toward my roomies Barb and Maryanne, who were both nurses. "What do you say, ladies? Can we get it?"

"Absolutely. I'll text the lead doctor right now," she answered.

Barb frequently traveled to Bangladesh from Australia to assist with cleft palate surgeries, and as a Days for Girls Australia team leader, she had not only brought DfG kits for communities they served with but had worked with a local leader to coordinate Ambassador of Health training for the more than eighty local individuals that I had trained earlier that day.

Don seemed only slightly reassured, promising to send the medication he had picked up to my hotel in New York as backup so it would be there when I arrived to speak at the United Nations, just in case. "But I really think you should just come home now and skip the Asian Women's Conference and UN. Don't you?"

"I'm literally surrounded by nurses and doctors here. I'll only be in Hong Kong for two days, and the conference is an important opportunity for Days for Girls. We may not get another chance. I'll be fine, really."

He looked unconvinced. "How'd the training go today?"

"It was brilliant," Barb answered. "You should have seen us all practice teaching each other."

Just as we had finished the AWH training, two young women approached me in their bright colored saris. One said, "I never wanted to have a baby, because I was afraid I might have a girl-child and she would go through what I have. But now I pray to Allah that I may have a girl-child, and I will teach her what we have learned and that she is strong and beautiful and can make a difference." Her friend nodded in agreement.

With their permission, I hugged them both.

—

The team had breakfast together the next morning as we planned our full day ahead. Sabera, a local leader and Barb's local partner who was coordinating our DfG activities, arranged a short television interview to promote menstrual advocacy and for the two of us to introduce her work with Days for Girls in Bangladesh. Afterward, the drive to the edge of the slums north of Dhaka went by quickly. We pulled in just before several of Sabera's influential friends arrived. She had convinced them to join us in hopes of gaining long-term support for the program.

She climbed out of the vehicle eager to greet them. "Thank you for coming. The girls will welcome your support." Spotting the teacher of the nearby school who had been waiting for us, she called out, "We are here!"

Soon 110 girls approached from somewhere alongside the road we had just turned down and gathered under the ornate scallop-trimmed tent set up for them. Their matching school uniforms, purple three-piece saris, fluttered as they hurried to the tarp laid out for seating.

Sabera welcomed them, introducing everyone before launching into the health education she had just learned. I snapped a few photos of the girls' attentive faces as they listened. Barb commented in a whisper that she would never have thought 110 girls could be so quiet. Sabera's passion was the self-defense portion of the curriculum. People often emphasize the part of the education that most sings to them, and for her it was self-defense, though she covered it all: periods, reproductive wellness, and more, just as she had learned.

Afterward the rest of us moved among the girls as they carefully removed the items from their colorful DfG bags before practicing folding and unfolding one or two liners, placing them in their protective shield to create a pad. Snapping and unsnapping the wings of their pads around their brightly colored new "knickers."

"That's exactly right!" Barb said, cheering them on.

The girls nearest us waved them high above their heads.

Soon they were singing, "We Will Overcome," first in Bengali and then in English, before switching to upbeat traditional songs as music played from a boombox nearby. The girls started dancing, becoming a braided bob and weave of purple sari happiness, the scalloped edges of the tent overhead swaying with them in the breeze. They grabbed our hands and pulled us in. An instant happy memory of sunshine, purple, and laughter.

A year later, when Barb and fellow nurse, Maryanne returned on another surgical mission they dropped by to visit the same school. "A few of the girls recognized us and ran up to say they hadn't missed a single day of school since the training," Barb would report. "We asked how it went with what we taught them. They said they had taught their parents, too. The older girls joined us to teach the younger girls at their school."

For now, reluctantly, we said goodbye and the girls returned to their school. I wanted to follow them down the path to the place the girls were from. "There may be a couple hours before dark," I said, noting the still strong daylight overhead. "Could we make a brief stop at the slums where the girls live?" I wouldn't be with them later in the week when they did more distributions there and I was eager to see for myself what they had described in great detail. The shanties sounded like the ones in Kenya I was familiar with.

"Are you kidding me?" Maryanne said, laughing. "Not a chance. We're exhausted. You're going to kill us with this pace. But we could stop at the fabric supplier you wanted to see on the way back."

The wholesale fabric supplier was in a cinderblock building with many stories, resembling a small mall. We took two staircases up and entered the fabric store. The men behind the glass cases were happy to assist. We touched the fabric samples they pulled from shelves. They had more options than most areas I'd seen.

"How much flannel fabric do you usually have in stock?" Barb asked.

Under the flicker of the bare fluorescent tubes, my ears started ringing, one of the signs of neurological trouble for me. But it made no sense. It was the wrong time of month. I didn't have a headache. I felt my forehead. It felt like I might have a slight fever. The infection! Illness can be one of the triggers of the disorder that had stayed quiet within me most of my life.

Barb's doctor friends had gone to the trouble of locating the prescription at a Bengali local pharmacy and hand delivered the needed prescription to me the evening prior. It looked perfectly packaged. But a full day after starting the antibiotics, there was a slight metallic taste in my mouth, and I felt worse before starting to feel the familiar threat of seizure.

"I think I better go back to wait in the car," I said.

"No worries. We're done here," Barb said.

She and Maryanne came too, stopping to talk to a group of military cadets. I struggled to smile as the team bantered, the car only twenty feet away from where we stood. My vision started to tunnel as I walked toward it.

"Let's go have dinner," Barb said behind me.

I couldn't answer. Things slowed. I recall opening the door, managing to slide onto the back seat.

"Celeste, your seatbelt."

Darkness.

—

Don had insisted on having a personal talk with both Maryanne and Barb before the trip, explaining my disorder. I am always embarrassed as he shares the details: "If she starts slurring her speech or glazing over, or trembling, get her to a safe place to rest. It can look frightening. It doesn't happen often. But I wanted you to know. If it happens, don't take her to the hospital. You will be tempted to. But she just needs her emergency med, then let her sleep it off. Give her water if she wakes up. She's always thirsty after. And you will be shocked the next morning when she is back to normal. Above all, call me if anything happens."

They promised.

Maryanne laughed. "You're a bit over the top about this, eh? We're Aussie nurses. No problem."

Don got the call at four in the morning his time. He sat up at the edge of the bed.

"It's bad," Maryanne said. "We were able to walk her back to the room, but the seizures are getting worse. We think we should take her to the hospital."

"Let me see her," Don said.

They were on FaceTime, and at Don's request Maryanne pointed the phone camera at me.

I didn't hear any of the conversation, but Don said he spent the next fifteen minutes trying to assure them.

Sometime in the early hours of the morning, I woke up sore and thirsty. Barb was at my side within moments. "Water?"

"Thank you."

"What are you thinking to ever travel alone? Those are some serious seizures. You scared us," Barb said.

I negotiated with them all. "Look at me. I'm almost back to normal. I'm okay now. These stops ahead are important."

Reluctantly, miraculously, Don rescheduled my flight to Hong Kong to allow a day of rest before flying again.

—

My travel mates were amazed at how normal I appeared the next morning.

"I wouldn't have believed it if I wasn't seeing it for myself," Barb said.

"Good thing. There's a lot of road ahead of me," I replied. "Thank you for taking such good care of me. Keep up the good work here," I told Sabera. "Reach out anytime. I'm at your service. See you at the UN in a few days."

Sabera was traveling to the United States to see her son and had offered to join us a few days later on the DfG menstrual advocacy panel at the UN's Commission on the Status of Women. Her driver dropped me off at the airport. I had insisted that they not miss their next appointment.

There were few women anywhere in sight inside the airport, certainly none that appeared to be traveling alone. I felt the stares of men as I walked to the ticket line pulling a large DfG duffel resting on top of my wheeled personal carry-on. My flight confirmed, the man behind the check-in desk took one look at the duffel I carried and announced that there would be an extra $400 in luggage fees.

"Are you sure?" I asked. "It's the exact weight listed on your website, a little lighter actually."

"It's a new policy," the woman beside him assured me. No, I couldn't pay with my card. This fee had to be paid in cash. They smiled, but this was obvious extortion.

"I don't have any taka left and really need this to go with me. Is there any way that you could waive the new charge for a nonprofit effort just this once?"

"No. It must be paid in cash."

"No cards?" I felt the fever I had been battling since the day before gaining ground again, but it wasn't anger.

"Taka only."

The airline desk staff assured me that there was a cash machine, but the only one they had was on the basement level. Pointing to a man who moments earlier was offering to push my luggage trolley for tips, they said he could show me the way. The man led me toward a dark corridor. Don was on the phone with me as I puzzled through what to do. The last thing he heard me say before the signal broke up was, "I don't want to do this."

The duffel was heavy with AWH flipcharts for a training I would be conducting at the Asian Women's Conference in Hong Kong following my address there. On every trip we scheduled numerous opportunities to leverage the full value of any travel. Expert now at fitting all of my personal belongings for each trip into my backpack and a single canvas-sided carry-on that was now down to three wheels, I had reserved the space in the duffels for DfG flipcharts to help train new Ambassadors of Health, an important part of why I had come. The duffels had to come with me. I tell women all over the world to trust their feelings. I would not have advised others to follow a stranger down a dimly lit hallway, but I felt I had no choice.[31]

As it turned out, the cash machine worked fine and the gentleman was, well, every bit a gentleman, accepting the tip I offered him as we returned to the check-in line before going back to offering trolley assistance to others. I took a deep breath and got back in line.

The time of departure was now nearing when I finally made it back to the front of the line. Holding out the wad of cash, I asked for a receipt. The two behind the desk seemed flustered, looking to a new man who was now standing beside them. "Oh! What is that for? Your duffel is complementary." Too tight on time now and, to be honest, too tired to elaborate about their former demands, I

---

[31] The next time I encountered this issue legitimately on a trip, I asked if the business class tickets came with baggage allowance and, having been affirmed that was the case, upgraded a member of our team for far less than the cost of the extra luggage fee would have been. There is more than one way to get there with your luggage.

hurried off to my flight still holding the wad of Bangladesh currency that I would have to exchange later. Nauseated, the metallic taste still brittle in my mouth, I slumped into my seat and buckled up. I was asleep before takeoff.

—

The flight attendant welcoming us all to Bangkok startled me awake. It felt like minutes since departure. I looked out the window too late to see any approach and turned off my phone's airplane mode to text Don as I do every time I land: "Touchdown." Unbuckling, I waited in my seat for the passenger next to me to join the throng pushing toward the exit before grabbing my own bag out of the overhead bin. A wave of dizziness went over me. No worries. The rest of my luggage had been checked straight through. All I had to do was roll my three-legged bag to the gate, and after an easy five-hour layover I would fly to Hong Kong where I would be picked up.

I looked for a display screen to indicate the gate. Nothing. I called Don as promised. "Hey! I made it. I'm not sure what gate I'm headed to, but I'm looking." I felt more feverish now, my bag suddenly too heavy. The white walls of the airport seemed to fade in and out. Every gate seat was occupied. I tried to sound cheerful. "Hold on. I'm looking for a plug-in. My phone is going dead."

"Celeste, you don't sound good. Your speech is slurred."

"I'm just looking for a power outlet. I'm going to sit down by this pillar for a minute." I slumped against one of many towering columns. "I . . . I . . . don't feel well. I'm just going to sit . . ."

"Celeste? Is there anyone near you?" Don asked, his voice rising.

I struggled to form my words. "It's . . . What? Don, it's okay. Just . . . wait . . ." The white walls around me seemed to turn to mist. I struggled to keep my eyes open. Gone.

—

Don was in our living room back home. He looked out the window at the rows of dahlias, lobelias, and colorful lilies: tiger, trumpet, starburst. All names that he did not remember, though he loved seeing them sway in the yard—reminders of my love for gardening when I was home. He tried to picture where I could possibly be in an airport he had never seen. It wasn't until the fourth number he called at the airport in Thailand that he got a live person. "My wife is sick. I was just talking to her and the phone went dead. She is sitting at the base of a column." He was not aware that the corridors of the airport were lined with pillars like a forest of white giants.

"Sorry, sir. We don't have any personnel to search for passengers, and this is a non-announcement airport. We cannot put out a call for her."

"But this is an emergency. Please." They hung up.

He started looking for flights. There were none available until the next day, and even then it would be a full additional day before he could get to Bangkok. Not wanting to frighten our children, he didn't call any of them. Instead, he sat looking out into the now dark sky and wept. Hours later, he tried to calm his mind, which was filled with unbidden images of loss, traffickers, and coffins. He stared at the phone for the next five hours until it finally rang.

I had opened my eyes to find I was still propped against the column. My bag was still at my side. I had no idea what time it was. Ignoring the stiffness I felt, I set off to find an outlet to charge my phone. It came to life with a flurry of texts from Don.

"I'm sorry," I said when he answered my call. "I was out. I'm fine now . . . It just took a while to find a place to charge my phone. I'm okay, but I missed my flight. Barely. But I missed it."

I could only hear sobbing on the other line. It took minutes before he could compose himself.

"You're alive!"

"I'm so, so sorry, Don."

"Oh, Celeste. Please just come home."

"Sweetheart. This time someone will be waiting for me. Please, Don. It's important or you know I would come home. I can do this. We can do this. I promise I will never try to fly alone after this. I love you too much to put you through this again. But these events will make such a difference. I can do this."

The silence on the other end of the line stretched on a long time before he answered. "I'll reschedule the flight to Hong Kong and call Julie to tell her your flight has changed. You should rest up and charge up. Promise me that you will call me the minute you are in your seat for takeoff and when you touch down. I won't be able to sleep until you do."

When I touched down in Hong Kong, Julie Cook and a whole group of her friends were waiting for me. Julie snapped a group selfie and texted it to Don. "I promised him," she said.

Don says that it was the best photo he ever received. My eyes were only slightly misaligned (his barometer for how I was doing) and my smile was a little crooked, but in the photo I was surrounded by friends and people who loved me. He knew I would be safe now. He cried himself to sleep.

—

That night, as I brushed my teeth, I stared at the antibiotics bottle. Could the meds be counterfeit? The pieces came together in my mind. If they were, it was no one's fault except for those greedy enough to risk lives for profit, leaving innocent people and even health providers victim to their scheme with counterfeit, copycat pills and packaging that can be nearly identical to the real thing. Not just inert and ineffective, they are often toxic. I dropped the bottle into the trash.

The speech and AWH training went well in Hong Kong, and new champions and chapters of Days for Girls as well as vital future team members all resulted from the event. The chapters formed there went on to reach thousands and thousands of girls, stretching to new communities and local leaders.

When I landed in New York City three days later, the hotel concierge passed me a bag with a small box inside, the antibiotics that Don had sent ahead for me. Perhaps this one would work. I took one, swallowing it with a full glass of water, before retreating to our room where I fell to sleep almost immediately.

Leah woke me a few hours later. It was time to meet for dinner with the other global delegates of Days for Girls gathered for the panel at the UN's Commission on the Status of Women. We chose a small Italian restaurant. They had arrived from Nigeria, Bangladesh, and Uganda, grateful to represent the girls and women in their countries and Days for Girls. We all felt honored to participate. For the next two days they would all share their stories in every event they attended and remind the world how much the periods, strength, and dignity of girls matter.

The UN's New York City headquarters is located in the Turtle Bay neighborhood of Manhattan. A row of national flags wave above the street at the entrance. We had applied for our passes months before, and now we checked through security before entering the courtyard that stretches to the waters of the East River.

As we gathered on the other side of the scanners, Leah handed a stack of Days for Girls business cards and flyers to each of our team. I asked, "Is everyone still okay with our plan to divide and conquer?" We would reach more people if we attended different sessions to network until we reconvened at the next session DfG was featured in. Everyone chattered happily as we captured the moment in a photo just outside of the main entrance, in front of the bronze globe-like sphere, golden in the sun. We walked in together.

Inside, greeters queued us up into lines organized by alphabet. Their badges indicated the languages they could translate. Judging by the flurry of diverse people in colorful traditional garbs or business dress from around the world, they were all going to be needed today. It was a global hive of people with purpose, and today that purpose was the UN's Commission on the Status of Women.

The UNFPA[32] menstrual awareness meeting was a first for Leah and me. It was not in the opulent wood-paneled UN general assembly room but in one of the smaller conference rooms down one floor and a few polished marble hallways away. The growing queue of people waiting outside the room boded well for the issue at stake.

The woman next to me wore a silken sari. She smiled in response to my greeting, quickly sharing that in India this was a pressing issue.

"I'd love to hear more," I said.

She explained that some of the new disposable options available to them weren't comfortable but that P&G (Proctor & Gamble) was now giving away three-month samples of pads. She was pleased.

"Do the women have a way to get more after the three-month supply?" I asked.

She looked perturbed. "Well, perhaps. And maybe not. But at least they have something for a time. It is better than nothing."

"Would you like to see our DfG pad?" I asked. She turned the winged pad in her hand, admiring the colors, then questioned whether cleaning them would work culturally. We discussed the importance of individual options, including single-use products and the power of invitations to take on the stigma and taboo women face through education. Then the innovation behind our pad design.

---

[32] United Nations Sexual and Reproductive Health Agency.

"These might work," she said, looking thoughtful. "Do you have a card?"

They opened the doors to the room as she tucked our small trifold brochure into her satchel before walking inside.

I took my place at the large oval wooden table. A small translation ear cuff was on the console in front of me, and I slipped it on and dialed the language selection from among perhaps a dozen selections to English. I couldn't resist shifting it to different languages—different voices, different cadence, the same message. And this time the conversation of this table of delegates from around the world was dedicated to both menstrual wellness and to sharing the stories of those most affected by period poverty. I took notes as the delegates around the table shared their many now familiar stories of the plights of women, girls, and menstruators who have to go without basic care products and vital education. When the dialogue came to me, my contribution was briefly in confirmation of the global evidence of all that they had shared and the positive results of including everyone in communities in menstrual wellness conversations. I ended on the effectiveness of allowing products to be designed based on the feedback of those we serve. Several of the presentations focused on the value and difficulty of monitoring and evaluation, something exceptionally complicated when you are tackling a taboo subject. We all shared materials and contacts. At last, menstrual wellness had a place at the table at the UN. Momentum continued to grow.

Memorably, as we left, people in the hallway parted respectfully as four delegates from Sierra Leone walked confidently shoulder to shoulder in their unmistakable traditional dress, tall regal headdresses, and dramatic sleeves. They were not the only impressive women to choose the strength of their traditional apparel that day.

Severina Lemachokoti was standing in front of Norman Rockwell's iconic ceramic collaged mural of people from many nations, which reads *Do unto others as you would have them do unto you*, when I met her. The mural was as colorful and captivating as her Maasai beads, traditional headpiece, and bright Maasai red kitenge dress and sash, not to mention her brilliant smile. Severina is a long-standing advocate of both the strength of indigenous peoples and the reduction of FGM/C.[33] We became fast friends, and she instantly stepped in

---

[33] Female Genital Mutilation/Cutting.

to champion for the menstrual movement as well. She currently serves on the boards of both Days for Girls International and DfG Kenya.

In the days that followed, she joined us at several of our four remaining panels. At one of the gatherings, Days for Girls delegates each rose to share the stories and strength of their own experiences and communities. Among them were Dr. Ugo for Nigeria, Sabera for Bangladesh, and Chris Mutalya, a Rotarian specializing in Water and Sanitation, and board member for DfG Uganda. We sat side by side at the front of the room, each rising when it was our turn to speak. Attending was another menstrual policy champion, Jennifer Weiss-Wolf, in the room that filled to capacity. Questions and comments flowed readily from the standing-room-only gathering and continued in the hallways after the session. Later, Leah and I conducted AWH with a room full of delegates from around the world who elected to join us to become DfG Ambassadors of Women's Health.

Next was a meeting with New York's U.S. Representative Grace Meng, who had just taken a historic stand for menstrual equity in her role as a politician, to my knowledge, one of the first to do so. Then onto the opportunity to hear directly from women who shared the shame of limited access to pads in prison, and having to ask guards for each one, in some cases being asked to show proof that they had used the last one. The attendees brainstormed on possible ways to improve options, a discussion that proved the dilemma to be multifaceted and including issues that ranged from security to pads being used as contraband and for coercion. We finished up with a quick meeting with a commission for menstrual advocacy in New York City who reviewed the impact of offering free menstrual supplies in the bathrooms of a school in Queens. They reported a rise in school attendance, and that the initial hoarding they anticipated did not happen. It appeared that students were taking only what they needed when they needed it.

And finally, I was headed home to Don.

—

In truth, there had been no monumental declaration. Though I had long envisioned and worked toward a moment of recognition of the issue at this level, being at the UN was, in the end, another series of moments. But maybe that's the magic of it. The power is in the connections. More arms linking. Change happens not with grand referendums, but step by step. It's great to have the issue on the world stage. Important, even. But those taking action—a girl helping others go to class, a volunteer changing lives and finding their own changed as well, a doctor teaching health and wellness, a person who speaks up wherever they are, a volunteer changing lives while lifting their own—when they link arms, they hold the movement of change in their own two hands.

Volunteers were reaching more and more communities and girls, and all along the way they remained on the lookout for more local leaders wherever they lived to assist in leading the program and more organizations to collaborate with. Enterprises were being established. Sadly, some were one-time wonders; others flourished with inspiring dedication. Each bringing their own unique understanding and determination.

On the flight home, I worked out more ways to standardize the training of trainers and how to delegate even more of my work, although training is one of my favorite activities with Days for Girls. I knew that if we were going to grow even faster and support that growth without breaking my husband's heart, I needed to work smarter, not harder. I needed not only to delegate more, but to relish the rhythm of rest as a strategic part of work. It would take time. When you are determined to do whatever it takes, it is easy to run faster than you are able. It was time to find ways to sustain. This trip had been an invitation to breathe. The global truth was everywhere: menstruation matters, and our champions and advocates were multiplying. There were more and more of us all over the world, capable and passionate about making the shift. It was time for me to shift my role and make more of the work easier to scale.

Only months later, we had complete videos and text for online training for the AWH education. My focus shifted to our educational resources and raising more funds to back them all up, and even more communications to highlight their strengths and successes.

Chapter 53

Periods Don't Cause Banana Blight

When you take a stand, it actually does shift
the whole universe, and unexpected,
unpredictable things happen.
—Lynne Twist

Guyana, South America, 2018

"AUNTY JAGUAR!" THIS IS THE NAME THE PEOPLE OF PARUIMA IN GUY-
ana call Miriam Lancaster when she approaches their village. If you happen to
meet her, be sure to ask why. I guarantee that her blue eyes will twinkle when she
tells you.[34] Tall and thin, her quiet strength hints at her fifty years of nursing but
leaves her rank of captain in the U.S. Public Health Service a delight to discover.
One would not guess that she lived in Guyana as a child where her father, a doctor, had been a medical missionary during some of her childhood.

Miriam couldn't stop thinking about how the women of her childhood village needed DfG after she heard my TEDx talk on the topic. Despite a debilitat-
ing autoimmune condition and some difficulty walking, Miriam was determined
to return to Paruima. While iritis was destroying her eyesight, her vision of
starting Days for Girls in Guyana was clear. She could see herself returning to
remote rainforests and Paruima to start a DfG team there.

The *Lonely Planet* travel guide described Guyana as dangerous, not for the

---

[34] The villagers told Miriam that when she sleeps she sounds like a jaguar!

faint-hearted, not a tourist destination, and "only for rugged 'Indiana Jones' types," but Miriam sees it for what it is, stunningly beautiful and her first home. Though getting to remote Paruima is not easy. There are many delays, and it is expensive. The first leg from Georgetown is via a single prop airplane. If you are lucky, you can catch a ride with the mission plane, though a recent crash of their small single-engine Cessna, specially outfitted for jungle travel, leaves that option currently unavailable. The flight generally makes several stops at various villages because it not only serves to carry cargo but is also the only air ambulance serving the vast expanses of the interior, carrying indigenous people into Georgetown for medical emergencies. Once you land at the tiny Paruima grass airstrip, you have to crawl down a river embankment so steep that it is impossible to do otherwise, cross the river in a canoe, climb up an even steeper embankment, then stop at the little police building and get permission to enter before hiking to wherever you are staying. Miriam goes anyway.

She says, "I believe that when we say 'Every Girl. Everywhere. Period.' we truly mean it." By the time Miriam completed her first one hundred DfG kits for Paruima on her tiny 1937 Singer Featherweight sewing machine, she had also formed a chapter and taught many to join in, advocating far and wide. "Someone has to go to those remote faraway places that aren't on anyone's radar, but where the need is great. 'Everywhere' means everywhere."

That's how we ended up in Guyana together and stuck in a remote location on one of those Indiana Jones–like roads. We were headed to remote Guyanese communities in a vehicle loaned to us by gracious friends. We hired Miriam's long-time friend Ron to be our guide and driver. Ron had bravely recommended driving us to Bartica, located along the Essequibo River, and was now pouring what was left of our drinking water into the overheated radiator. It was not enough.

"This be de kind a road that stick to de car," he said in "Creolese" while doing typical Guyanese "suck teeth," a mannerism that seems to interchangeably indicate emphasis and frustration.

The vehicle had forged on for miles before coming to a halt, at last overheating after plowing through the portion of the road that was now unavoidably axel-deep silt. Tangles of darkening rainforest stretched on either side of the single-lane road. We had not seen another vehicle since we passed a huge logging truck stuck several miles back, far too big for us to assist. There was no cell signal, and no sign of help.

Olinda, another of Miriam's long-time local friends and new DfG volunteer recruit traveling with us, remained unruffled. "Things always work out in Guyana."

Deep silence settled in around us.

"I'll bet there's water just a few feet into the rainforest. We could fill our water bottles and come right back," I suggested.

"No. That is not a good idea," Olinda said. She and Ron were adamant.

We stared down the middle of the desolate road.

"Are we lost?" I asked.

"No, we are in Guyana," Ron answered.

"How far do you think it is to town?" Miriam asked.

"Town?" Ron said, looking around deliberately before answering. "Still far. No water bottles. D'ere always be water bottles on de ground near town."

Made sense to me.

A short way down the road was a single mud puddle, most of it more pudding-like than liquid. I offered to use my LifeStraw water bottle to filter it for water enough to cool the radiator. Ron looked concerned. None of us were convinced it would really work, but it was worth a try. It took almost an hour, but brown sludge was slowly transformed to sediment-free water one half cup at a time until we had enough to infuse the radiator. I'll admit that I didn't have enough courage to "clean and reuse" as advised on the bottle instructions. That was the last time that I used that particular LifeStraw water bottle, but it had fulfilled its purpose well and far exceeded expectations. We made it far enough down the road to impose upon a stranger for more water. It was enough to get us to Bartica.

In Bartica, we had two quick but important meetings with local authorities. One of the Ministry of Education and Interior dignitaries explained that he had just been talking to his staff about what to do for menstrual care when girls were in school. He approved of our engagement to deliver menstrual health education at a local school that Olinda had prearranged for us. But before we left, he said, "What about Days for Boys?" A comment that resonated as our Men Who Know education was not yet widely distributed. I took note, promising to introduce it to

the team in Guyana. With enthusiastic and important permission given, a half
hour later we arrived at the school as promised.

Olinda was fully prepared to serve as the Ambassador of Women's Health
that day, having reviewed, discussed, and practiced her Days for Girls AWH
education delivery all along the way. She warmly greeted the school director.

"It will only take us a few minutes to gather the girls. We knew you may be
coming. We have few visitors; the girls are looking forward to this," the school
director told us.

The covered open space we stood in felt more like a miniature auditorium
than a classroom, but it protected us well from sun and rain. I imagined that it,
like so many other open classrooms I had stood in, would be loud in the rain.
We heard the girls' cheerful chatter before they crossed into the room through
the double doorway framed by colorful, hand-drawn posters. Dozens of girls,
teachers, and community leaders soon sat on the floor, quiet in anticipation as
Olinda shared knowledge that dispelled local myths surrounding menstruation.
"You *can* wash. You *can* eat meat during your period. You are strong every day
of the month." They unpacked their kits to practice how to place liners into the
shields and learned how to wash and care for them.

A local leader underscored the wisdom of our including a bag to do pre-
rinsing of soiled liners, explaining that they take great care to never rinse blood
in the rivers, not wanting to do anything that might attract piranhas and kamudi
(anaconda) to their area of the river. Having women avoid the river during menstruation was not a myth, nor meant to demean, it was a safety measure here.
And having something to use to care for their cycle meant that they could be
productive and protect their environment in a way that worked for them. Piranhas and kamudi concerns I had not heard anywhere else in the world, were
already addressed by an element of design that had been recommended by others
for other reasons which applied with equal importance in this setting as well.

Ron dropped us off on his way back to Georgetown so we could return to
where we were staying by water taxi, a long narrow covered boat with eight slim
benches inside. Passengers lined up along the wooden dock, buckling their provided orange life vests before stepping down to duck into the rocking boat. The
water taxi splashed its way upriver to the next inlet, stopping only long enough
to spill and receive more riders before bumping its way to the next island or inlet.

Miriam pointed out that there are 365 islands along the Essequibo River—one for each day of the year. Some only large enough for birds to seek refuge on. We splashed our way farther along the shoreline filled with mangroves. It was hard to believe that it had only been two days since we had arrived. It had already been a good trip and it had just started. Olinda and Miriam would return by water taxi again with more DfG kits just a few weeks later.

All our days in Guyana were filled with meetings, advocacy, and adventure, all with one goal in mind: to give communities the tools to shift stigma to health and freedom. Two of many experiences in Guyana stand out for me.

Kaieteur Falls

Early breakfast included eggs and "pine juice," a Guyanese light "tea" made by boiling the core and rind of a freshly picked pineapple until it is juiced out. The resulting tea is then cooled to drink. I fell in love with pine juice. I drank three tall glasses before I ate the poached eggs and a curry squash vegetable dish our friend and gracious hostess Michelle offered. She laughed at my enthusiasm for pine juice. Because she was born in Guyana, it is a common staple for her. She chatted effortlessly as she continued to chop, stir, and serve her family, which now, luckily, included Miriam and me. Having successfully convinced her that I love doing dishes, she had just sat down to work on her florist orders when a call came in: a friend's single-prop plane flight to Kaieteur Falls had two last-minute passenger openings. It would be a quick trip, only a few hours long, but the chance of a lifetime. Miriam and I could only bring a few DfG kits and a flipchart in our backpacks in case they were wanted there, but that was it. Of course, we said yes!

The clamoring plane engine made it difficult to carry on a conversation, but there was little need. All six passengers were mesmerized by the river below, curling in and out of thick rainforest that was broken only by the river itself. A few sections of the river were mysteriously even more turquoise and beige than the rest. I shouted, pointing to the swirl of colors, and gestured, "What is that?" Gold mining. Mining operations use arsenic and mercury to flush out gold in dredges that float in Guyana's rivers. Local indigenous boys are hired to direct hoses at the river bottom, vacuuming sand and potential gold to sluice boxes, swimming in the very chemicals that leave entire sections of the river transformed from vibrant blue to rancid brown and a creamy sort of turquoise. It is said that even birds die when flying over some areas. The practice had been outlawed, but we were looking at the proof that it continued in the remote areas of Guyana.

No one needed to point out Kaieteur Falls. The largest single-drop waterfall by volume in the world, its enormous bowl of water shimmered, thundering over red rock 741 feet down to the Potaro River below.

Several local guides waited as we touched down. Our guide, Tim, passed us each a bottle of water, offered us bug repellant, and then headed down the trail. Almost instantly he was pointing out flora and fauna. He explained to us that Guyana is one of the most ecologically diverse countries in the world. There is more diversity in one kilometer than any other place.

Almost as if in response to his words, colorful birds called out overhead and small creatures scattered away from otherworldly plants as we approached. We walked beside him under enormous trees, some so tall that we couldn't see the canopy top in places.

Tim stopped, peering inside a giant bromeliad plant, its broad blades almost as tall as he was. He shone a light to reveal a small amphibian. "There. Do you see it?" We couldn't miss it. A tiny golden frog of poison dart fame crouched far below. Tim knew exactly where to find it; these frogs spend their entire life in their ideal plant world, which provides an ongoing source of fast food: bugs that slide down the leaves into the frogs' watery home. "De gold frog be jes like me. He never leave dis place," Tim said with pride.

We heard the pounding water of the falls long before we saw it. One more turn and there it was, unbelievably close, and one of the most beautiful and spectacular waterfalls in the world—right here in Tim's backyard. The water of the river wove unhurried past flowering reeds at the pebbled riverside just a short distance from its furious drop. We didn't hurry either, lingering in a place so full of sights, sounds, and fragrance that attempting to take it all in stretched the capacity of our senses. I closed my eyes to slow it all down, focusing on the smell of orchids, leaves, and rich soil that rose swirling in air tinged with the mist of the falls. Only then did I reopen my eyes to the intense green surrounding us.

As we turned back, the thunder of the falls faded remarkably quickly behind us. Tim asked us where we lived and what we did for a living. His eyes widened when we told him our reason for being in Guyana. He explained that his people needed Days for Girls. It was a three-day walk away and involved crossing the river, but miners had found his people and had brought disposable single-use menstrual pads with them. At first they gave pads for free. In time, when the girls were accustomed to using them, the miners withdrew them, demanding sexual favors in exchange for more.

In one of the most remote places in the world. Even there, people with periods were exploited.

It had become a health problem. Tim's sister, a nurse, struggled to know how to help.

I really thought that maybe this place had found a solution that worked for them, perhaps a unique leaf that was absorbent and soft, or some other suitable local solution that would leave only health education necessary. But no. Loss and exploitation due to lack of health education and menstrual resources had reached even this rare place.

Tim would be returning home in four days and could deliver the news of this option himself. We shifted our focus and spent a lot of the rest of our time together going over the AWH flipchart with him so he could pass it and the example kit on to his sister. Several months later, Miriam arranged for a guide from Tim's village to take fifty more DfG kits to Tim's sister to distribute.

There are no accidents in where our paths take us when we make it a habit to surrender our days and say yes.

As we flew back to Georgetown, we were equal parts pensive and grateful about what we had just experienced and eager to deliver the AWH course to another friend's village the next day.

Abeola's Story

When we arrived at the next village, a large group of people were in a heated discussion. Our host, who arranged today's DfG distribution only days earlier, asked us to feel free to look around while he intervened. We wandered around, marveling at the orchids growing in the tree limbs not far above our heads. These flowers were gathered to make beautiful fragrant displays to welcome visitors to hotel lobbies. We continued exploring as the heated discussion went on.

We wouldn't know until later that day how important our timing had been.

Nearly everyone at this community worked at the beautiful flower and fruit farm where we were invited to conduct an AWH education session and kit distribution. We met the women under the sway of coconut palms, in a clearing that would serve as our classroom, surrounded by lush tropical forest and exotic flowers. As women gathered, we were asked if anyone could have one of the DfG kits without attending the education. Miriam assured them that education was important for wellness and that the kits wouldn't be as effective if they came without care and usage dialogue. They needed to know how to use the washable kits well so the kits would stay healthy and last for years to come. In response, we were asked to wait a few more minutes.

Soon several more women arrived dressed in formal attire, one all in white. A wedding that was about to take place was postponed long enough for some of the wedding party to hear the DfG health and safety education and receive their kits before proceeding to the wedding. Among the attendees was Abeola. Especially attentive and eager to learn about Days for Girls, she stayed afterward to ask more questions and offer to help. Our hosts, who owned the farm, told us her story. It was the very topic of the stormy discussion happening as we arrived.

Abeola worked hard at the local family flower farm and banana plantation every day. She could always be counted on to be at work and do her best. When banana blight hit the farm, the villagers hadn't heard that banana blight was occurring throughout South and Central America. In their minds, someone was to blame for the crop failure. Abeola became highly suspect because she was always at work. Which meant she didn't take days off during her period, which meant she farmed while menstruating. Someone thought they once saw her bathing in the river near the banana trees, too. They decided Abeola and her period was the reason the bananas were dying. People in the village had already started to shun and shame her. The heated discussion we had stumbled into was about what punishment would be sufficient for Abeola in order to stop the banana blight!

Instead, that day all the village, including the *toshao* (chief), learned that neither women nor periods cause banana blight. Abeola would tell you that women's health education is a life changer. She and three of her friends asked to train to become Days for Girls Ambassadors of Health. "We need to teach everyone at the village of our fathers."

Six months later, Miriam returned to Guyana, focused on DfG Ambassadors of Health training. The women were determined to share what they had learned with surrounding villages and traveled several hours up the lush tree-lined Demerara River by small boat to reach out with more DfG kits and education. This was the first of many trips.

I'm often reminded of Abeola. She was an accomplished basket maker, and one of her beautiful baskets skillfully woven of pine needles sits on my desk, a gift of thanks for the education that freed her from being seen as a blight on her community and allowed her to help her community understand more about their health.

—

What happened to my friend Miriam's vision for the far more remote Paruima? She returned to Paruima and started the first DfG remote team there in Guyana. It happened just like she dreamed. In her mind's eye she had seen herself meeting with the village council, teaching sewing classes, walking the jungle paths to distribute kits, and swimming with her long-time friends in the Kamarang River, though it mattered in ways she hadn't yet predicted.

Chapter 54

The Part That Saves Lives

Education is the key to unlock the golden door of freedom.
—*George Washington Carver*

Guyana, South America, 2015

IN GUYANA, AS IN MANY AREAS, WHEN YOU DISTRIBUTE KITS AT A school, it's not just the girls that attend. Mothers, aunts, grandmothers—all the women in the village gather (unless they are working on their cassava farms). They love that their new soft menstrual solutions are also colorful. Talk about ovulation, the time they are "most likely" to become pregnant, is a hit. Many women and girls stay after the formal education to go over their menstruation calendars to make sure they know how to identify the time each month they are ovulating. For years, Paruima has been begging for doctors to come and provide vasectomies. To my knowledge, no doctor has been willing to undergo the arduous travel and perform surgery on kitchen tables with the river being the only usual running water and flashlights or sunshine the only light to operate by.

The women are very diligent about learning how to track their periods and don't leave until they "get it." On one occasion, hours after the last woman left the schoolhouse, Miriam walked two miles down the jungle trail to the house of a dear friend where she was staying. She sensed someone was chasing her. Sure enough, a man was running after her. When he caught up, he said, "My wife told me you are teaching about *uh vo lat ers*. Please teach me! I want to learn."

At first Miriam had no idea what he meant.

"My wife and I have five children, and she is pregnant with the sixth. She is having trouble with this pregnancy," he explained. "We try to be careful. But she keeps getting pregnant." In fact, she was long overdue now and the baby was transverse.

Miriam sat with him beside the village *futebol* (soccer) field and went through the flipchart, teaching him to help track his wife's periods. On Miriam's flight back to Georgetown in the tiny mission plane, the man's wife, Salome, and their one-year-old daughter were on the plane. Salome was going into town for a C-section. Miriam was afraid Salome might die in flight, but she survived. All these years later, Miriam has kept in touch with her. Salome was the first woman in Guyana to receive a Days for Girls postpartum heavy flow kit—and is still using it six years later. She hasn't been pregnant since she and her husband learned about *"uh vo lat ers."*

A couple years ago, Miriam sent me a video taken by a young Arekuna videographer, Chris Elliman. It was a video of the Paruima Days for Girls sewing team leader, Yvonne, and her husband John. They were doing a distribution of one hundred kits in the village of Waramadong on the Kamarang River. With the help of a translator (John, a former toshao chieftain from Paruima), the Arekuna and Akawaio girls at the boarding school thanked Miriam for bringing Days for Girls to the "Upper Maz," the huge Mazaruni River area where travel between villages is accomplished by canoes. Miriam's vision was coming to life, extending far beyond Paruima and the Kamarang River.

Nine of the ten regions in Guyana have received Days for Girls kits, though many more are needed. In addition to the team in Paruima, a DfG resource center in Georgetown is led by Danny Ramdeen, a talented sewing manufacturing manager who does DfG volunteer work in his off-hours. Their group raises funds through a monthly barbecue so they can keep sewing DfG kits for the more remote areas of Guyana.

Guyana is a post-colonial independent commonwealth country. It is historically and politically divided along ethnic, religious, and geographic lines that include some of the most remote areas on Earth. This has left deep cultural divides that largely persist today.

When Danny, a man of East Indian descent and Hindu faith, welcomed Dr. Pat, a black Christian Guyanese doctor, to the DfG center, his mother questioned his judgment. Danny answered, "In Days for Girls there are no divides." The historic division hasn't been easy to overcome, but the Guyanese DfG volunteers work together for the sake of their shared purpose. As of this writing, the leaders of Days for Girls from diverse Guyanese backgrounds were arranging a cultural exchange conference to meet and discuss their goals and how they will continue to expand their combined efforts to reach every person in Guyana who needs DfG kits, no matter where they live or who they are. It would not surprise me if the outcome of this conference went on to map the way forward for other organizations around the world, bridging enormous cultural divides.

—

My friend's clear vision, undeterred by failing eyesight, brought Days for Girls to Guyana. I'm delighted to report that with the help of a wonderful rheumatologist and ophthalmologist, Miriam underwent surgery for cataracts caused by ocular steroids and receives ongoing injections to suppress her overactive immune system. Her health and vision have improved. She says that Days for Girls saved her eyes, and even her life, because Days for Girls gave her purpose. Miriam calls her remission a "Days for Girls Guyana miracle."

DfG Guyana's leaders and volunteers continue to make many trips on the Demerara, Essequibo, and Pomeroon Rivers, and other shining tributaries, to bring education wherever they go. They have distributed DfG kits to more than four thousand girls and women. They have crossed many rivers to get Days for Girls health education and menstrual solutions to those who need them most as their part of reaching *Every girl. Everywhere. Period.* There is still a long way to go, and they are determined to cover every last canoed mile.

Chapter 55
An Unfortunate Liability

They told me their maturation lesson had been very short . . .
Their instructor turned to the boys and said,
"Your shoulders will broaden and your voice will deepen."
And then she turned to the girls and all she said was,
"You will have an unfortunate liability."
—Reported as experienced by Tiffany Larson

India, 2019

"THEY WILL NEVER USE THESE KITS. IT IS TOO LOW CASTE TO WASH and care for. They are probably throwing them away." Considering that the man who just said this was to oversee implementation of the Days for Girls grant from an influential global nonprofit organization that works to eradicate some of the world's most prevalent root causes of poverty, Rotary International, and that the grant was to create the local Days for Girls enterprise we were launching that very day in Agra, India, several of us froze. Speechless for a heartbeat.

It was Neha (pronounced NA-ha) who replied first.

Standing all of five-foot-two in her striped school uniform, her shiny hair pulled back in two long braids, she tapped the arm of the man who stood a full foot taller than her, an influential and esteemed business and Rotary leader, and said, "Excuse me. I have been using mine for two years. And I can go to school every day now because I have it."

It took uncommon courage for her to speak up. The next thing she did would have been incredible for any teenager anywhere in the world, but where she lives, it was also unbelievably brave.

Before I tell you what happened, allow me to share this small segment of a 2018 article from *BBC News, Delhi*:

> **India's uncomfortable relationship with periods is back in the headlines.**
> College students living in a hostel in the western Indian state of Gujarat have complained that they were made to strip and show their underwear to female teachers to prove that they were not menstruating.[35]

Why? Because they had stopped registering their period days with school authorities. Which meant some of them had to be "guilty" of breaking the rules.

> . . . women are barred from entering the temple and the kitchen and are not allowed to touch other students during their periods.
>
> At meal times, they have to sit away from others, they have to clean their own dishes, and in the classroom, they are expected to sit on the last bench.

A similar incident had happened three years earlier in northern India to seventy young women.

Menstruation seen as something to fear, a curse to feel ashamed of. Millions of women facing menstruation without what they need. The scale of the issue is truly mind-blowing. When I was last in India, a representative from UNICEF told me that more than one million women are forced to practice the isolation of chhaupadi there, often alone in the woods at night.

In the Beed district, an area known for sugarcane harvesting in rural Maharashtra, at least 4,605 women are reported as "wombless" for work. Thousands of women in their twenties to forties are encouraged to have hysterectomies, known as a surgery removing their *pishvi*, which means "bag" but is used to refer to a uterus. Removed because women with periods are seen as less desirable as laborers. Breaks are far apart and punishment is severe, including fines if they take time away from the field for self-care. So they remove part of their bodies and likewise are uninformed of the real physical and hormonal hazards and recovery

---

[35] Geeta Pandey, "'Period-Shaming' Indian College Forces Students to Strip to Underwear," *BBC News, Delhi*, February 2020. www.bbc.com/news/world-asia-india-51504992.

needed after the surgery. They are expected to get right back to the hard labor in the sugarcane field. They pay physically and go into debt to become permanently wombless for work.

Now, this is where choice comes in, not only for them, but for all of us. You can throw this book in anger. You can go back to your own life. Or you can find the silver thread of opportunity hidden here. From here, we can contribute to changing our world, a place to leverage for greater equity for all of us. The shift to shatter menstrual shame is something that we can all be part of changing together.

Thank goodness, there have been many advancements in India's dialogue about periods recently. Advocacy for ending period poverty is growing, from Bollywood's 2018 film *Pad Man* to the Academy Award–winning documentary *Period. End of Sentence.* to local leaders participating in programs like Days for Girls all over the world, including India. Many are coming to see periods as the natural biological function they are.

Robin, a Days for Girls Ambassador of Health, says she was once with a group of men in India getting approval to share our curriculum with their community. One of the leaders asked, "Is what you are saying true? If so, why does my wife have to stay in a shed?" Exactly. Knowledge is a game changer. And it's worth repeating that communities need to be part of the shift.

In 2018, the top court in a landmark order opened the Sabarimala Temple in the southern state of Kerala to women of all ages, saying that keeping women out of the temple was discriminatory. But a year later, the judges agreed to review the order after massive protests in the state, many of the participants women.

Does that mean that menstrual equity is not wanted and needed?

We don't think so.

Raju was one of the first men to help teach our education in India by assisting with translation. After helping to teach and distribute kits in the slums he said emotionally:

I didn't know my India. When I was with the young girls, I was the translator. I came to learn that the girls go through much during the time of their period. They use the ash of the wood. This was painful to me because I have a daughter who is the same age as the girls, and my daughter doesn't know where the pads come from because I buy them for her. She knows she will have what she needs. But the girls in the slums, they had nothing. They do not have toilets, they have to go to the General [shared sanitation areas]. One of the girls was asked if she felt shy and she said she does; the young boys keep watching her so she feels shy. She only goes once a day. What happens if they have diarrhea? How many times will she have to show herself to the boys? I came to know my India today.

In my experience, when addressing a taboo topic, it is especially important to invite inclusive conversations that are less about shame and more about opportunities to hear each other, learn together, consider what solutions work for all. That starts with the determined voices in the community that step forward first.

Let's go back to brave Neha. She lived in a culture where periods are so very taboo, and yet she did something amazing. She volunteered to bring her Days for Girls kit the next day for everyone to see, as proof that she was using it.

When she held up her liners and shields it was clear the items were used and well cared for, showing only the slightest sign of stains. They were soft and well folded. There was minimal sign of wear at the edges, but it was clear that there was far more usage to come. I photographed her shields, bags, and liners to document two-plus years of usage. She smiled when we asked to take a photo of her with Rosemary, who had written the grant that brought us there, and Sondra who would go on to assist with DfG's work throughout India. Both had instructed many Ambassadors of Health, including Neha. It is a photo that I cherish.

Two days later, at the community-wide celebration of the launch of the enterprise, I watched the man Neha had spoken to demonstrate with great enthusiasm how a Days for Girls kit works to the special dignitary guest and district governor of the area. The governor's response? "This is really good!"

One girl's courage led to powerful business advocates. If you ask me, I'd say the heroes of the day didn't all stand on stage receiving lanyards of roses and pearls. One was standing in the audience with her classmates.

Chapter 56

The Terminator

When girls are educated, everything is possible.
—Chief Theresa Kachindamoto

Malawi, 2018

CHIEF THERESA NEVER SAW HERSELF BECOMING A CHIEF. NOR DID SHE see herself returning to live again in Mtakataka in the Dedza district in a small house built under the shade of an enormous baobab tree. The youngest of twelve siblings who shared the blood of traditional rulers of Central Malawi, Africa, she is a dedicated mother of five who had chosen the equally rewarding path of using her education to serve as secretary at a college in Zomba for twenty-seven years. Then the president of Malawi called on her to become the chief after the deaths of her father and two of her brothers. The decision was not easy. Her life could be at risk if she took the position. She was already making a difference where she was. It took several years to convince her, but eventually, Theresa Kachindamoto was made paramount chief, with informal authority over 900,000 people.

Chief Theresa had many things she hoped her people could improve together. Her country has one of the highest rates of child marriage in the world. It is common for girls as young as eleven to be married off for a dowry price, carrying babies long before their own bodies are fully developed. Chief Theresa started leading intervention early in the cycle, asking communities to stand together to be mentors of other options for girls and families. She informed all of the chiefs in her stewardship, who conduct the traditional ceremony, that no further child marriages would be tolerated or she would strip their authority and annul any underage marriages she learned of, and she would send the girls back to school where they belonged. Chief Theresa kept her promise, earning this mild-mannered leader the nickname "The Terminator" after she annulled more than 1,500 chief-ordained marriages.

According to studies by UN Women and UNICEF, 46.7 percent of Malawi's girls are married before the age of eighteen.[36] Adolescent pregnancies comprise 29 percent of all births and 15 percent of maternal deaths.[37] The practice of child marriage robs girls of their childhood and education opportunities, condemning them to a vicious cycle of poverty. In 2013, it was reported that only 45 percent of girls remained in school past the eighth grade. There was little reason to believe those numbers had changed. Chief Theresa was doing something about that, and helping boys stay in school, too.

She also has worked to terminate the dreadful traditional practice known as "brushing off the dust" (*kusasa fumbi*).[38] After her first period a girl is "cleansed" by being blindfolded and forced to be initiated into sex with a paid older male village sex worker, known as a "hyena." The practice puts unsuspecting young girls at risk of infection and pregnancy, but it goes on.

After hearing of another "brushing" about to occur, this small-in-stature woman quietly arrived at the celebration dressed to blend in, settling in behind the blindfolded girls sitting in rows, awaiting their fate. The men's processional "hyena" stopped dead when someone noticed her sitting among the girls.

"What are you planning to do with my girls?" she asked. "Go on. Don't stop on my account."

The men quickly left, and the girls took off their blindfolds. "Thank you, Chief Kachindamoto! Thank you!"

When she told me about it, she looked at me with a coy smile, not quite breaking free of the moment that you could see was replaying in her mind.

---

[36] "The Situation of Children and Women in Malawi," *UNICEF Malawi,* accessed January 20, 2023. www.unicef.org/malawi/situation-children-and-women-malawi.

[37] "Maternal Health," *UNICEF Malawi,* accessed January 20, 2023. www.unicef.org/malawi/toics/maternal-health.

[38] This practice is also found in parts of Zambia, Uganda, Tanzania, Mozambique, Angola, Ivory Coast, and the Congo.

"At first it was difficult for people to accept, but now more people are understanding," Kachindamoto says. She has received many death threats and each time responds: "Go ahead if you must. But not today. I have important things to do today."

—

Kachindamoto finds sponsors to help pay the tuition of girls whose parents cannot afford to pay school fees. She convenes local leaders to serve as mentors and role models for the youth of Malawi. She pressures other chiefs to uphold higher standards of access to education for their young girls and boys or lose their jobs, but it is an ongoing battle.

Chief Theresa came to mind as we geared up to celebrate Days for Girls' tenth birthday. Volunteers and enterprises around the globe were joining hands for an ambitious special event we called the Global Girls Festival. It would take a lot of coordination, but we could do it. When the idea first came to me, I asked, "What if for our tenth birthday we could reach 100,000 girls and women in one day?" After all, a year earlier, Days for Girls Nepal had reached 5,000 in one day with one team. With global efforts, I was sure we could certainly do it. The idea, like so many that I have, made several team members want to faint. I backed off temporarily, sparing them panic until I could go into feasibility mode before returning with the idea anew, complete with spreadsheets. After consulting with our team and getting further input, it was decided that a more reasonable goal would be 100,000 in twenty-eight days, although it would still require a lot of work and an aggressive timeline.

When I shared the vision with a friend, she didn't flinch and instead said, "Let's do it!" She and the dōTERRA Healing Hands Foundation stepped in to help with funding that would serve as an anchor for assurance to enterprises and chapters around the world, allowing many others to support the effort as well. Two women tackled managing the project: a friend, Laurie Baum, and a Global Health Organization fellow joined us, tackling some of the massive amount of coordination. Leaders everywhere joined in.

Although she already had made amazing strides as an advocate for young girls, Chief Theresa originally learned about Days for Girls during the campaign. As part of the effort, I asked Beria Michembo, a Days for Girls enterprise leader in Malawi, if she could connect with Chief Theresa to see if she would like to join hands with us as part of our efforts.

Beria traveled down long roads to bring the news of Days for Girls and the challenge to the chief and her people. The motorcycle she was a passenger on crashed just three kilometers short of her destination. She rose from the ground with small lacerations on her face and hands, but she climbed back on, continued her journey, and was rewarded by the renowned warmth of Chief Theresa's humble greeting at her home. A monkey scurried back and forth on the porch as Beria and Chief Theresa met.

Chief Theresa said, "God sees the cry of his people. Twenty minutes ago, I was with the girls who were complaining that they need pads to manage their periods at school; here you are now."

Beria soon forgot her injuries as Chief Theresa explained that most girls miss school during their periods because they say they "do not want to show up their menses to the boys. They struggle with life; they feel that God loves boys only in such a way that He brought the period to girls only."

A few weeks later, Beria returned with Lindiwe of Days for Girls Eswatini (formerly known as the Kingdom of Swaziland), armed with DfG kits from their local enterprises. Lindiwe shared what the experience was like to reach Chief Theresa's girls:

> The chief wanted to reach nine hundred girls and women. I was to bring four hundred Days for Girls kits from the Eswatini DfG enterprise, and Beria would bring five hundred from Days for Girls Kasupe and Mangalala. When I brought the four hundred kits through the airport, customs was pressuring me about my bags but I explained what it was for and that they were meant for the chief so they let me through.
>
> The road to Dedza was so scary. Winding steeply down, down into a valley. I had never seen a road like this. It was worse than the road to Malagwane times ten. I thought, "I am going to die in a foreign country."
>
> The chief was under a large tree holding back-to-back meetings when we arrived. She was meeting with leaders about identifying boys who were finished with school but not yet employed. She had found a way for them to get training to receive licenses to drive so they could be employed in the near future. She

was very active. She was sure to point out things which we had in common as she took us to her office then to her house for refreshments. The walls of her office were well appointed with photos from her many travels; in each she wore her traditional beads, red robes, and leopard skin shirt, but I noted that in the photo in Eswatini, she wore the traditional clothes of Eswatini. She even greeted me like a Swazi, "*Sawubona*" (hello), turning to Beria to greet her in her own native tongue of Malawi. She is a leader who can connect with everyone.

Before traveling to the distribution location near the chief's home area we went together to the offices of the Ministry of Education, accompanied, as protocol, by a senior officer. Two journalists joined us as well, one for a radio station and one for a local newspaper.

We met the girls under the big tree outside her home. The chief was the first to talk; she introduced the men and women who are mentors in the community. She explained what we had come for. She reminded the girls, "'You are beautiful and you are strong. If you are educated you can build the future you want. Marriage is not a means to an end."

She turned to us, explaining that the girls were struggling to attend school because they don't have access to sanitary pads, but now they would have an answer. Then she invited us to teach.

Beria and I taught the education together, me in English and Beria in the local language. The girls listened so carefully as they sat under the tree that we didn't even need a loudspeaker. They cheered when they saw their DfG kits and learned how they worked. Chief Theresa cheered, too.

Four hundred girls received the first Days for Girls kits and Ambassador of Women's Health education about what a period is and how to use their DfG kits and stay healthy. The rest of the DfG kits were stored in the chief's personal office until several weeks later when a second distribution and AWH education event took place.

The hills on the way home didn't seem as steep, nor as hard.

Beria followed up a year later, reaching out to call the chief to arrange for monitoring and evaluation. She was surprised that Chief Theresa answered herself on the first ring: "When I introduced myself again, she said, 'Oh yes! Beria from Days for Girls. I remember you very well.' This made me super excited and energetic for the call. I explained the reason I made the call. Her response was, 'Girls' eyes are now always on the chalkboard not at their back looking to see if they are okay when menstruating. They are now focused.'"

Community after community around the world were also part of the celebration, reaching tens of thousands of women and girls. It wasn't easy, but together DfG champions of all kinds in many different countries shouldered the task of distributing one hundred thousand kits in twenty-eight days. Each individual they reached had her own story. Each kit also had its own story of how it reached her. We completed our audacious goal by Days for Girls' tenth birthday, November 1, 2018, proving that neither distance nor difficulty nor apparent unlikelihood could stop the Power of We! Once again, we learned what we could accomplish together—wherever we stand and whatever it takes.

Chapter 57

The Women of the Cloud Forest

When the villages work together,
we will turn this world around.
—Quechua Proverb

Pisaq, Peru, 2019

SEVEN WOMEN SAT WAITING SIDE BY SIDE, PERCHED ALONG A STONE wall at the crest of the mountain peak, far above the terraced green valley below. They were dressed in brilliant colors: traditional full skirts and flat caps, like graduate mortarboards with colorful frills that ruffled in the wind. They were early, although they had traveled far by foot along narrow pathways at altitudes so high that not even the rainforest could grow there, only short grasses amidst solid stone. My lungs wrestled with the skinny air at 13,650 feet above sea level as I dropped the duffel of supplies at the building door and hurried to meet them. They sat in silence.

I turned to greet them. "*¿Cómo estás? Mi nombre es* Celeste." No response. In fairness, I was speaking Spanish, and these were women of the cloud forest who speak primarily Quechua. Not Spanish. Living above the mountainous rainforests of Peru, there was only a small chance they would understand me. But this was different. There was not a flicker of response other than their colorful skirts and caps waving in the next gust of wind. I sat on the wall with them, honoring their silence.

Don, Calvin, and Emily were offloading their duffel bags, following the counsel not to hurry when you are new to this altitude.

Judy, director of DESEA Peru and a native Peruvian who works with

Andean communities in a variety of wellness initiatives, is intimately familiar with, and trusted by, the community. When she called everyone in, the women quickly rose to go inside where a few more were waiting.

The Quechuan nurses of DESEA had practiced AWH training with us for a full day prior, commenting that they knew the details of the curriculum but hadn't realized that they could have fun teaching it. They were already set up and prepared to instruct. After brief introductions that always include getting permission to photograph, I retreated to the background, taking photos and video footage, while the local women taught about health, how to use DfG kits, handwashing, and safety. They delivered it flawlessly and yes, they even had fun.

The women practiced the fold and snap of their new washable pads. I couldn't understand the Quechuan phrases that passed between them, but it felt like they were celebrating together. Later, they translated one young woman's comments for us, explaining that she had to walk to school for hours. Not having anything for her menses meant that the miles of staining moisture would chap and irritate her legs, risking infection for lack of adequate protection. She would now have what she needed, and she hoped to teach others what she had learned, too. The women were engaged and asked many questions, although for the most part I could only guess what they were asking based on which page of the flipchart the nurses turned to. When the nurses started talking about self-defense, the women laughed and followed every move. The nurses called me to the front. "They have a question for you. They want to know why they are learning this. Who is it they would protect themselves from? Our village is like a family. No one would ever attack anyone else."

This was the first time I had ever encountered a comment like this. My mind retraced all of the communities where being attacked wasn't a matter of if, but when. I paused, taking in the beauty of their statement. I hoped that this would always be the case for this community.

On our last trip to Peru, my oldest son, Devin, was translating, listening intently as a woman sent by her village became emotional when she learned what her community had sent her to retrieve from us: kits and health educational resources. She reported that several girls had been attacked when they came to Cusco from the rainforest in search of work. She explained that they had everything they need: food, water, community, and, recently, even education. The girls only came for money to . . . Devin had stopped translating. We all leaned in. Devin, who had occasionally told me that if I invested the amount of time and energy that I put into Days for Girls, I could create a thriving business that supported Days for Girls and still have more time left for family, could now hardly speak. "She says they come for money to buy pads," he said at last. "The last girl's father had explained that he wasn't able to provide pads for her. That's why she left the protection of her village. Just pads." We were all speechless now. After we finished the training and the woman was ready to return to her community with the pads and education, Devin slowly walked at my side. "Mom, I get it now. Keep going. Don't stop."

What these women of the cloud forest were reporting was significant. I looked into their faces with hope and saw they were sincere. "In case you ever need to defend yourself, your body will remember," I said. "And in the meantime, you can have fun with the dance of it." After translation, they laughed.

The self-defense portion of our curriculum has been included almost from the very beginning, growing in priority as we heard stories of women and girls being attacked and exploited in every corner of the Earth. We knew that the content had to be practical, effective, and simple to replicate. It also needed to deliver value with minimum risk of triggering trauma. In time, it was interactive and easy to implement, and included an important question to answer with confidence: "Where are you strong?" Something we should all be asked to consider.

In one school in Jinja, Uganda, the headmaster told us how vital permission to defend themselves had turned out to be. Two girls in their school were walking home when a man in a car offered to give them a ride. They remembered to "trust their feelings" and said no thank you. After one of the girls turned down the path to her family's thatch hut, the stranger pulled up alongside the remaining girl, insisting she get in the car. When she refused to get in, he pushed her into the ditch next to the road.

It's important to note that in the same community a year earlier, the head girl of the school, their brightest, had been found alone, unchaperoned, in a room with a local male primary schoolteacher. They were not embracing. They were simply in the same room unchaperoned.

The girl was punished with a one-year jail sentence. No more school. No more bright future. It was 2014, rather than another century as one might assume.

Nothing happened to the teacher.

Now, a year later, another girl's life hung in the balance. Only this one was doubly vulnerable, in a ditch and under attack. But she had an advantage. She had learned body literacy. She had already decided whether she had the right to defend herself. She knew where her body was strong (elbows, knees, heels, palms of her hands, and, of course, her mind and resilience). Importantly, she also knew where her attacker was weak. Her counterattack to the groin left him howling. His cries were what brought community members running to see what was wrong. By that time, she was out of the ditch. Safe. She survived, body and spirit intact in her community.

Messages are as important as the practical defense moves that come with them. Our SAFE lesson is just minutes long, but it teaches S for SURVIVE— because *you* matter. Not just physically, but in mind and spirit, too. A is for always be AWARE of what is around you. F is for FEELINGS matter; trust yours. And E is for EXIT with friends (try not to go it alone; stay with others).

Psychologist Amy Cuddy has a phenomenal TEDx talk about how your body is listening. Confidence, calm, and endorphins are boosted when you physically pose, standing strong. The girls and women learned that too. To trust their feelings, walk tall and strong. Be a loud storm if you are in danger.

When I teach self-defense we have fun, but I know how high the stakes really are. I was lucky. I survived. Not just physically, but emotionally, and spiritually determined to go on. Trauma has real consequences, and hope can be a superpower. This part of our curriculum invites everyone to decide to survive, whether they have already experienced trauma in the past or are learning to know how to protect themselves and others in the future. No matter what is ahead, behind, or in the present, hope, survival, and determination to recover remains a choice that we can make.

—

The women of the cloud forest had another strength: the power of community. As the DESEA nurses finished the education and presentation, two of the local women leaders stepped forward, their colorful apparel individual and unique. One wore the signature flat frill-edged hat of this community. Another wore a tall wool-brimmed hat and a simple sweater over her broad, colorful skirts indicative of another community. They spoke at length while all listened intently. I listened as well; though I could not understand their words, it is always important to me to be present and attentive to communication. I thought I heard my name within the unfamiliar dialect. Impossible. No one had said it since our introductions to the group over an hour ago. Then I heard it again from the second woman to speak. One of the nurses gestured for my friend Emily and me to come forward. "They wish to also thank you for bringing the kits." As she spoke, all the women looked us directly in the eyes. These phenomenal women had recalled an unfamiliar name with strange phonetics, retained and echoed in this moment. An impressive feat left us feeling deeply honored to be seen by them.

Later the translator explained that one had said, "We learned so much today. We now know how to take care of our bodies to protect ourselves from infection . . . We are excited to go home and teach our daughters . . . We are happy to have these kits. We want to teach others. We are very grateful."

We took a few more photos together, the women's DfG kits, as colorful as their dresses, swinging beside them in the wind. Then they disappeared in different directions more quickly than seemed possible.[39]

---

[39] In October 2022, Judy of DESEA showed Kayla-Leah and volunteers returning to Peru with 400 more DfG kits that DfG Ambassador of Women's Health curriculum had become part of their ongoing program offerings with or without kits, but they were pleased to receive more. New local Quechua instructors had been trained by the original Quechua nurses and delivered engaging DfG education impeccably. Judy reported that in the cloud forest communities that they serve there were now only a few hundred more left to reach with kits and education. DfG volunteers plan to return and support the local leaders there in reaching them all.

Chapter 58

What We Fear More than Death

*Humility is not thinking less
of yourself, but thinking of
yourself less.*
—Rick Warren

Seattle, Washington, November 15, 2019

"THERE YOU ARE, CELESTE!" AKHTAR BADSHAH SAID, RETAINING, AS
ever, the bounce of a tall college student, rather than what one might expect from
the former senior director at Microsoft. In the world of development, this man is
a big deal, but his manner is genuine and warm. Author and esteemed university
professor, today he was in his role as Global Washington's president of the board
of directors. Turning to the volunteer registrars at the international conference
center, he introduced me: "You may recognize Celeste Mergens, today's honoree
for the Global Hero Award." They offered congratulations as they handed me
my packet. The phenomenal past winners were listed in the booklet, including
Akhtar himself, Bill Gates Senior, and others whose work I admired. I smiled
and introduced Don and a few of my now grown children who had walked in
behind me, and I wondered, *How did I get here?*

Akhtar and I walked together to where the award luncheon would be
held, talking about . . . I don't know what, because my head was now filled
with an unrelenting feeling that any minute now, they would change their
minds.

Days for Girls has brought me occasion to meet many dignitaries, and I have had the great gift of receiving many awards on behalf of Days for Girls, but suddenly I felt like an imposter in this place.

Several of the large foundations in the area had overlooked Days for Girls, misunderstanding our hybrid design that equally engages stakeholders around the world, both through volunteers and social entrepreneurship. And now I would receive this award in front of some of them, which could have felt like vindication but that day left me feeling instead an enormous sense of responsibility to represent the mission and, just as important, the plight and strength of those we serve and serve with at Days for Girls.

In recent years more and more organizations are recognizing the importance of menstruation to the seventeen UN Global Sustainable Development Goals, "a universal call to action to end poverty, protect the planet, and ensure that by 2030 all people enjoy peace and prosperity."[40] Menstrual equity touches on no less than a solid six of the objectives: 3. Good Health and Well-Being; 4. Quality Education; 5. Gender Equality; 6. Clean Water and Sanitation; 8. Decent Work and Economic Growth; and 12. Responsible Consumption and Production. It also helps communities engage in ways that work for themselves, and supports local leadership.

—

Before the event, there was time for tea, greetings, and meeting fellow keynote speaker Raj Kumar, the Founder of Devex. Don sat at my side. My children took up almost a whole table in one end of the room.

It's interesting to note that according to the National Institutes of Mental Health, fear of death ranks *below* fear of public speaking for 70 percent of the population.[41] But to me it feels like crowd surfing: trusting people you don't know yet to catch your message, watching the light of awareness grow in their eyes. As mentioned, I typically give more than fifty addresses a year,

---

[40] "The SDGS in Action," *United Nations Development Programme*, accessed January 20, 2023. www.undp.org/sustainable-development-goals.

[41] Pat LaDouceur, "What We Fear More than Death," *MentalHelp.net* (blog), accessed November 23, 2022. www.mentalhelp.net/blogs/what-we-fear-more-than-death/.

and a few of them have been in front of as many as forty thousand people. This time, although my checklist of points to cover was nearly as familiar to me as my phone number, the closer we came to the event starting, the more the sequence of details seemed to jump around in my head like droplets on a hot oiled skillet. I sent up a prayer, then reminded myself that I only had to connect, not be perfect. I envisioned finishing and everyone having that familiar *aha* of recognition, gathering afterward in support. But still, little of the checklist came back to me.

"Please join me in welcoming to the stage this year's Global Hero Award winner, Celeste Mergens of Days for Girls International."

Don squeezed my hand as I rose from the table. I barely heard the applause as I walked up to the platform, reminding myself: *Deep breath. Be authentic. Be in this moment. Be interested in these people who care. Lose the list.*

For some unexplained reason I have a fear that is not likely to top many lists: fear of being full of myself. This is going to sound like hyperbole, but I would honestly rather die than feel like I am more important than anyone else. Praise from others brings an interesting crash of gratitude for the affirmation, and absolute awareness of the truth that every advance is only possible with the contributions of many. Add to that a compelling desire to reflect gratitude back to the individual—if they have the ability to understand and empathize with something others cannot even consider, that says a lot about them, not about me. Then there is the profound truth that they can't see good in others unless it is reflected from somewhere within themselves. It actually does take one to know one.

When someone asks if I feel so proud of the accomplishments and awards, I answer sincerely, "It is a privilege to do this work. Technically, I'm the really good listener who pays attention, shows up, and keeps working. It is those that we are reaching that matter most." This time as I stood at the podium, I saw in my mind the smiles of Kgotsu in Zimbabwe, the courage of Neha in India, my daughters and sons who were sitting nearby smiling, and Don, who was beaming ear to ear. I felt the importance of us taking on something that some communities fear more than death, menstruation as a perceived curse, and the power in the shift.

I took another deep breath and started my address.

Feeling calm now, I shared the stories we had outlined as well as one that I had been told not to share. (I even told the audience that I wasn't supposed to share it.) I forgot to thank the team. I always thank the team. But not that day. On that day it was all about the girls and how important and effective it is to reach them. The standing ovation was for them.

Chapter 59
The Price of Pencils and Pads

Learn from the people.
Plan with the people.
Begin with what they know.
Build with what they have.
But with the best leaders,
When the work is done,
The task accomplished,
The people will say,
"We have done it ourselves."
—Lao-Tzu

Bomet County, Kenya, 2019–2020
I WAS ABOUT TO LEAVE FOR DŌTERRA'S 2019 INTERNATIONAL CONVEN-tion where forty thousand people were about to hear more about Days for Girls. It took three hops to slip on my favorite pumps while simultaneously reaching for my cell phone. It was Anita Byegon calling. The first DfG Ambassador of Health for Bomet County, Kenya, and a dear friend, she usually only called for our weekly leadership team meeting. This had to be big news. I was right. This call was not her usual happy update.

Trigger Alert: Suicide

Jump ahead to the bottom of page 282 if you wish to avoid this potential trigger.

A fourteen-year-old Kenyan girl named Jackline had just committed suicide after being period shamed in class.

Earlier in the day Anita's cell phone had pinged with WhatsApp and Facebook messages from all over her county; the loss had just been discovered. Having just finished a DfG distribution education session, she rushed to make the four-hour drive to the school in Kabiangek, located in Kenya's southwestern region.

The people of Kabiangek were now tearing down the gate to the school in anger, shouting in protest, or standing in vigil in their grief.

Anita was told that the teacher, seeing the stain, had called Jackline dirty and ordered her to leave the classroom to stand outside against the wall while she looked for pads in the office. There were none. But Jackline had already run home. Her mother, a quiet, petite woman, Beatrice, said, "She had nothing to use as a pad." With no other option, she instructed Jackline to get the water jug and a rope to lower it into the river, clean herself up, and get back to class. The community found her hanging from the very rope she had been instructed to draw water with.

Not every person who is shamed commits suicide. But pervasive shame and stigma all over the world are a grim reality. Kenya's government has been a global leader in attempting to address menstrual inequity; they had been funding single-use disposable menstrual pads since 2011, an initiative that has at times been controversial due to reports of not reaching all schools, or running out of pads long before the school year ends, but their leadership has still been far ahead of most countries. Kenya also ended menstrual product taxes in 2004, a forward-thinking initiative that many countries, including the United States, are only just considering. Still, strong menstrual stigma persists throughout Kenya.

In this case, you and I couldn't be there to help. Anita could.

With Jackline's passing, Anita and friends called on their local community to commit to drawing a red line against menstrual shame and stigma for all of Bomet County and across Kenya in honor of Jackline. Jackline's mother joined them.

As Ambassadors of Women's Health, Anita and others expanded their conversations, calling for others to stand beside them in ending gender violence and shame. Anita met with local government and community leaders. Her team held educational rallies for hundreds of people at a time. They contributed to radio and TV broadcasts. Anita declared, "With proper education no teacher would shame like that, and no students would either. With proper supplies they can count on, this will never happen again."

Funding came in from Days for Girls supporters as well as the dōTERRA Healing Hands Foundation to support additional global efforts, including Kenya. In March 2020 more than thirty enterprise leaders from across Kenya gathered with Jackline's mother. Anita and friends readied to reach thousands with education and DfG kits in a matter of days.

"Two girls were selected from each school to be trained as Ambassadors of Health and serve as liaisons between students and administration. Working with the government's Gender Office, we reached over five hundred schools across Bomet County with the four-day training that covered various aspects of Days for Girls Ambassador of Women's Health including menstrual health management, ending gender-based violence, and life skills," Anita said.

These girls, like those around the world, reported managing their menstruation with whatever they could gain access to—leaves, torn blanket pieces, feathers, moss, stones, trash, torn sheets, two pairs of knickers. They, like so many others, reported that single-use pads left them not having what they needed at times or choosing to wash, dry, and reuse the same single-use pad for their full cycle, leaving them more vulnerable to infection. Or worse, exploitation.

A focused woman who is a mother, Anita works long hours managing both her enterprise and local advocacy; she feels this work is one of her life callings. "I am so glad that we could do something to help girls and women have safe, beautiful, and long-lasting alternatives they can count on month after month. I loved seeing the smiles of the girls and getting their assurance that they are going to break the silence on menstruation and they are now Days for Girls Ambassadors in their various schools within Bomet County. I am so humbled to see these girls ready to reach out to so many others to break the shame."

—

For Alice Wambui Mwangi, another dear friend and DfG Ambassador, and "Smile Star'D" Days for Girls enterprise owner in Nakuru, Kenya, Jackline's story hit close to home. Alice remembers that when she got her first period she was also sitting in class. She said, "I was in a room with three hundred students, a very congested room. We shared a desk, four students per desk. It was sunny, dusty, and windy outside when I realized that I had stained my uniform."

A bright student, she was often called on to come to the chalkboard. The teacher chose that moment to call her up. Alice didn't respond as usual. Her teacher, six feet tall, held a stick in his hand as he walked to her desk. Instead of hitting her with it, he slapped her face with his open palm. She stared down at his black shoes as he demanded that she go to the headmaster for disobedience. Rising, she quickly turned her skirt around to cover the stain with her books. But it was too late to hide it. Her classmates laughed. Alice went home and stayed there until her period ended. She was fortunate to be resilient enough to return to school again and again. "I tried using pages from my composition book and textbooks, tore part of my mattress, bedsheet, blanket, and some special leaves that were used as toilet paper in old times, which some people use even today. Nothing really worked, and that wasn't the only time I was punished or shamed, but I didn't give up."

One of fourteen children, she could only attend school if she managed to find a way to get a scholarship to secondary school and then college. She did just that, determined to be a force for good; today she is a vital Ambassador of Women's Health and leader with Days for Girls in Kenya and beyond. She represented Days for Girls at the African Youth Summit in Addis Ababa, Ethiopia, in April 2019. She advocates with diplomats for menstrual equity and tirelessly teaches communities in remote villages about their health. Her Days for Girls enterprise fills the orders of international visitors wanting DfG kits for those they serve, as well as local and nonprofit organizational requests for kits. Alice, and all those like her, is building community conversations as well as supplying girls with DfG kits.

She shared a favorite photo: "You see in the photo this girl has her sweater around her waist. She had started her period a day before the campaign; she didn't have sanitary pads. Her parents depend on hand-to-mouth jobs with less pay. They couldn't afford to buy pads. Now because of Days for Girls, this girl could smile again." Alice's smile is bigger still. Today her enterprise has reached more than 55,000 women and girls and offered health instruction to more than 80,000 community members.

—

I met my friend Khayanga Waskike, another Kenyan DfG Ambassador of Women's Health and enterprise owner, when she lived in Canada and traveled to our DfG offices. She has a strong and joyful presence, laughing easily, and she too is all in when it comes to ending period poverty. Khayanga explained, "When I was a young girl, I used to hunt for the thinnest splattered cow dung and then shake out the bugs before breaking it into pieces to use for a pad." Born and raised in Musembe a village in Lugari, Kenya, and later moving to Canada, she returned to her homeland after retirement, determined to make a difference. "I knew there would be many needs to be met, but I didn't think cow dung would still be used for menstruation. I was shocked to find that people still didn't have what they needed. My search for solutions led me to Days for Girls."

For Khayanga, Days for Girls' policy that health education for the entire community is just as important as the pads is vital. "Everyone must know that periods are natural. When my period came the very first time, I was in the bush fetching firewood. When I got home and saw blood stains on my clothes, I thought a stick had pricked inside me from careless tree climbing and left me bleeding. When it didn't stop, I got very scared. I told an older friend from the home next to ours. She told me that it was a very bad thing that happens to girls. She said that it was a taboo and that I should be very careful that nobody should find out, not even my mother, and especially boys. My private period journey started right there. I never did speak with my mother about it until we started the Days for Girls Lugari enterprise where my mother sometimes volunteers as a packer for the kits. It was during the AWH training for the staff that she herself opened up and spoke about periods. She was eighty years old then. I was shocked though delighted that we can both talk about something I feared to share with her throughout my life until this Days for Girls enterprise was launched and we both got comfortable talking or even listening to talks about menstruation in each other's presence."

Since then Khayanga not only helped facilitate the legal enterprise registration process in Kenya but also was a pivotal part of gathering other DfG leaders at her compound to practice quality manufacturing and education, all with funding from Days for Girls supporters. Her Days for Girls enterprise employs sixteen people and has reached more than thirty thousand community members, creating and providing DfG kits to more than seven thousand women and girls.

—

In honor of girls like Jackline and the importance of ending menstrual shame, on March 2, 2020, the leaders of DfG Kenya all came together. Forty-two DfG Ambassadors of Health and enterprise leaders from all over Kenya traveled long distances to gather in Bomet, again with the help of dōTERRA and Days for Girls supporters. For two days they shared best practices; drilled each other, reinforcing confidence for health training and presentation; discussed quality manufacturing measures; and readied for the official launch of the campaign in which they intended to "draw a red line through menstrual shaming." DfG chapter founder Kayla-Leah, her son Rider, and I passed out supplies while Anita and Khayanga paired everyone up, each planning to take on various sections of the AWH flipchart. The room was filled with happy chatter and last-minute instructions as we filed down the stairs to load into buses and vehicles headed for the first of three large school-based community meetings.

The bus ride went by in a flash. We were all too excited to notice time. We were focused on each other. I was one of the last off the bus and couldn't help but smile at the many Ambassadors all dressed in matching orange Days for Girls golf shirts, filing to the designated school fields centered between rows of classrooms. It felt like a team arriving at a sporting event. And it was: they came to tackle a serious taboo with confidence and clarity. Jackline's mother, the media, and hundreds of students and teachers were waiting for them, filling the open grass fields, their desks and benches brought outside. Within minutes dozens of local DfG leaders had banners up and were ready to go.

The headmistress welcomed us. The mayor welcomed us. Jackline's mother spoke before returning to her chair just in front of the row of over thirty DfG Ambassadors that stood shoulder to shoulder in their bright orange shirts. Dedicated women and men who had been actively advocating for menstrual equity in their own counties came together in honor of Jackline and offered an invitation to change things together. This was her community. They wanted to start here.

Introductions rang out over the noise of the crowd. "I'm Charles from Bomet."

"I'm Elizabeth from Maasai Mara."

"I'm Katini from Goshen."

"Noel from Narok."

"I'm Jacob."

"I'm Agnes."

Nearly the span of Kenya was represented. Students murmured audibly in response. It was so moving that my voice caught in my throat as I was invited to give my thanks to those assembled for hosting the launch of the campaign. By the time the Kenyan DfG Ambassadors of Health came forward two by two to present sections of the health education, we were all glued to their movements.

"Are you ready to celebrate wellness?"

"Yes!" the students answered.

"Who here is ready to be a champion for ending menstrual shame?"

"I am!" students shouted.

Two of the local Ambassadors of Health, Brenda and Robert, took on puberty to applause. "Your amazing body transforms . . . What changes as you grow from child to adult?"

"We grow taller!" a boy in front answered. More answers followed. Many laughed as Brenda walked with swaying hips to give the hint that one change for girls is their shape changes and hips widen. "This change is not just on the outside; it is also on the inside and does not finish until about age eighteen. This is the reason that if you wait until after you are eighteen to have a baby, your body will be ready and you are more likely to have a healthy baby and a healthy mom. Your body is still growing until then." That single data point alone, along with the way it is taught, is truly significant.

In many places girls are candidates for marriage as soon as they start menstruating, and even earlier. Tell global girls that the biggest cause of death for girls between ages fifteen and nineteen years is complications from pregnancy and childbirth, they will likely roll their eyes. After all, their mother may have been a young teen when they were born. She may have a friend who has given birth very early in her teens. But if you tie the facts to what they can see in their own experience, logic takes the lead. Now they recall friends and family who passed during childbirth at young ages. Our curriculum doesn't make them wrong; it bridges their experience, connecting with new facts. Bonus points for the laughter and engagement.

Two other Ambassadors instructed on women's reproductive health. Ambassadors bring a sense of wonder as they interact with gatherings as small as ten and as big as hundreds. Covering menstruation, how the cycle works, how to chart it, how babies happen, preventing sexually transmitted infection, handwashing, self-defense, and even avoiding human trafficking, in just two hours. Ambassadors Christine and Noel brought extra laughs as they invited everyone to join in learning a few self-defense principles.

Soon youth were gathering to play games aimed at breaking menstrual stigma: bouncing a red balloon within a circle of youth trying to keep it from hitting the ground to show how it takes a village to support healthy menstrual attitudes.

A row of students and teachers formed to sign the menstrual pledge: *We are drawing a red line against menstrual shaming. No more lost days. No more lost lives. No more lost dignity. Period.* Local media captured the moments.

In the fall of 2020, on the anniversary of Jackline's death, they took on thousands more county by county, with the goal of reaching every county through engaging full communities, strategically. They reached 44,193 Kenyan women and girls with Kenyan-made kits and education when no one could bring kits made elsewhere due to the COVID-19 pandemic. These amazing ambassadors connected with at least triple that number in community member engagement as well. Social entrepreneurs led within their communities, providing jobs through their enterprises to sustain the supply and advance advocacy.

They are still standing up for menstrual equity. Right now. Today. Together.

Chapter 60

Time in the Zone

We look up at the same stars
and see such different things.
—George R. R. Martin

2020

"WE ARE CANCELING OUR ORDER." CRUSHING NEWS FROM THE KENYAN official to the social enterprise leader who had worked for months to fulfill this order—first pitching the opportunity to the official, then preparing for a large community-wide menstrual wellness campaign that included many students receiving locally produced Days for Girls kits and education. She had been organizing, budgeting, and finally rallying her seamstresses to make many kits in preparation ever since. Now this news.

"Why? What happened?" she asked.

"I just learned that Days for Girls kits were given down county. We have set aside the funding, but we will be seen as foolish if we use our small community budget to pay for what is being given freely to others."

Not for the first time, a hardworking chapter had generously and unintentionally sent volunteer-made kits with a partner to the wrong location—where an enterprise had been thriving.

We had reached the tipping point even before we expected it.

—

I often said that one day we would reach this day where enterprises would be taking the lead in places where chapters had "seeded" the market, and local

leaders would join in and carry on; that we would have, in essence, worked ourselves out of a job and into a support role. There would still be more work to do,
but the shift would signal a real victory, leaving chapters and teams to target
volunteer-made kits in places where menstrual conversations and solutions still
needed a kickstart, while also advancing advocacy, enterprises, and emergency
interventions.

I had been describing our volunteer and enterprise programs as two arms
that work together, wrapping the globe to reach Every Girl. Everywhere. Period.
Each arm advocating where they live to end period poverty and shame, effectively reaching every corner of the planet, including Antarctica.[42] Our hybrid
model isn't the easy way. It requires a complexity of organization that would not
be needed if we settled for either volunteer engagement or entrepreneurship, but
I could see the benefits and importance of both working together. Thankfully, a
lot of others see it too.

As our organization matured, we began to see the chapters, teams, clubs,
offices, and enterprises not as two arms, but as a continuum of impact. All are
important, and volunteer efforts often lead to the better outcomes of the other.

But a hybrid model can be confusing. While some loved DfG because of it,
many fell into one camp or the other. Some objected to any kind of selling: "If
they can't afford disposable pads, what are you doing selling pads anywhere?!"
Others objected to any kind of giving: "Do-gooders cause harm." We were ap-
proaching our mission from both means of engagement, as appropriate, inviting
partners and governments to step beside both enterprises and chapters in supporting local jobs and leadership to break the stigma and increase menstrual
product access.

We were in essence pioneering a franchise powered by crowdsourcing—
listening and attempting to glean and share best practices as we went. Some of
our enterprise innovations worked well, and some of them were challenging.
Giving everyone standard templates was effective. Translating proven resources

---

[42] Years ago two female scientists took DfG menstrual cups with them to Antarctica, a solution
as practical for them as it was valuable to DfG in raising awareness when they tweeted from there
about us. Although we could technically report that we have reached seven continents, we still say
six since this was a one-time intentional effort.

was effective. Giving large notebooks of instructions? Expecting long reports? Not so much, of course.

At first, I thought we were helping people to be the "Avon ladies of menstrual health," but it became clear over time that wasn't what we were asking at all. We were asking them to be the chemist creating the lipstick: to predict how much colorant they would need to order before they needed it, and to package and *then* market and sell. Yes, they had the advantage of the Days for Girls' brand and products, proven curriculum, and reduced material costs thanks to bulk global purchasing.[43] But even our offices in Uganda and Ghana were instructing social enterprise candidates differently depending on who was teaching, despite our efforts to be consistent. We were working to standardize our training to be as precise and consistent as our sewing patterns, instructions, and flipcharts. That wasn't easy.

All the Zoom meetings, global local leadership cooperation, and beautifully created handbooks, outlines, and slide decks were helping . . . and yet sometimes not. This puzzle was *Tetris 3D* on level 12. How do you create consistency across the globe when people come to Days for Girls leadership with all different strengths? What if a person has passion, respect in their community, sewing skills, but no experience saving resources for sustainable supply purchase? How could we offer ways to learn the skills they needed to help build something that would take time to grow? How do you teach skills like accounting, forecasting, and reporting, in dozens of languages, to those who in some cases have not had the resources to be concerned about being financially literate, let alone skilled at it? And how do you do it in a way that leaves them confident and does not take them from their families?

It took time for Days for Girls social entrepreneurs to see their leadership role in creating community buy-in, and encouraging nonprofit and government support in purchasing their programs and kits, rather than expecting to fully rely on the support of Days for Girls International. Add in perhaps the most

---

[43] While Days for Girls utilizes and encourages as much local purchasing as possible, we have found that for some, items have a lower cost and better consistency of material quality when purchased strategically in large wholesale quantities through valued partners. Groups utilize whichever is best suited to their situation.

interesting puzzle of all: the same community challenges could be seen completely differently depending on the individual.

For example, a DfG social enterprise leader working with the Maasai in Kenya declared, "They don't want to talk about periods. There is not much water. They don't have money. This is impossible." In contrast, another, whose enterprise was only a county away, within the same culture and very similar issues, would tell anyone who would listen quite the opposite. "Talking about periods is new here so everyone needs us! Our pad design saves them money and doesn't use much water to wash! That's important to them. It's perfect. These things are selling like you wouldn't believe!" When they didn't sell well at one market, she decided that the spectacle of a man selling pads and panties might draw a crowd. She hired someone eager to help. She was right; the market grew.

The same issues. Very different responses.

One was determined. She focused on the possibilities she needed to reach her goals, and not the obstacles. How do you look for, discern, and nourish that trait? In my experience, seeing possibilities even in the face of hardship is one predictor for both success and resilience.

We needed to mentor enterprise leaders further in confidence, marketing, and business skills while standardizing our training so that best practices could be shared more regularly.

Thanks to Days for Girls supporters, we were able to hire a team member to help research, establish, and implement additional training and standards of qualification for applying to be an enterprise so that we could help them better succeed. It was a process that took a lot of additional inquiry and was met with some dismay. Everyone wanted to just start.

We shifted to training in cohorts instead of on demand, which allowed our small team to focus on more systems and standardization. The tricky part was doing it without making things more complicated. Genius is in simplicity. We were determined, measuring our impact and pivoting as needed along the way, improving our monitoring and evaluation as we went.

A surprising need came into focus. World-renowned social impact specialist, Jane Reisman, lent her expertise to help us capture excellent monitoring, learning, and evaluation (MLE). To do that we had to start by working together as a global team to build our *Theory of Change*, a document that pinpoints our exact

core objective and how we plan to reach it. This process helped us to know what
to measure and what success is. You might think that it would be simple, something like girls attending school. But it's not that easy. School attendance has
many factors. And Days for Girls pads and education benefits the entire community, including every person who needs absorbance protection: people with
periods, postpartum mothers, women with fistulas (who need them every day),
and we have reports of women (and a few men) who use them for stress incon-
tinence. Global DfG team members convened, creating massive colorful charts
that pinpointed the stakeholders, impact, and details that capture our work and
strategic method. The results rivaled the webs seen in crime specials, connecting
the dots to every suspect and every possibility. In this case, every word and activity was scrutinized. The results? A single sentence. Success for Days for Girls
means *shattering stigma and limitations associated with menstruation.*

Then came the work of color coding the world map to make it easy to know
what areas were open for volunteer-made kits and which were not. At the instruction of our remarkable programs director, Tiffany Larson,[44] our team member Leyla Isin-Xiong took this project on with complete commitment. It would
take a year of puzzling, listening, and systemizing with a global lens to codify
our zones of activity:

- Red zones—they've got this! Period. Only locally made kits go here.
  Local leaders fulfill the need for their entire country. A true victory.
- Orange means we can handle this together. In orange zones, enterprises
  are the primary supplier of kits wherever possible, but if no enterprises
  are active nearby the location seeking DfG kits, then kits sewn by
  chapters and teams may be distributed. Still, wherever possible, local
  DfG-certified Ambassadors of Health deliver the education. Their presence, ability, and visibility as exemplary leaders are priceless to others
  who see their example as potential for themselves. Their ability to speak
  local dialects is almost equally ideal.
- Blue zones represent wide open territory for chapters to expand the

---

[44] After years of the gift of working with her and seeing her genius and dedication in action, I am
pleased to announce that Tiffany recently stepped into the role of CEO.

reach, further advocacy, and build future markets while on the lookout for local leaders who can help grow the work from there.

The zones are our commitment and belief in the strength of every community. We continue to lean into sustainable change, in pursuit of our goal of more community self-reliance. Chapters, teams, clubs, and Days for Girls International's organizational efforts support enterprises in every way they can, a process that now requires even more communication.

Days for Girls enterprises around the globe celebrated the positive impact the zones have for their communities and economies. When Alice Wambui Mwangi heard the news in Kenya, she practically jumped for joy. "This will uplift and empower locals," she said. "The men and women who work at the enterprises earn an income that way. Which helps put food on the table, pay school fees for kids, and provide for their family's basic needs. It's such an important thing."

In Malawi, DfG enterprise leader Yamikani shared that her DfG enterprise members were doing so well that in one case a single mother of two who was hired after her husband had abandoned them was now purchasing a home of her own with funds from her work there. That enterprise was founded by a DfG team leader, Penny of Mansfield, Ohio; both women were committed to protecting local efforts so those kinds of successes could continue.

Ultimately, the DfG impact zones position DfG and our incredible network of advocates, supporters, enterprise leaders, and volunteers to accomplish even more while respecting and elevating local communities as the menstrual health champions, change-makers, and thought leaders that they are.

—

So, everyone loved the new zones, right? Wrong. For some it was incredibly threatening and even arrogant. What made us think that less than thirty enterprises could cover all of Kenya? Were we abandoning our vision of Every Girl. Everywhere. Period?

"Celeste, I can't believe you are in support of this. We can't abandon them now!" said one leader, a dear friend who had dedicated years of her life to DfG. She misunderstood the opportunity to support local leadership and further our mission, and fought with all her might for her beloved Kenyan friends in the red zone.

The passion we all held was now dividing us.

We tried to explain that this was the victory we had always been working toward. That what we were now calling the red zone was a win-win: women and girls experiencing period poverty would have increased access to menstrual health solutions and education, and our enterprise members would earn income to improve their livelihoods, grow their businesses, influence positive social and political change, and ultimately reach more women and girls. But that meant no more remote volunteer-made kits in those areas. Enterprises would exclusively supply DfG kits as well as menstrual health education there. Volunteers and partners were encouraged to purchase directly from enterprises. By partnering with and supporting enterprises in this way, all stakeholders can double or even triple their impact.

Leyla had to repeat the reasons for the zones again and again, rising early and working well into the night to reach every time zone. She and the team created presentations, documents, and videos, and they met virtually with people all over the world to answer questions, patiently responding to fear and concern with calm. Most in our global family of impact understood and advocated for the change, too, but it took a lot of dialogue before a few who were vocally and visibly rallying opposition to start recognizing that this wasn't turning our backs—it was trusting and backing up strong local leadership.

I understood the dilemma more than they knew.

Days for Girls was growing up. I had studied and learned all along the way to continually grow my capacity with the organization, as had many on our team; we were willing to work within the global schedule of others while holding firm to our commitment that the focus of the work we were doing was singularly about those we serve. The challenges, and even the awards, became more reason to hold that focus strong. Yet what was now required of me seemed far more challenging.

Now I had to entrust some of the most beloved parts of my role to others. I had to let go of even more—and like some chapter and team leaders, I found this particular change difficult. It was time to back away from things that I had traveled the world to listen, learn, and become expert in. Would others care about the lessons learned as much as I did? Could they take in all that we had learned as context and then keep listening and building from there with their own additional wisdom gained from the field?

Shortly after Days for Girls started, I had the very strong prompting that sewing was not my role at Days for Girls—*back away from the sewing machine.* A prompting so strong I had to consciously set it aside when I took on sewing a long white blessing dress with a scalloped hem and matching bonnet, or a turtle costume for a grandchild.

The cycle to choose to let go had come calling again: to trust more of the specialized pieces of the work to others or risk limiting the future scale of Days for Girls. We had the remarkable gift of tens of thousands of volunteers who are as talented as anyone you could hire, and who worked longer hours than any employer could ask. Now we needed additional, very particular skill sets. And it was important we hired for those needs.

I let go of the entire program side of our organization. My favorite part. For me, it felt like dropping a precious not-yet-perfected masterpiece constructed by the work of artisans around the world. Brilliant in design, but still needing completion. So much was at stake; yet there was so much possibility. I let go, trusting that somehow the new team members would ask the right questions and strike the right balance between learning, knowing, creating, and holding so much possibility. I did it! Standing only slightly ready to jump back in to rescue any pieces that might be dropped. But I knew in my heart that I could count on the strength and commitment of the team.

In the minds of some of our important volunteer leaders, we were asking them to do the very same thing: to drop the very thing they had worked on for years. We were asking them not to take kits to the orphanages they had serviced, perhaps for years; we were asking them to now purchase kits from the local enterprise—made by somebody else. But many were passionate about the place they were delivering to. They wanted to deliver what they had made. The passion for which they had sacrificed their homes to storage, the days building teams, educating, advocating, sewing, and fundraising to reach more girls, rising to the occasion with a level of skill and commitment that stunned newcomers visiting our regional conferences. We said Every Girl, and they were as determined to get there as I was. So how could we possibly ask them to just trust that someone else would get there? Someone else would figure it out. What if others weren't as determined? What if no one ever reached a girl they would have reached?

Statistics upheld the wisdom of our trust in local leaders.

In 2018 DfG reached 23,452 women and girls in Kenya. Of that number, 19,647 kits were made by chapters and teams, and 3,805 were made by enterprises. In 2020, we recorded the most kits distributed in Kenya in a single year: 44,193. Of those, 40,961 were made and distributed by enterprise leaders there. Many were supported by fundraising from chapters. By 2021, Kenyan enterprises reached 80,882, their biggest year ever. They could do even more with more support and are readying for the potential of large government contracts while staying nimble and personally supporting their communities.

By ensuring that distribution efforts aren't duplicated between enterprises and chapters and teams, we were creating an even stronger network of DfG programs working together in harmony to turn periods into pathways.

Global COVID-19 restrictions underscored the wisdom. While chapters and team partners were suddenly unable to travel due to the pandemic, DfG enterprises were there on the ground, responding to the needs in their communities.

Chapters and teams began partnering with the enterprises to continue reaching women and girls.

Some examples come to mind.

Eruption in the Orange Zone

In the Democratic Republic of Congo, ten kilometers from Goma in the North Kivu province, the ground was still rumbling long after Mount Nyiragongo erupted in 2016. The deadly volcano had destroyed over 3,600 houses as well as schools and marketplaces. DfG chapters and teams responded to assist local DfG social entrepreneurs in the emergency. Following the eruption, thirty-four chapters and teams from around the world raised nearly ten thousand dollars in a matter of one week to sponsor kits made by DRC and Rwanda enterprises as well as emergency supplies to reach the women and girls and communities as soon as possible.

Pivotal Partnerships in the Red Zone

Other chapters formed partnerships with local social enterprise DfG leaders. They pivoted to purchase kits from an enterprise toward their ongoing local partnerships to honor commitments made before the zones. Teams like the Provo, Utah, team, together with the Stanwood-Camano Island, Washington, chapter, coordinate ongoing fundraisers to support the Kolkata, India, enterprise's community outreach efforts. Jenny, of the Rotary Passport Club of Melbourne, Australia, reported on their sponsorship of kits for Kenya. "This is fantastic to have these connections as we develop projects and connections that can assist so many people throughout the world. I think that Days for Girls partnering with Rotarians makes so much sense. Sometimes, as with Alice Wambui Mwangi, it is about finding funds to support a distribution, sometimes it is about the connections. I also see worth in taking a project such as the one we decided to do as an opportunity to also raise awareness of needs amongst people here in Melbourne. Many have no idea, and it is important for people to understand issues across the globe."

The enterprise leader they supported used the resources to reach a boarding school where five hundred girls were attending because they were avoiding the cut of FGM/C or narrowly sidestepping being child brides. Their chapter was "raising awareness of a place where girls sometimes have no choice over their bodies and their future!"

Outreach in the Blue Zone

Homaira lives in the blue zone in Afghanistan where there is not yet a Days for Girls enterprise. Her first period was a scary day for her. Like so many, she had no idea what was happening to her body. "I couldn't stop crying," she said.

Here's what World Vision reported:

Given the sensitive nature of menstruation in Afghanistan and entrenched cultural beliefs, menstrual hygiene management is difficult to address there.

With the support of Days for Girls International and World Vision Australia, however, World Vision Afghanistan assisted 1,000 women and girls in Herat's IDP (Internally Displaced Persons) settlements to manage their menstrual periods. This was delivered through menstrual health awareness sessions (Days for Girls Ambassador for Women's Health Education) and the distribution of Days for Girls Menstrual Health Kits. These partners reported that "this menstrual hygiene management approach has been critical for empowering women and girls."

Homaira said, "In the past, I felt I was filthy and that this blood was a sign of impurity because I had no idea what this blood was for and why we had to experience it for seven days per month. Now I . . . no longer experience shame from menstruation because it is a sign of a healthy body."

The approach shared in Days for Girls Ambassador for Women's Health Education has also helped dispel myths. According to Homaira, "We were previously told to avoid vegetables and bathing for the duration of our periods in order to prevent infertility. Now we know how to take care of ourselves during the period."

Maryam, age thirty, was told by her grandmother, "Do not wash yourself after using the toilet because it causes infertility and do not walk because it will damage your uterus." Maryam said, "Now I know that these myths were not only harmful, but also jeopardize our health in the long term."

Pari Gul, age sixteen, is another participant in the Days for Girls project. Access to sanitary pads was a challenge for her. "We are a large family so we can barely afford to buy food. I have five sisters and all of them have to buy sanitary pads each month, which is costly for us, and we cannot afford it. I remember one day when I didn't have sanitary pads. It was time to go to school, and I didn't want to miss school. I had a brown scarf that I really liked. I cut it into pieces and used it as sanitary pads. I cried a lot over missing my scarf. It wasn't the last time. I had to do the same with my other clothes too," said Pari Gul, with tears in her eyes. Now she has the DfG kits. "I am very happy now. I can use it multiple times, which is very easy, without paying money for it. I have shown the kit to my friends and they have sewed the same sanitary napkins in order to reduce the cost of buying sanitary pads from the market."

These students turned unresolved menstrual management challenges into strength, sharing their stories and helping more of their community to claim their days back, too. When overcoming generations of stigma, that's especially important and remarkable, and so are they.

Chapter 61

Cambodia

If you are planning for a year, sow rice;
If you are planning for a decade, plant trees;
If you are planning for a lifetime, educate people.
—Chinese Proverb

Cambodia, 2019

"I KNOW WHAT YOU ARE TRYING TO DO, BUT IT IS NOT GOING TO WORK."
The unusually tall and imposing Cambodian master teacher clearly had every confidence he was right.

Bad news for us.

The half-dozen additional designated master teachers looked mildly curious sitting in student desks in the comfortable cinder block classroom we had been assigned by the Ministry of Education, Youth, and Sport (MoEYS).

The teacher continued, his long legs casually crossed at the ankle, extending far beyond the too-small desk he sat in. "If we talk about this, the students will mock us. The teachers will think us mad, and the parents will be angry at us." None of his colleagues made any motion, but they seemed to agree by virtue of the fact that they now sat staring at Monie, Leyla, and the rest of us in the same way he did.

We were off to a shaky start.

Thankfully, the day before, Monie, who was leading Days for Girls Cambodian efforts with skill and dedication, had introduced us to her good friend, Yin Sopheap.

Sopheap is a revered founder of an exceptional school campus for thousands of students in Cambodia. You sense the pride of the students there as they hurry between palm tree–lined pathways to their classrooms. After we visited his campus, he had volunteered to join us for our master teachers' kickoff meeting. Now hearing their concern, he offered to address them. We couldn't understand the Khmer he spoke in, but his confidence and ease were obvious. Soon they were laughing and nodding in agreement.

He turned to us with the same cheerful demeanor. "I have explained that when I was a young man I didn't know what was happening to my body as I grew. I didn't like getting hair. I was embarrassed that my body was starting to do things without me telling it to. Once I had to hold my arm down on my lap while others went to recess, waving them to go ahead. I stayed until it settled down." He laughed, then continued, "I tried to find books about what my body was doing and eventually understood. But it was terrible! Imagine how much harder it must be for young women. I wished someone would have taught me. I think everyone should know what is happening with their bodies, don't you?"

He ended by inviting Monie to return to the front of the class.

—

Days for Girls came to Cambodia because of Tiann Monie.

Monie had suffered the hunger and devastation of Cambodia's Killing Fields genocides during the four-year period in the late 1970s when dictator Pol Pot facilitated the murder of 1.7 to 2 million educated Khmer. Pol Pot's regime promised peace and equality; instead it divided families, forced labor, imprisoned innocents, and starved millions. You were a threat and most at risk of torture and mass killings if you were educated or political, or wore eyeglasses. Somehow Monie survived. Although she had studied in France, she managed to suffer the hunger and devastation of the Pol Pot "simple life" without being executed as so many were. Later she returned to Phnom Penh determined to help restore her country.

Now Monie was showing us her beautiful city. The tuk-tuk we rode in had tassels along the top and a carefully curated row of bamboo shoots braided in decorative twists in the windshield. We turned down the road adjacent to the shimmering riverway bustling with activity under blue skies. She was taking us to the first of two memorials of the Killing Fields.

We entered the rows of buildings at Tuol Sleng (S-21), the main political prison, where suspected enemies of Angkar were sent. People were incarcerated, tortured, and interrogated there before being starved or executed for their brilliance. In one room dozens and dozens of faded collaged photos hung in framed billboard stands, a stark record of only a few. Innocent people of every age and gender—teachers, children, officials, doctors, writers—all seen as representing a threat to growth and equality. I wanted to run from the room, sickened by the tangible loss and violence. I forced myself to stay, stopping the tour audio to look into the faces to honor them before retreating to the bench outside, feeling short of air. No country thinks genocide is possible until it happens. How do we make sure we see that the things that unite us are stronger than the things that divide us?

While we listened to the atrocities that had happened in the past, children played in a nearby school playground, yards away. A bell rang, prompting them to return to their classrooms. I felt the relief of knowing that education turns the tides.

Monie was committed to doing everything she could to strengthen the educational opportunities that had been decimated by that era. A woman who loves science, she created school programs through her highly regarded Cambodian nonprofit CRESO. Her recommendation of Days for Girls is as influential as her dedication.

Maria Hicks, a DfG Australian volunteer and winner of the Order of the Australia Medal for her service in Cambodia and beyond, had introduced Monie to Days for Girls and kept the conversation going. I met Monie when Maria arranged for her to attend a DfG Ambassador of Health regional training in Pennsylvania. Between the two of them, Days for Girls' work in Cambodia had taken root as firmly as the vines entwining the carved stone temples of Angkor Wat. Others were now joining in.

One of them is Aviv Palti, an astute Australian businessman, and his daughter Jessica, whose phenomenal social entrepreneurship program in Cambodia added Days for Girls to their work in a big way. They call it Project G (G for Girls). It is managed by student leadership. Aviv says, "Many organizations get attracted to the beautiful kits but fail to understand the life-changing impact of thorough and connected education. Before we started Project G, part of the team's 'research' was to attend other workshops—what we found [before Days for Girls] was weak, incomplete, and ineffective education . . . Giving a gift alone is not empowering; the right education is."

They would know. Project G has an incredible team of young DfG Ambassadors of Health. They teach every student at every school they go to, always including everyone holistically. Their delivery of DfG education is exemplary. So good that our first full day in Cambodia was spent videoing their extraordinary young leaders in action. Leaders like Sinoun and Heng whose inclusive leadership invites everyone on their team to make decisions and participate. Their engaging footage would serve as both example and clear evidence of just how interactive the lessons can be. We added the footage from Project G to a video of Sopheap sharing his story of why everyone needs body literacy. Between the two, we hoped they would be evidence enough to encourage teachers to overcome the fear of discussing periods.

—

Leyla Isin-Xiong was prepared to do the in-service for the master teachers over the next few days. She had come directly from Laos where she lives with her husband Valee, who works in Luang Prabang and regularly visits his family village in the mountains. They had both worked on Days for Girls projects for a while now. One of the most meaningful events for Leyla was a distribution in Laos two years prior that reinforced for her the incredible power and strength of knowledge. During the distribution, DfG Laos leaders, LyLy,[45] Soua Vang, and Tarn Khounvilaila conducted the Ambassador of Women's Health curriculum and distributed DfG kits to a classroom of girls. The three youngest girls sat in the front row, absolutely mesmerized; they hung on every word the local leaders shared. At the end of the session, the girls approached LyLy, Soua, and Tarn with excitement. "We can't wait to get our period now," they said.

Getting menstrual health knowledge *before* getting their first period is a game changer. The girls said they now felt prepared for it with their new understanding and DfG kits. Leyla wanted that for all the girls of Laos and Cambodia, too. This first pilot curriculum was planned for fifth graders throughout Cambodia.

Although her flight from Laos had been shorter than ours and she was in a

---

[45] LyLy regrettably died unexpectedly in 2020.

familiar time zone, Leyla had been putting in long hours balancing in essence two roles: curriculum expert, for which she has a degree and experience, and international chapters director, and she was feeling the stretch.

All these months later, everyone's effort was about to pay off.

Crisp blank notebooks and curriculum manuals filled with swirling Khmer script were placed at every desk for the next stage, training the master teachers.

Introductions complete, Leyla moved to the front of the room. "Let's start by reading the first page together. One paragraph each."

The first teacher started to read, but halted, looking up hesitantly.

The second teacher started but also stopped short. "These words are out of order and make no sense."

All the teachers nodded.

I stared at the neat rows of swirling font as if I could confirm either way.

Morina, the third-party MLE representative in the room, had just collected the master teachers' completed surveys designed to assess current knowledge and help measure the impact of the training long-term. She paused to take a glance at one of the manuals. She confirmed, "It is true. This happens a lot with translations, but this document is impossible to understand." Somehow, despite months of effort, the translated printing was garbled.

The teachers looked ready to leave.

"No problem," I assured them, quickly collecting the specialized Days for Girls curriculum that had been entrusted for months into the hands of a highly recommended expert Khmer translator. A translation done *after* Monie, and our Global Advocacy Director Diana Nelson, and Leyla had worked on the modules for almost a year. We didn't know how it happened, but we had a bigger issue at the moment: a classroom full of teachers ready for the next instruction, and no flipchart and manual as planned.

The man who first declared "this would not work" spoke again with more confidence still. "Anyway, you don't need to do this. The Ministry is working on a curriculum."

Leyla and I looked at each other. "Yes. This *is* it," she said.

We were there at the invitation of the Cambodian Department of School Health of the Ministry of Education, Youth, and Sport. A big name for a department with a large scope of impact. We were partnering to pilot and test a version of our DfG health curriculum specific to grade levels, along with a story activity created by the nonprofit WASH United. MoEYS had tried other curricula but was not seeing uptake. After observing DfG's interactive sessions, they had invited us to pilot with them. The plan was for these master teachers from Ratanakiri, Mondulkiri, and Kratié provinces who would go on to teach other teachers to feel confident instructing about maturation and periods. It mattered very much that this went well.

Tenacious flexibility is a long-held premise of success for DfG. We would need it that day. I suggested that we shift to the Ambassador of Women's Health segment, one portion of the specialized curriculum, and my favorite part to do. We used the projector we brought for the images. Morina offered to stay and translate live. Next Leyla moved ahead with activities planned for the next day. Activities that included string and popsicle sticks—practical everyday items that teachers could engage with even if they have few resources. It all worked out phenomenally. So much so that when Leyla and I held a fun quiz at the end of the AWH section, our originally skeptical master teacher was the first to put his hand up and answer to get a prize. For each question, his hand shot up in the air, eager to answer, at one point with such force that he nearly knocked his whole desk over, answering correctly, "Three!"

Much to our relief, by the end of the day all the teachers were smiling and interacting. It had gone well though not at all as planned. We saved figuring out what to do with the manuals for after the day's activities. But we would somehow need to have a solution to our mystery manual translation problem within the next two days.

—

There is no large office printing store in Ratanakiri province. Not even a copy machine. Certainly nothing after dark, but my friend Kayla-Leah, author, TEDx champ, and DfG chapter founder, who has the equivalent of a black belt in friend-making, asked our tuk-tuk driver if he knew anyone who could help us print ten flipcharts after working hours and before 9 AM tomorrow. It turned out that he knew someone to ask, and he called them on the spot. Would they be willing to take on an emergency early morning printing job if we emailed it to them by daybreak? He would get back to us.

To celebrate the day going well and to thank him, we had invited Sopheap to dinner, informing him of our translation problem as we dined on traditional Cambodian and Italian food with his son and friends at their favorite restaurant. Sopheap recommended one of his team members to assist us, a brilliant young man named Saron. It was 7 PM. A half hour later, Saron arrived at our hotel ready to assist.

Our tuk-tuk driver friend called. Much to our relief, the printer had agreed to start at 5 AM to print and bind ten flipcharts that would need to be back to us before 9 AM. Now to complete a task in two days that had taken an expert several months.

We devised a plan: divide and conquer. Monie and Maria Hicks would complete plans for a school sanitation project that they were working on. Meanwhile, Saron and the rest of us would work on the flipchart and manuals. There was no way he could retranslate the flipchart overnight alone. Not to mention ninety-six pages of curriculum to be redone as well—within two days. Huddled up at a table in the hotel dining area, he tackled the first pages of the flipchart and the rest of us took on wrestling with Google translation to do the remaining pages as well as the first twenty-six pages of the lesson plans. Word by word, Google translation is often a problem. But the trick is to take one phrase at a time, translate, then reverse translate, changing the phrase until the meaning matches in both languages. It took creativity and tenacity, but in three to four tries we could usually get very close before moving our attempts into the master Google doc we all shared access to so that Saron could correct and refine it. Our "starters" gave him enough information to be able to complete the translation more quickly.

We worked very late, and then he went home to keep working on shared documents from there. Through the magic of Google shared docs, we continued page by page inching forward together though apart. Our four personal Google icons hovered at the top of the page until just before sunrise.

The flipchart file made it to the printer just in time. At dawn they confirmed that they had arrived to find it in their email. Saron sent a WhatsApp message: he was going to sleep now but would continue to work on the manuals for the master teachers in Phnom Penh when he woke up.

After breakfast Monie and her daughter, Nathalie, went onto the school project as planned. Leyla, Maria, and I went back to the master trainers, and Kayla-Leah took the tuk-tuk to the printer's shop.

We dove into the next round of activities. By the time Maria brought in lunch for everyone, Kayla-Leah was still out. An hour later she arrived with a stack of brand-new Khmer flipcharts fresh off the press. Just in time. "They didn't have a collator," she said. "Each page had to be fed in twice by hand."

The newly translated flipcharts were met with the teachers' approval. By the time they started practicing how to demonstrate snapping a DfG pad onto panties, one of the men pulled the panties with pad onto his bicep. "These make girls strong," he said.

Next we needed to complete the manuals for the master teachers and college instructors who would receive the training two days later. Manuals that would be reviewed by the Ministry of Education and representatives in Phnom Penh.

Nathalie had to head back to an important meeting with the Ministry, so we took public transportation back. The road passed green rice fields and broad sparkling rivers as we made our way to the city. Our feet rested on someone's bags of grain along the floorboard. We stopped at a market for lunch where the offered fare included interesting stuffed pastry, chicken feet soup, fried insects, and pig knuckles. We went for dragon fruit (my favorite) and a pomelo, which resembles a large grapefruit, only less tart. One more stop and we could get back to translating.

Plans for the night shift were worked out over dinner on the rooftop deck where the twinkling lights of Phnom Phen stretched into the distance, the spires of ornate temples outlined in the moonlit sky. Amazingly, Saron had worked throughout the day and was nearly finished but would not have time to review nor proofread any of it.

The Days for Girls curriculum has been translated into thirty-plus languages around the world. We know from experience that it is best to have at least one additional set of eyes to review, doubly true considering what had just happened. Now what? Maria asked the woman at the hotel lobby desk if she knew anyone who could help us. She did! "I used to translate for the UN for three years. I get off in an hour. I can help after that." Another Days for Girls miracle. She stayed several hours before confirming that it was accurate, recommending only a few small changes. Saron had done a remarkable job.

Side by side throughout the evening and into the night we pivoted to focus on formatting each page, adding icons to differentiate types of activities and creating culturally relevant covers for each manual. By morning it was all miraculously ready for print. This time we would have the luxury of giving the printer almost a full day to complete them. Off to a quick meeting with administration at the college, and then we would finish preparing for the big day. -

The next morning Maria left in one tuk-tuk to pick up the freshly printed large classroom banners each new Ambassador of Health teacher would need. Kayla-Leah got in another tuk-tuk to pick up the manuals and additional flip-charts. She was just returning up the stairs with the box of manuals when she crossed paths with the college director himself.

"Oh! Are these the manuals from the new course? May I see them?"

He thumbed through the pages intently. She held her breath. He reached for the second manual, his brow furrowed, and browsed a few more pages.

"Excellent. Most translations have bad luck. This is one of the best I've ever seen."

—

Upstairs our welcomes wove straight into the new video featuring Sopheap, the Project G youth leaders instructing, as well as video footage of a local medical student giving instructions from the manuals in Khmer so all the instructor segment introductions would be standardized as well. All were created in time for the next session to begin. Miraculous, I know.

This group of master teachers was so eager to learn that we couldn't even complete back-to-back points of the Ambassador of Health education without a torrent of questions. It doesn't get better than that. But we finally offered a compromise. What if we went through the entire flipchart once without questions? They could determine how many of their questions were addressed in the education they would soon offer. Then they could tell us if anything was missing, followed by discussion, questions, and thoughts.

Afterward, one of the teachers raised her hand, not with a question but a statement. "I am fifty-seven years old, and I never learned this. Until today, I thought men menstruated too . . . I can't believe I haven't learned this before.

I'm so happy to learn this important information, and I believe everyone in my country should know this."

After the day's interaction and instruction, everyone took their Khmer manuals and flipcharts home. When they returned the next day, they had already started using their new resources. One woman reported that she taught her children from the flipchart. Her father-in-law was nearby so she invited him to join them as well. They all learned together. Another of the teachers said that she had shared the story activity with her daughters, feeling it was perfect for young girls. Both teachers enjoyed talking with their families as a result. They loved the engaging combination of activities and stories. Days later, training complete, certificates in hand, everyone was eager to get started teaching.

A few weeks later Leyla returned so that she and Monie could do two weeks of follow-ups with the first master teachers who hadn't received all the materials earlier. They were fired up for action. As they finished the practice drills, the lead teacher pounded her fist into the desk. "We need to get permission to start training teachers immediately."

When the Phnom Penh master teachers heard the team was following up the next week in Ratanakiri, Mondulkiri, and Kratié, they insisted on joining to lead the delivery of the training themselves. They don't usually do that. But they said the content was too important and their endorsement would ensure support. They were so committed that they were willing to travel and be away from their families for a week to do it.

They sought and received permission from the teacher training college and the MoEYS within an unprecedented twenty-four hours. Because it was them asking.

Permission granted. Funding secured. The first of the schoolteachers ready and eager to welcome them, the master teachers were ready to go.

The COVID-19 pandemic hit. The schools closed.

Laos borders were closed, and Leyla was diverted to Australia. Over a year and a half later, she was still waiting to go home to her husband. Her husband's village chief said, "Your wife has left you. I will find you another wife." Over and over again Valee assured him it was not by choice that they were apart. They spent hours talking on Zoom. In March 2022, they were at last united in Cambodia, and in September of that year Leyla was finally able to return home to

Laos. Her "two-week trip" was finally over. She is still working hard for global menstrual equity with Days for Girls and on the Cambodia project where the work continues and is expanding. The outcome has been as bright as everyone had hoped.

I am happy, we get to know a lot, it's kind of experience, when we grow up, we won't be nervous, if there is no menstruation, there won't be human on earth.

—Female student in Ratanakiri

I will tell my younger sister, so she won't be scared, and she will know how to take care of her body.

—Female student in Mondulkiri

Here are a few highlights from the MLE data for teacher training in Cambodia.

Can a girl play sports during menstruation?
Pre-DfG Education: only 41.2 percent said yes.
Post-DfG Education: 91.2 percent said yes.

What are the phases of the menstrual cycle?
Pre-DfG Education: 0 percent answered correctly.
Post-DfG Education: 100 percent answered correctly.

What is the average length of the menstrual cycle?
Pre-DfG Education: 74 percent answered correctly.
Post-DfG Education: 97 percent answered correctly.

Chapter 62

Resilience

A good half of the art of living is resilience.
—Alain de Botton

March 2020

INSTANT MESSAGES WERE BOUNCING AROUND THE GLOBE FROM MY WhatsApp, the modern global walkie-talkie, way more effective than the ham radio I dreamed of building as a child. Each office leader answered with their own status and potential strategies tinged with the uncertainty of hourly change since the pandemic struck.

DfG Uganda's country leader Diana Nampeera was messaging tonight. The familiar three dots bobbled in the response line as she recorded her WhatsApp message. "Riots are growing. We're still okay for now. Samantha's fiancé has a permit for his vehicle to be on the road so we are able to move out to purchase and deliver basic staples, beans, coal, and sugar for team members who can't come in yet. We just don't know how long the lockdown will be. I'm trying to get permission for us to keep working, but travel is expensive and risky for our teams right now. We're trying."

I messaged back. "Could anything help some of your team stay temporarily in place at the office so they can continue to have income and meet your goals without as much risk? Would bicycles for transportation help?"

"No bicycles," she answered. "But we could purchase some mattresses and bedding and turn some of our storage areas into temporary dorms and continue our safety protocols here."

"Brilliant." Thanks to our supporters, her team was off to get mattresses along with more staples shortly thereafter.

What she didn't say was that her own health was failing and over WhatsApp we couldn't see that her eyes were slightly yellow and her stomach nearly constantly ached. Local doctors diagnosed her with an ulcer and the pandemic made follow-up less accessible.[46]

—

Our entire team redoubled our communication. Global leaders responded in ways that ensured everyone was as safe as possible and ahead of an invisible curve no one could be certain of anywhere. We wanted to hear what they were going through wherever they lived in the world. In fact, we were counting on it to keep the pulse of the organization and allow us to focus on opportunities rather than obstacles.

Thanks to generous supporters we were able to allocate funding for the full spectrum of support, from food staples, to bicycles to get to work when public transport was closed, to resources given to our office leaders so they could make faster decisions and stay locally responsive to the rapidly changing conditions. And then there were the funds that could be allocated for enterprise leaders who could still work within their communities.

Days for Girls leaders had been on the front line responding in the ways their communities most needed them, too. Enterprises were given the chance to propose funding for up to $500 to meet the needs in their communities in any way they saw fit.

What did the enterprises ask for? In Kenya, one enterprise asked for only $40 for emergency response, enough funding to make lunch for their team and ingredients to make soap. They sold the soap to increase community wellness, bought more lunch and soap ingredients and repeated, growing it over and over until they could open up and start sewing again.

---

[46] She was popping antacids but continued her work for menstrual equity for almost another year before they discovered that she was battling liver cancer. Tragically, multiple surgical interventions proved ineffective. She continued her leadership with Days for Girls until her final days, speaking at a virtual UN event just weeks before her passing in 2022.

An enterprise in Mombasa asked for funds to improve a latrine so they could keep working to make more menstrual kits. They had been borrowing a church bathroom during the day before social distancing demands temporarily closed the doors. They needed a latrine close by so they could keep working effectively.

Alice Wambui Mwangi explained that her enterprise went door to door. "When the government announced the lockdowns, the news didn't reach many of the small villages we serve. Some people thought that rural communities would be okay, that it was an urban problem. They thought the virus wasn't a risk to them. We went house to house, maintaining social distance and explaining about COVID-19 and how dangerous it is." Alice and her team set up water buckets on fences as handwashing stations and provided soap, using the supportive materials the DfG education includes: demonstrations on how to effectively wash hands.

Country shutdowns were happening everywhere. Days for Girls supporters had already quickly come together to create a Rapid Response Resiliency Fund to meet the needs reported by DfG leaders all over the world. We geared up a communications response—*Periods Don't Pause for Pandemics*—and shared it globally through our advocacy efforts.

Did it work? According to Alice, "The shift in direction gave us a way to help but it also provided new revenue opportunities including making masks and pads to expand our enterprise despite the pandemic. We were able to keep twenty people working and paid, and they are learning how businesses need to be flexible. And of course, we were helping our communities make sense of the pandemic and helping them through it with education."

Several enterprises became government-certified in making masks for their countries, which led to further DfG kit purchase opportunities as well. Some were called on by local governments to lead food distribution as a result of their status as trusted leaders in their communities. They brought their advocacy tool kits and menstrual resources too. The proactive efforts built trust for even bigger partnership opportunities for menstrual equity responses in their communities.

DfG Zimbabwe regional leader Chipo Chikomo got twenty minutes' notice to provide one hundred masks for the World Health Organization. She was ready and able to deliver. Her enterprise was almost the only location where masks were available because of her prompt pivot and ability to meet the urgent need.

Police in Zimbabwe enforced mask mandates and quarantined those without masks in their homes. People who usually sold items for day-to-day survival were left without income or a place to live. Many had sought refuge in the rubbish dump, and the population of people trying to scrounge something to eat while staying below the radar of the police was growing. The police took their enforcement of curfews and masks seriously, beating one seven-year-old boy who wandered outside during curfew so severely that his back was broken.

Chipo had the supplies her team needed to respond, but masks were only part of her team's response. She arranged to go to the Chikurubi prison where she was granted special permission to offer AWH education, DfG kits, and masks to women. "This is more than work," Chipo said. "When you understand it's part of your purpose, you constantly dream of ways of improving and going beyond the normal call of duty."

DfG Ecuador's enterprise was self-sustaining before COVID-19 hit, and wondered how they could keep it going when the open market they sold pads at closed due to the pandemic. But local authorities granted them permission to stay open, the only booth given an exception. They asked for funding to meet with remote village representatives who would deliver the education and DfG kits to those women of the rainforest who were isolated.

In Nepal they participated in an emergency public response, offering DfG pads with care and usage explanation as one of the emergency supply options.

In Rwanda, the Rwamagana enterprise was certified by the government to make masks. They went on to not only provide masks but also were granted special permission to offer education and distribute DfG kits even in lockdown. Officials considered menstrual care to be urgent due to rising cases of teen pregnancies attributed to girls exchanging sex for pads. Similar reports of rising child pregnancies were coming from other countries as well. Because their local enterprise leaders provided health insurance and savings programs for their employees, keeping them working while reaching more girls created multiple facets of ongoing benefits.

The pandemic highlighted a long-held ethos of our organization that even though partnership and collaboration are extremely valuable, it is the community that is best equipped to respond to local needs. When borders are closed, only those within them can directly respond to the needs. Established relationships continue to be fostered and trust flourishes. This was reinforced with each report that came in.

Perhaps one of the most dramatic examples of DfG first responses was in Lebanon. An enormous rush of gray smoke suddenly split the sky above the port of Beirut. It was August 4, 2020, at the height of the pandemic. Khayrieh Al Assadd, country coordinator of DfG Lebanon, was standing in her kitchen far from the waters of the bay so she didn't see the smoke from the fire, but she felt the explosion seconds later when flame and ballast sent a mushroom blast of impact from explosives stored at the port. It was the largest nonnuclear blast in history, measuring 3.3 on the Richter scale; it was felt across Turkey, Israel, Palestine, and as far away as Europe. An estimated 300,000 people were left homeless by the force of the explosion.

Khayrieh rallied local enterprise leaders, who responded almost immediately. Wearing their official Days for Girls vests, they walked in the heat past debris where houses once stood, taking care not to get cut by the broken glass shards that seemed to be everywhere. They brought people they encountered water, soap, cleaning materials, menstrual pads, and masks that were now needed to help protect lungs from fallout ash as well as COVID-19. People had lost family, friends, their homes, and any sense of security. The team spent time listening as well as passing out supplies. Having someone who listened and cared seemed to help as much as the water, soap, and cleaning agents they gave out to help clean up the blood. So much blood. They kept going.

Over and over people said these enterprise leaders were the first to bring aid. They kept going through the heat of the day, grateful to be able to help. As they continued, they coordinated with other NGOs so they could avoid replicating services and reach more people.

The explosion pushed the economy over the precipice that COVID-19 had led it to. Supply chains collapsed on the way down. The need for DfG enterprise washable pads rose to even higher levels beyond the refugee work the team there had already been doing so well for years.

DfG local leaders and project partners in Lebanon reported on the tremendous need for more DfG kits and health education in refugee settings. Khayrieh said, "Most refugees can't afford pads because they need to spend what little money they have on food and medicine. They use old white cloth or old T-shirts instead, but the problem is they are too shy to wash this and hang it out to dry. This isn't safe for their health. DfG kits provide a wonderful alternative . . . as they are multicolored, don't look like pads, and they are safe to use! The AWH education is just as important because it teaches them information that most of them don't already know. It makes them more relaxed and confident, and it breaks down taboos and stigmas. It has a lasting impact because they can pass the information on to their daughters, who will then pass it down to their daughters."

Those who couldn't access single-use pads needed a more sustainable option and choices that worked for them, washable pads or menstrual cups. We were hearing that increasingly from people and places all over the world.

Chapters and teams rallied to join the Lebanon enterprises in their Emergency Response Project,[47] raising U.S. $26,414.48 to sponsor the cost of additional kits to be made and distributed by the Lebanon enterprises and reach girls right away after the Beirut explosions. A total of 23,115 women and girls were reached (20,815 chapter and team kits and 2,300 Lebanon enterprise kits).

Because of the twin efforts of our phenomenal local leaders and chapters sending resources for refugees, in the last quarter of 2020, while other organizations were struggling to hold ground, Days for Girls reached almost 250,000 more women and girls, reaching a total of almost 2.1 million women and girls by the end of the year. Not because of a large grant nor any huge endowment, but because of everyday people all over the world who came together to do what had appeared to be impossible.

When volunteers couldn't get kits to most global distribution sites, they

---

[47] "Addressing Menstrual Hygiene and Health Needs of Refugees: Sustainable Menstrual Hygiene Products Offer a Critical Solution for the Sexual and Reproductive Health Needs of Syrian Refugees in Lebanon," Anera (blog), accessed November 27, 2022. www.anera.org/stories/addressing-menstrual-hygiene-and-health-needs-of-refugees/.

pivoted to meet an unexpected need: face masks. They pivoted to rally their skills and materials into action, creating over one million face masks while N95 masks were in critically short supply all over the United States and beyond. A challenge for which they won the Organization of the Year Award, but quietly just kept sewing, soon returning to the practical health needs they had been meeting all along.

Chapter 63

The Power of Knowing

I can be changed by what happens to me,
but I refuse to be reduced by it.
—Maya Angelou

Malawi, 2020

EUNICE'S STORY IS SADLY A FAMILIAR ONE. "YOU ARE NOW IN THE COM-pany of the bad," her guardian told her when she began bleeding as a preteen. The whole family started mocking Eunice: "She is probably sleeping with boys." Bright, inquisitive, honest, and very literal, Eunice was adamant that she was not. But no one would explain what was happening except to say it would be with her the rest of her life. Her stomach hurt; she was nauseated. Was this really the rest of her life?

Her guardian spoke in riddles to her. "Do not walk behind a man. Do not associate with uncircumcised people."

Friends at school told her bits in fits of whispers. "This thing happens to some girls of a certain age but other girls it does not happen at that age."

"You must stop putting salt in relish during this time, or you will make everyone sick."

"You are now dirty. You can only be cleansed by a man, but you must be careful."

Nothing was clear.

A man on a bench tried to take advantage of her. She escaped his grip and ran to tell her guardian. She was slapped. Nothing happened to the man.

Only a few months later, she was sexually abused by a neighbor. If her guardian slapped her for sitting next to someone, imagine the consequences of telling her family about this attack that left her feeling like her whole body had been stolen? Eunice kept quiet, and when she started missing her period, she was grateful it had stopped. Four months later, she wondered what was moving in her stomach. She shared her concern with someone. They told her she was pregnant.

She tried to kill herself with medicine. She tried to end the baby growing inside her. Nothing worked. She tried again to end her life, but both she and the baby survived. Eventually she gathered enough courage to inform her guardians about the abuse and her suspected situation. She was kicked out of her home and sent to the home of the very neighbor who had abused her. Eventually her parents took her back, but now she was alone everywhere she went, even when she was with them. She knew her status: fifteen-year-old dropout, bringer-of-shame with no possible future.

Soon the bulge of the baby was so stretched that she could watch the jut and roll of the baby's movements. "It won't be long now," her mother said as she left for errands. "If you feel anything strange, go tell the neighbor."

What did strange mean? Eunice wondered. But after all their harsh responses, she didn't dare ask more questions.

While her mother was away, her water broke and trickled onto her bare feet. She went to her neighbor, who asked, "Are you in labor?"

"What is labor?" Eunice asked.

"Do you have pain?" the neighbor asked. Eunice said no, but the neighbor took her to the clinic anyway.

A clinic vehicle transported her over bumpy roads to the government referral hospital, dropping her off alone. She stood in line swaying.

The nurse that checked her in was busy, but Eunice asked the question bursting from her body. "Will you please tell me how babies are born?"

The nurse stopped what she was doing and called two other nurses over. "Ask that again," she said. When Eunice repeated the question, the nurses looked at each other before laughing so hard that one nearly knocked down the simple IV post that stood dusty and limp nearby. "You will find out soon enough," she said, still laughing.

Eunice prayed that God would be with her and comfort her. She felt a calm come over her even as the pain grew big enough to deliver a son.

On that day, alone in that place, she didn't know that she would go on to not only raise a strong, intelligent son but also graduate from college, work for a president, be an administrator at a college, and help girls all over Malawi to not have to go through what she did. She said, "I don't think that I can change the world, but I think that I can change the world of one person."

She takes that commitment seriously.

Today her advocacy for women and girls all over Malawi includes Days for Girls.

—

Eunice's first Days for Girls enterprise is in the third stall in a single-story stucco strip of roadside shops along the road at Sankhari village. Inside, the space is well organized, very small, and brimming with production. There you can purchase handcrafted cloth earrings, necklaces, purses, and even shoes. The room is 90 percent filled with the chatter and hum of six people making DfG kits. Window openings let in light and dust with equal ease, but the space is solid and has electricity and the power of passion.

Stacks of soft deep purple flannel are finished with a serger sewing machine into DfG absorbent liners on one side of the room, and the other side is focused on cutting fabric that is layered into shields ready for sewing. The five women and one man there will cheerfully tell of their successes. Eunice and the other DfG Malawi leaders, Yamikani and Mabel, all serve to help keep women out of destitution. Helping vulnerable women is the driving force behind their enterprises as well. For each of them lifting communities is important, but just as important is the mission of health education and menstrual equity. They work together in decision-making, garnering supplies, fulfilling orders, and taking on big projects.

When the pandemic hit, it hit all of them, not only their enterprises, but also those they were trying to reach. As shutdowns worsened, the leaders did all they could to resource materials. DfGI's team had been working to appropriately get donated funds to all of the enterprises, but it wasn't easy to keep up with the changes all over the globe.

Melani, our DfGI enterprise program manager, mentioned that the Malawi enterprises needed supplies. When I sent Eunice a quick check-in on WhatsApp, she replied almost instantly. "The place where we usually get our fabric is expected to close any time now. But if I had the funding, we could purchase enough fabric to keep us going for months. People would be able to keep working. But it would have to be here very soon."

It was nighttime for the team members in the United States, and I would need to contact someone to make a wire transfer happen. It was good that the allocated funds were available, thanks to DfG supporters. I spent the next hour on the phone, maxing out small mobile funding transfers until the system locked me out, just short of the full amount Eunice had asked for. Meanwhile, she messaged Mabel and Yamikani to confirm the materials they needed to stock up on, and communicated with Melani to see what other areas had similar needs. Then Eunice headed to town in hopes of purchasing local Malawi kitenge and supplies. While she drove, she canvased shops over the phone to ask them to reserve fabric for the enterprises. Shops were reluctant. "What assurance do we have that you will buy this much?" She answered the same question for shop after shop while weaving through backstreet traffic. "You know us. We purchase from you all of this time. Please, do us this favor. I'm on my way now."

Things were even more chaotic at the Lilongwe Old Town shopping district called Bwalo la Njobvu.[48] Finding a parking spot is always challenging, but this time the parking pile-up was like a tangled ball of steel wool made of cars, tuk-tuks, and bicycles, almost impossible to navigate with the growing crowds. A car pulled out of an almost-spot and Eunice rushed in, quickly paying a young man to watch over her car before hurrying into the pressing crowds toward familiar shops.

Protests broke out in the dusty narrow passageways of wholesale buildings and the roadway packed with hundreds of formal and pop-up shops. People wrestled over toiletries and hardware with equal fervor. Many shop owners were forced to close to protect their remaining wares. Eunice called the shops that were expecting her again and again, though they were having trouble hearing her over the shouts and honking. "Please stay. We are coming." Navigating the chaos of crowds, traffic, and protests, she made the rounds to all as promised, miraculously acquiring nearly all the materials she needed before winding her way back. Thank goodness the shopkeepers sent people out with her to help carry all the

---

[48] Literally translated, it means "ground for elephants."

material. As she pulled out, traffic was snarled to a stop. Eunice was locked in her car while fighting surrounded her, but she calmly waited, knowing that the contents of her car didn't look nearly as valuable as they were. She had the fabric to keep the team's enterprises going so they could continue their work.

This fabric was for menstrual kits and masks. It would keep people working and keep people safe. Yamikani arrived to pick up the fabric for her enterprise workers. They couriered materials to Mabel. Soon the colorful kitenge was transformed into quality masks and additional Days for Girls kits.

It paid off. Expats and diplomats came to know that if you wanted a quality mask, a Days for Girls enterprise would have what you need. Visitors asked, "What do you usually do?" The answer inspired orders for more than 3,200 DfG kits in addition to what would over time add up to more than 11,000 masks sold. They made plain masks, branded corporate masks, monogrammed bridal party masks, and did so while others didn't yet have supplies. Because of the resourcefulness of the Malawi team and the efforts of DfG supporters, their work there didn't stop. The teams also became emergency responders, teaching and helping people stay safe and get what they needed.

Eunice's reputation for integrity and commitment to women's health and her country brought Days for Girls to the attention of the First Lady of Malawi. Committed to girls getting education opportunities and having all they need to give them confidence and safety, First Lady Monica Chakwera became an official ambassador of menstrual health with Days for Girls and announced the commitment with a gathering on International Menstrual Hygiene Day on May 28, 2021. Through the committed efforts of Eunice and so many others, a global intention came to life in local action.

Chapter 64

The First Lady, the Minister of Gender, and the Royal One

Stronger than any army is
an idea whose time has come.
—Victor Hugo

Malawi, International Menstrual Health Day, May 28, 2021[49]

THE FIRST LADY'S OFFICE WAS THROUGH THE GARDENS AND UP THE broad exterior stone staircase, then past the tall white columns of the portico entry. Eunice had arranged for a pre-event meeting. Her Excellency, Monica Chakwera, sat behind an elegant desk as we entered the room with its vaulted ceilings and classic art. During the formal introductions, she struck me as equal parts intelligent, elegant, and humble, and instantly one of my new favorite people. It was easy to see why she is so beloved in her country. Her commitment to elevating education for girls is recognized as indefatigable. After greetings and refreshments, she shared her prepared comments, highlighting her commitment to the girls, her country, and menstrual health. But there was also bad news: due to serious unforeseeable circumstances, she would regrettably have to travel for an emergency, unavoidably missing her own event. Her expression was sincere and solemn as she delivered the news.

Two days later, as we turned down the dirt road toward the school where the national celebration of Menstrual Health Day would happen, the road was still being shoveled and smoothed in preparation for their honored guest. I wondered

---

[49] It's referred to as Menstrual Hygiene Day as well.

if they knew that another strong woman, the Honorable Patricia Kaliati, Minister of Gender of Malawi, had agreed to represent the First Lady at the event in her stead. As we arrived, festive music was already playing, though the Minister had not arrived. The crowd was almost a thousand people strong and growing—students, teachers, community members, leaders, parents, and performers encircled the three tents.

Cabinet and tribal leaders from around the country as well as a huge local crowd had gathered at the rural Thema Secondary School. The crowd stood to attention as the Minister of Gender's black Land Cruiser approached, pulling in past towering eucalyptus trees onto the campus. Eunice gestured. "Come, let's greet her," she said.

Honorable Patricia Kaliati's full title is actually Minister of Gender, Community Development, and Social Welfare of Malawi. One of the most powerful members of the cabinet, she stepped out of the car and was immediately surrounded in greeting by dignitaries and chiefs who parted in two rows as she walked toward the school headmaster's office.

Entering the simple office, she sat in one of the wooden chairs next to his desk, just arm's reach from the entirety of the school's chemistry lab, a small open cabinet containing a few glass beakers and several bottles filled with powder or liquid. She signaled for the dozen or so representatives designated to follow her in to be seated, then signed the guest registry with a large flowing script, a greeting in commemoration of this important day. Passing the registry for the rest of us to add our own signatures, she turned her full focus on the headmaster, speaking in English. "How many students attend here? And how many girls have dropped out due to forced child marriages?"

"Of one hundred seventy-six students, thirty-five girls have dropped out for forced marriage since the school year began. Ten in this calendar year alone."

"This is not acceptable. It is unlawful . . ." She said, then shifted to the local language.

Eunice, who was sitting beside me, whispered in my ear, "She is telling the headmaster to take action, and the senior chief that it is his responsibility to ensure that all chiefs in his area keep the law and protect the girls." Others answered questions in a language that I could not understand, but one thing was obvious: the Minister's message was understood.

A few minutes later the Minister rose, the others following her out. She paused at the booths set up by the partners of the First Lady of Malawi's Foundation, Shaping Our Future Foundation (SOFF), an initiative determined to reach five thousand girls in a pilot program with Days for Girls that was to launch concerted efforts toward countrywide menstrual equity. Media cameras rolling, local Ambassadors of Women's Health ceremonially exhibited DfG kits and education. Loma, as representative to the First Lady's Foundation, said a few words, and then our partners at Plan International shared their efforts and commitment before we all followed the Minister in a procession toward the center tent. She paused to greet the six hundred or so girls who were standing dressed in their respective school uniforms, white shirts with blue skirts, green skirts, or red dresses. They waved back. She took her central seat of honor behind a low table topped with flowers and small flags of Malawi.

Eunice had been working for months with the leaders of Days for Girls Malawi and Diana Nelson, Days for Girl's advocacy director, a tall, soft-spoken woman whose balance of decorum and astute sense of strategy are a superpower for building alliances. I first met Diana when I spoke at the Asian Women's Conference. After the conference she became a volunteer, then a part-time assistant for chapters. A communications major in college, and already living in the circles of diplomats thanks to her husband's roles at the United States Agency for International Development (USAID), Diana proved to be far more than a natural; she is the Picasso of abstract connections, expertly painting pathways for connection and win-wins. Eunice and Diana were the perfect complements for blazing the trail with the First Lady's office as well as with other members of the cabinet.

Thanks to the First Lady's commitment to piloting this Days for Girls partnership, nearly every cabinet of the government was present. Even the military supported period equity that day; Yamikani had convinced local chiefs to reach out to the military to donate the chairs and the three large tents for the First Lady's event.

My assigned seat was under the central tent, between Honorable Patricia Kaliati and Senior Chief Theresa Kachindamoto. The music faded as Priscilla, Principal Communications Officer in the First Lady's office, welcomed everyone, introducing the troupes of student dancers from three schools whose dance-off swooped in and out, weaving past each other as fellow students drummed. Chief

Theresa, wearing a belted burgundy coat and sash over her bright traditional dress even in the heat of the day, joined a group of girls as they sang, smiling and stomping in sync with them just before the string of prepared speeches of the dignitaries started.

Three speeches in, it was Eunice's turn. For this important occasion she had abandoned her business dresses, opting instead for the strength of tradition, wearing the special traditional cloth designed for the day as a headdress and wrap. Stepping from the shade into the sun, microphone in hand, she eloquently recognized the day, the partners, the dignitaries, and all those in attendance.

Yamikani and I were up next. I paused, breathing in this moment filled with sun, leaders, community, girls, and so much possibility, and silently prayed I could be equal to it. In addition to Yamikani's work in overseeing the details of the day with Mabel and Eunice, she had been busy serving as translator in the local dialect. Now she would translate my speech. Although she was confident, bold, and comfortable with any of the languages spoken there, the dialect of this community was Yamikani's own. One of the dignitaries, noting the ease and perfection of her dialect, was disbelieving. "No girl from here has ever gone on as you have. It is not possible."

"You're wrong. I am proof," Yamikani had replied. Her father had done all he could to ensure that she got every opportunity for education, although it took a great deal of sacrifice. Now she was here, a leader in community development, founder of a DfG enterprise, and one of three primary organizers of the work of Days for Girls Malawi.

"Do you feel it?" I asked the still growing crowd. "The importance of this moment?" The women trilled. I continued, "Imagine a day, not too long from now, when we will look back and celebrate that on this International Menstrual Health Day we declared our vision for a clear end to menstrual poverty."

I looked into the faces of those gathered around us as Yamikani translated. I continued and deliberately kept my own speech short. Today was their day. "In thanks to this moment, and those gathered here, as well as those we collectively represent, this great country can make the very real consequences of period poverty a thing of the past. It can be done when we have the courage to acknowledge the truth that the people of this great country, those gathered here, and our entire world were all born of the miracle of menstruation. Periods are a healthy and natural part of every person's existence in this world. What are we afraid of? By speaking up and addressing menstrual equity, we build strength for this community, country, and our world as a whole. Today, your arrival here declares that you are no longer afraid and can decide that the days of shame over menstruation are behind you. It is an honor to stand with your community as you declare that the strength of all your days for all of your people is a powerful force for good. Thank you for choosing to be part of the turning point."

After she finished translating, Yamikani said to me, "You just came out and said it! You have undeniably challenged the taboo. I gave extra care to cover translating every word."

I had no doubt. She's amazing that way.

Just before the next speaker finished his speech, the PA system went down. The sound guy went into a flurry of cords and tape—it was clear it could be a while. The speaker spoke louder before abruptly finishing. Honorable Patricia Kaliati rose from her seat. "I'll do it," she said. Leaving her prepared speech notebook on the table in front of her, she stepped into the middle of the field, her gold lace blouse glinting in the sun.

The gathering had grown even larger since we started, but now the crowd went silent.

The Minister's powerful extemporaneous call to action rang through the field. The moment is emblazoned in my heart, and I recall many of her words still. "Mothers, you must stand up for your girls. Their education will return strength to you far into your future. Do not trade their future for trinkets in exchange for their early marriage, keep them in school. Teachers, do not look the other way when men come for them. And keep your hands off your students as well; they are your responsibility, not yours for the taking. Fathers, leave your girls alone. Do not believe the witch doctors when they tell you that defiling your daughters will cure you from HIV or make you rich. It will not. Only weak men hurt girls. And no more beating women. If you want to hit someone, come hit me!" As she was imposing and substantial, the traditional wrap around her hair making her seem even taller, I doubted anyone would offer to take her on.

For more than half an hour, her voice rose passionately as she called on every stakeholder in the community to stand up for girls, end child marriage, and keep girls in school. "Men, leave the young ones alone. If your wives no longer look beautiful, it is because you have put them down. These girls should be with those their own age. What kind of man are you if you must go after young ones?"

One of the local television camera men looked up from the lens and over his shoulder at the crowd, his surprised expression shifting quickly to a smile.

The Minister of Gender gave the senior chiefs a deadline. "I expect that by June 1st you will have guided all the chiefs in annulling all child marriages. Do I have your commitment? Good. Then I will expect word of your successes. If you want help on knowing how to accomplish this, approach Senior Chief Theresa Kachindamoto."

Chief Theresa gently nodded her head, her soft smile unchanging.

Next, the Minister spoke to the girls themselves who were still at attention. "Your future is through education."

Eunice directed Chief Theresa and me to join the Minister of Gender on the field where she was declaring to the girls that if you wanted to be a leader like these women, you need education. Another trill of celebration rose. She called out the Members of Parliament, teachers, and leaders from the crowd to come forward in support of the girls. One by one leaders joined her at the center of that circle of a crowd of a thousand or more people, all coming together to stand with her as she declared support for their First Lady, the girls, and the community.

Women's voices rose with another traditional trill. A small breeze swept up a sunny swirl of snippets of grass and leaves that caught my attention as it whirled just to the right of the group of girls. The lean funneled column reached fifteen feet high before showering over them, confetti-like. I smiled, wondering how many noticed this dusting, not in the tradition of the "hyenas" who preyed on them with their ceremonial "dusting off" and "cleansing," but this time in a moment when everyone in their communities was challenged to stand with them. The symbolism struck me as they swept the bits from their hair.

The microphone came back to life. Honorable Patricia Kaliati continued her comments in short order before calmly returning to her seat to cheers from the crowd. A Member of Parliament took the moment to ask her for things for the community, stating that we should provide changing rooms next to the latrines for the girls. What a perfect thing for the community to provide in support of their girls receiving kits and education. People could come together, a few bricks each, and quickly create a changing room of their own making for each school.

The Minister said, "Days for Girls is in great hands and I know that the girls of Malawi's lives will be changed." She pledged renewed support of Days for Girls and the First Lady, and the Days for Girls leaders in Malawi. It wasn't just talk. She shifted tradition that day by asking many high-profile men and women present to give out DfG kits to thirty-five girls, symbolic of the more than six hundred who had received them over the past few days and the promise of almost five thousand more to come.

Afterward Eunice said, "Having the men pass them out broke the stigma. That one action showed how Days for Girls works for equity on many levels. They stood up for periods with us!"

There were more symbolic gifts, more traditional dances, media interviews, and greetings of congratulations. No one seemed in much of a hurry to leave, though many had come long distances and had far to go before dark. It was a good day for girls.

Chapter 65

For the Girls

May your choices reflect your hopes, not your fears.
—Nelson Mandela

Malawi, 2021

THE CELEBRATION WAS NOT OVER. DRUMS AND DANCING PLAYED ON AS the Minister departed. Traditional Big Dance Spirit creatures in their wild, oversized monster costumes chased children who ran away squealing. I paused, giving a nod to the circle of seven chiefs huddled in conversation over her assignment to them. Some wore fez caps, one wore a crowning fringe of feather, or perhaps it was the frill of a pelt, I could not be sure, but they all looked up and smiled before returning to their discussion. Chief Theresa stood surrounded by a circle of girls near our vehicles. Days for Girls Malawi team members chatted easily with each other as if it were just an ordinary day. But it was a day for Every Girl. Everywhere. Period. A day filled with messages I hoped everyone could hear.

Celebrating period equity had become, as it so often does, a clarion moment that connects many things of importance.

We were not alone in celebration. It was International Menstrual Hygiene Day, and a multitude of organizations, groups, and events all over the world were raising awareness about period poverty and calling for menstrual equity with the slogan: *It's time for action.* People were taking action within their own communities, reaching thousands with more knowledge and resources around the world in a single day, declaring it as only the beginning of their commitment.

As a result of the school-based programming launched in Malawi that day, baseline and post-program survey data identified increased menstrual health knowledge among participants, and positive changes in confidence and attitudes surrounding menstruation.

- At baseline, prior to participation, 25 percent of students "strongly agreed" and an additional 19 percent "agreed" with the statement that a girl was dirty during menstruation, compared to only 3 percent and 2 percent respectively after participating in the Days for Girls program.
- Prior to doing AWH with DfG, 47 percent of students "strongly agreed" and an additional 25 percent "agreed" with the statement that menstruation should be kept a secret, dropping to just 2 to 4 percent after our programing.
- Since receiving their DfG kit, 97.9 percent said they feel comfortable when they use it.
- Since receiving their DfG kit, 97.5 percent said they feel comfortable and confident about being at school when they have their period.
- Since receiving their DfG kit, 97.7 percent said that during their last three menstrual periods, they could do all the activities they normally did when not having their periods.

This kind of data is coming in from all over the world.

Who would have guessed that something so simple would have such far-reaching effects?

In Kenya, where girls have been so vulnerable to the boda (motorcycle) drivers who ask girls to barter their bodies in exchange for pads, the Boda Girl project there highlights the cross-cutting benefits of addressing inequity head on. The project assists these girls to become licensed boda drivers, certified as official Community Health Workers, and as DfG Ambassadors of Health, who provide kits, menstrual health education, and rides to school for girls. A project turning vulnerability into strength. A win-win-win for the girls.

The need is still great; an estimated 500 million women and girls lack access to everything they need for menstrual care. That number represents a quarter of the menstruating population on Earth. It will take all of us to change that. Those who menstruate need reliable options. Making those solutions benefit local livelihoods and leadership is not the easy way, but we have found that it is a powerful endeavor worth the commitment. There is little funding applied to menstrual wellness, even though the need is clear and the results are remarkable. Small steps are making huge strides.

Awareness is growing. The shift to menstrual equity starts with courageous conversations. Now, you too can be part of the shift. There are a lot of things that are hard to change in this world; menstrual inequity isn't one of them. We can solve menstrual inequity in our lifetime—if we do it together.

—

That night in Malawi, I was too happy to sleep, sending up prayers and meditation for hours: gratitude for the blessing of being there, gratitude for those serving all over the world, joy for the beauty of connection, and joy for the leadership that brought us together. Gratitude for the quiet ones, the trilling ones, the serving ones, and the possibilities ahead. I was there. Having attended so many events, this one felt different.

Can you feel it? The power of what happens when communities stand together for a purpose. The ripple effect created far and wide was tangible to us on that day.

We do not live in a single-issue world, and there are many causes that merit tremendous focus. Imagine if we each stood where we feel called, not in fear, but in hope. We don't have to agree on everything. In fact, it's best that we don't. The world needs your unique strength and insight.

After the big event, I kicked off my shoes and walked barefoot in the sand beside the women of Days for Girls Malawi and stood hand in hand with Chief Theresa on the shores of Monkey Bay.

I am no longer the girl without a home. I have filled three passports with proof of all that we have in common: proof that we have the power to change our circumstances. The warm glimmer of that sidewalk in the state park so many years ago led to determination not in pursuit of adventure, but rather to partner to build solutions. At my core, complete trust that what I learned back then is true: circumstances don't define us. Determination can. All over the world, I have witnessed determined and inspired action.

Today I would tell that woman in the park who asked where my shoes were that it is not what we wear on our feet but what paths we take with them that matters.

Big challenges are big opportunities in disguise. Dare to hope for the change you yearn to see in the world, and go after it. While it is easy to see all that divides us, I celebrate the miracle that the world can choose to walk toward a day when we all have the full possibilities of Every Day. For Everyone. Period.

Imagine all that is possible. Together.

Epilogue

MONTHS LATER, A WHATSAPP MESSAGE CAME IN FROM YAMIKANI OF the Malawi team, who had traveled on down many treacherous roads far from the place I had last seen them:

Aug 5, 2021

As the team was packing up to go, after our kickoff event at Chilimbondo Primary School ground, a group of boys lingered around. One of the girls that had attended our AWH training and had received the Supreme Kit was walking past the boys.

"Mwalandila katundu (You have received a package)," one of the boys called out.

His friends jeered rudely.

The girl was not embarrassed; instead she faced them and said to their face,

"Nalandira kumene (Yes, I have received). I will proudly carry it without shame because I have learnt today that menstruation is not something to be ashamed of. I need to embrace it and be proud of it because I am fearfully and wonderfully made."

She then strolled away, a victory smile on her face.

This made the team proud, to know that we have made a huge impact on the life of this girl who could be so brave.

Days for Girls Outreach Today

584 chapters; 119 enterprises in 31 countries; 280,105 refugees reached; a total of 145 countries and more than 2,908,947 individuals reached with DfG kits . . . and counting.[50]

---

[50] As of 6/1/2023.

Acknowledgments

WRITING THIS BOOK WAS A GLOBAL EXPERIENCE. IT WOULDN'T HAVE been possible without the generous willingness of so many to share their stories. While I wrote this on planes, trains, and in corners and at desks around the world, I have many to thank for not only encouraging me, but also proofreading, listening, leading, cheering, and sharing their own strength. Like Days for Girls itself, it took all of us to bring this book to life. My amazing husband, Don, and beloved family Devin, Gentree, Dane, Brandie, Ashley, Brandon, Breanna, Raymond, Autumn, Reed, Kim, and the Turtles, who stood beside me all along (even when we were apart) and who read and listened to more versions of this book than I can count. Without you, I would not be who I am and Days for Girls would not exist. Jim and Andy Clay, this is "all your fault." Rob and Debbie Young, the world is a better place because of you. The list of champions of Days for Girls that I am blessed to call friends would be as long as this book. Here are many who gave feedback, edits, and encouragement as I completed these pages: Kayla-Leah Rich, Miriam Lancaster, Taylor Birch, Molly Mansker, Alexa Renehan, Toni Robino, Terry-Lynn Stone, Neil Gordon, Camille Fronk Olsen, Jen Kelly, Doug Wagner, Sister Marilyn Lacey, Tiffany Larson, Anne Wairepo, Sandy Clark, Leah Spelman, Gina Grimm, Liz Greer, Ruth Anne Shepherd, Jane Lubale, Karen Waite, Brittany Burke, Ann Rodman, Louise Colonnier, Gloria Buttsworth, Vida Peterson, Candace Stanford, Kitty Harmon, Maya Khaitu, Leyla Isin-Xiong, Eunice Chimphoyo-Banda, Deb Lund, Cynthia Kersey, Kirsten Berhan, Laurie Baum, Cynthia Forbes, Kassidy Sorenson, Jessi Messner, Andrea Estebaranz, Diana Nampeera and Dr. Sybilann Williams (we miss you, dear ones), Dr. Karen Harris, Janine Keblish, Jacquie Scott, Jessica Williams, Ann Lewis, Diana Nelson, Cynthia Covey Haller, and my editors Vy Tran, Laurel Leigh, Elizabeth Degenhard, and Alyn Wallace. Special thanks to Melissa Ambrosini who introduced me to my literary agent Bill Gladstone, who introduced the manuscript to Glenn Yeffeth of BenBella Books, who said yes to the book and DfG within two days. To the global family of Days for Girls, if only each of your stories could be shared. I had to choose a few to represent you all; I hope and pray that you feel represented here. Let's be honest. It's impossible to capture the miracle of you.

About the Author

Photo by Ashley Christensen

CELESTE MERGENS IS AN INNOVATIVE THOUGHT LEADER WHO HAS founded several successful organizations, including her passion, global award-winning Days for Girls International. Days for Girls was named by the *Huffington Post* as a "Next Ten" Organization poised to change the world in the next decade. They have reached more than 3 million women and girls and communities in 145 countries with menstrual wellness resources and health education.

Celeste is a sought-after speaker and consultant with over 50 events on average every year. She has been named *Conscious Company* Global Impact Entrepreneur's Top Ten Women, a Global Washington Global Hero, and Washington State's America Mother of the Year. She is also an AARP Purpose Prize winner and Women's Economic Forum's Woman of the Decade. She has been featured in Oprah's *O* magazine, *Forbes*, and *Stanford Social Innovation Review*.

She is happily married to her best friend of over 40 years, Don Mergens. They love being with their six adult children, children-in-law, and grandchildren.